LET'S PLAN A PARTY!

LET'S PLAN A PARTY!

40 CREATIVE IDEAS for SPECIAL PROGRAMS IN YOUR CHURCH

DEE TRAVIS
LYNNE REEVES

REGULAR BAPTIST PRESS
1300 North Meacham Road
Schaumburg, Illinois 60173-4806

Let's Plan a Party! is dedicated to both our families,
who have been so encouraging and helpful in
getting our book accomplished and who help plan,
organize, and cook for many a party!

Recipe Contributors: Benjie Anderson, Sheryl Bolton, Lela Burkhalter, Phyllis Burkhalter, Loy Christensen, Tammy Christensen, Mary Clayton, Della Collum, Carolyn Crigger, Julie Crill, Carmen Dahl, Zaylene Danley, Yvonne Hoag, Kris Hoakison, Barb Houg, Jennifer Hoyt, Barb Kuyper, Sue Maitlen, Jana Matthiesen, Rosalie McAlexander, Judy Miller, Crystal Musmaker, Robin Peters, Marlyn Rectenbaugh, May Rectenbaugh, Sherry Rectenbaugh, David Reeves, Lynne Reeves, Matthew Reeves, Chris Runyan, Judi Sauser, Ashley Scott, Dawn Shelley, Sharon Sorenson, Connie Standley, Donna Taylor, Betty Travis, Dee Travis, Jean Travis, Kelsey Travis, Mallory Travis, Meg Travis, Rachel Travis, Susan Walker, Deb Walter, Cheryl Wertenberger, Janene Wimmer, and Mary Ellen Wires.

Poem on page 37, "What Love Can Do," author unknown; from *Something Old, Something New* by Matilda Nordtvedt and Pearl Steinkuehler, Moody Publishers, © 1981. Used by permission.

Skit on page 64 by Sharon Sorenson. Used by permission.

Poem on page 69, "Time Is of the Essence," by Irene Foster; from *A Mother's Heart* by Jean Fleming, NavPress.

LET'S PLAN A PARTY! 40 Creative Ideas for Special Programs in Your Church
© 2004
Regular Baptist Press • Schaumburg, Illinois
1-800-727-4440 • www.regularbaptistpress.org
Printed in U.S.A.
All rights reserved
RBP5303 • ISBN: 1-59402-079-5

Contents

BRIDAL SHOWERS

BABY SHOWERS

FATHER AND SON EVENTS

MOTHER AND DAUGHTER EVENTS

Bridal Showers

A Match Made in Heaven

Theme and Decorations

- Invite the ladies to a morning or afternoon tea in honor of the bride-to-be.
- Decorate in Victorian style with lace, beads, candles, old white fancy gloves, and pretty fans.
- Group ladies at small tables for an elegant atmosphere. Seat the bride and her family at the head table.
- Decorate each table with pretty vases filled with flowers. Set vases on lace doilies. Lean a fan against each vase.
- Serve hot tea in fancy china teacups.
- To create a formal atmosphere, use young ladies as servers. Show them how to carry muffins, fruit, and drinks on trays and serve the guests.

Food

- Triangle sandwiches
- Cinnamon Crunch Muffins
- Poppy Seed Muffins
- Blueberry Muffins
- Fresh fruit
- A variety of flavored teas
- Hot chocolate topped with choice of whipped cream, cinnamon, multicolored sprinkles, and crushed peppermint candies

Games

Match Made in Heaven

Call the groom ahead of time and ask him questions about himself and his bride. At the shower she will answer each question and see how close she comes to his answers.

Possible Questions

Does he have a nickname for her?
What is his favorite food?
If he could travel anywhere, where would he go?
On what day of the week did he propose?
What color are her eyes?
What does he like best about her?
How much did he weigh when he was born?
Where did they meet?
How many kids does she want?
What is her favorite restaurant?
Where and when was their first kiss?
Has he ever had a broken bone?
Do they have a favorite song as a couple? If so, what is it?
Would she rather get candy, flowers, or perfume for Valentine's Day?

Whose Heart Belongs to Whom?

1. Mary and _____
2. Clark Kent and _____
3. Rhett and _____
4. Abraham and _____
5. Jacob and _____
6. Ginger Rogers and _____
7. Lucy and _____
8. Isaac and _____
9. Ananias and _____
10. Beauty and _____
11. George and _____
12. Wilma and _____
13. Adam and _____
14. Boaz and _____
15. Romeo and _____

Answers

(1) Joseph; (2) Lois Lane; (3) Scarlett; (4) Sarah; (5) Rachel; (6) Fred Astaire; (7) Desi or Ricky; (8) Rebekah; (9) Sapphira; (10) the beast; (11) Barbara, Laura, or Martha; (12) Fred; (13) Eve; (14) Ruth; (15) Juliet.

Matches Made in Heaven

Have one or two ladies share stories of when they played matchmaker and it worked.

Songs

"Matchmaker, Matchmaker"
"Let Me Call You Sweetheart"
"Tea for Two"
" 'Tis So Sweet to Trust in Jesus"
"Great Is Thy Faithfulness"

Devotions

A Match Made in Heaven

Everybody enjoys a good love story. Just look at all the books, songs, and films with romantic themes. In a good love story, two people find each other over distance and time. Usually they have to overcome many obstacles along the way. But love always triumphs in the end. Finding Mr. Right can be a difficult job. Only God knows who will be a good husband and perfect match for each woman.

Today we are going to look at a match made in Heaven, the love story of Isaac and Rebekah, which is found in Genesis 24. Rebekah willingly consented to marry Isaac without even seeing him. She left behind all she knew and loved and had great faith in God that He knew what He was doing. She trusted the Matchmaker of Heaven with her heart.

Isaac had faith in God too. What if his bride wasn't all he had dreamed of? What if the servant's idea of a wife didn't match his? But when Isaac looked up and saw Rebekah coming, he must have been pleased. He took her to his mother's tent (Sarah, who had died). Rebekah became his wife, and he loved her. God knew exactly what He was doing.

I am sure nobody here has a story like that. How did you meet your mate? What did you look for in choosing whom you would marry? God chose the best match for Abraham's son Isaac. Consider with me some of the qualities God wanted in His choice for Isaac's bride.

First, God's match for Isaac would be someone who believed in God. It was important to Abraham, Isaac's father, that his son's bride share their faith. They trusted in God and His promises. They wanted a godly woman of like faith and values. Abraham commissioned his servant to find a bride for Isaac. But he told the servant that the bride could not be a Canaanite. So the servant traveled many miles to find the best match for Isaac. It would be worth the long journey to find a woman who loved God.

When we want God's best in marriage, we must start with someone of the same faith, a man who trusts in Christ alone for eternal life.

Second, God's match for Isaac was a faithful servant. When Abraham's servant arrived in his master's home country, he was tired and hot, and so were his camels. When he saw Rebekah at the well and asked her for a drink, she offered to water his ten camels too. Right away he knew she must be the one for Isaac. She knew how to work hard and wasn't afraid of hard work.

Marriage is hard work. Love is wonderful, but after sin entered into the world with Adam and Eve, even keeping love aflame requires a lot of effort. Work at being supportive and honest; work at giving readily to your husband's needs. Be a faithful servant, willing to do your job and work hard at your marriage.

Third, God's match for Isaac had a willing heart. After Rebekah and the servant arrived back at the house, her father also believed this marriage was of God and gave his blessing. When her father and brother asked Rebekah, she replied, without question or hesitation, that she would go with the servant. I wonder if she had any idea what she was doing. I am sure she knew she could trust God's plan. She had a willing heart.

We, too, need to have willing hearts in our marriages—hearts that give up their own wills for the good of another. Rebekah could have selfishly asked for more time or to meet Isaac first, but she didn't think of herself and what she needed. She wanted what would please God. Our attitudes and actions need to please God in our homes. Be willing to say "I will do it" or "I will go."

No one knows better than God whom we should marry. He knows all about us. We can trust God with our desire for a good marriage. Even a match made in Heaven has to be lived out day to day here on earth. We need God's help in order to live this way. He gives us His Word, His Holy Spirit, and people to guide us down the right path. Trust Him for a mate who is a believer, is a faithful servant, and has a willing heart. Also trust Him for a marriage that is pleasing and honoring to Him.

Nametags

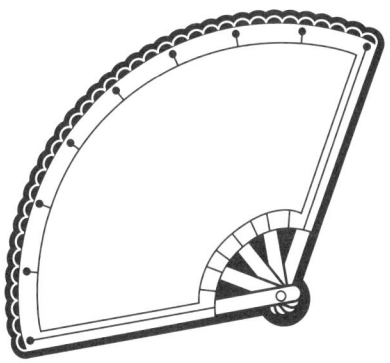

Prizes

- Tea towels
- Flavored teas
- Flavored hot chocolate mixes
- Jams and jellies
- Lace doilies

Recipes
Egg Salad Sandwiches

8 eggs
½ cup Miracle Whip
1 teaspoon prepared mustard
2 tablespoons sugar
Salt and pepper to taste

Boil eggs for 15–20 minutes. Drain and let cool in cold water. Peel and chop eggs into small pieces. Mix with rest of ingredients and spread on slices of bread. Cut off crusts and cut into triangles.

Ham Salad Sandwiches

1 lb. bologna
1 lb. hot dogs
Sweet pickle relish
Miracle Whip to taste

Grind bologna and hot dogs in food processor. Add sweet pickle relish and Miracle Whip. Spread on slices of bread. Cut off crusts and cut into triangles.

Cinnamon Crunch Muffins

3 cups flour
1½ cups brown sugar, firmly packed
2 teaspoons cinnamon, divided
½ teaspoon salt
1 teaspoon ground ginger
½ cup shortening
2 teaspoons baking powder
½ teaspoon baking soda
2 eggs, beaten
1 cup buttermilk
½ cup chopped pecans

1. In a large bowl, stir together flour, sugar, 1 teaspoon cinnamon, salt, and ginger. Add shortening; mix until crumbly.

2. Put $^2/_3$ cup of flour mixture into a small bowl. Add 1 teaspoon cinnamon and pecans. Set aside to use for the topping.

3. Add baking powder and baking soda to the remaining mixture; stir well. Add eggs and buttermilk; stir just until blended. Spoon batter into buttered muffin tins, filling each cup about $^2/_3$ full. Sprinkle muffins with the reserved topping. Bake at 375°F for 15–20 minutes.

Poppy Seed Muffins

1$^1/_2$ cups flour
$^1/_2$ cup wheat germ
$^1/_3$ cup poppy seeds
$^1/_3$ cup sugar
1 tablespoon baking powder
$^1/_2$ teaspoon salt
1 cup milk
1 egg
$^1/_4$ cup unsalted butter, melted

1. In a large bowl, stir together flour, wheat germ, poppy seeds, sugar, baking powder, and salt. Set aside.

2. In a small bowl, whisk together milk, egg, and butter until smooth. Add to dry ingredients and stir just until blended. Spoon into buttered muffin tins, filling each cup about $^2/_3$ full. Bake at 400°F for 15–18 minutes.

Blueberry Muffins

2 cups flour
$^2/_3$ cup sugar
2$^1/_2$ teaspoons baking powder
$^1/_4$ teaspoon baking soda
$^1/_2$ teaspoon salt
1 teaspoon cinnamon
1 cup milk
2 eggs, beaten
$^1/_2$ cup butter, melted
1 cup fresh or drained blueberries

1. In a large bowl, stir together flour, sugar, baking powder, baking soda, salt, and cinnamon. Set aside.

2. In another bowl, whisk together milk, eggs, and butter until smooth. Add to dry ingredients and stir until blended. Slowly stir in blueberries. Spoon into buttered muffin tins, filling each cup until $^3/_4$ full. Bake at 400°F for 15–18 minutes.

Dreamy Summer Nights

Theme and Decorations

- Hang sheer dark blue material with clear lights behind to look like a starry, romantic summer night.
- Sprinkle gold star confetti around star-shaped votive candles on dark blue tablecloths.
- Decorate with tropical flowers.

Food

- Coconut Cream Cake
- Pineapple Torte
- Tropical Punch
- Chocolate star candies
- Macadamia nuts

Games

Star Quiz

Answer the following questions.

1. What star is the name of a bird? _____
2. What star is called the sailor's friend? _____
3. What star is mentioned on a ship? _____
4. What star is used in a laundry? _____
5. What star means to move suddenly? _____
6. What star is found in a famine? _____
7. What stars are in the U.S. national anthem? _____
8. What is a little star (actress) called? _____
9. What star is found in water? _____
10. Who is our bright and morning star? _____
11. What star is used in a nursery rhyme? _____
12. What did Captain Kirk drive? _____

Answers

(1) Starling; (2) North Star; (3) starboard; (4) starch; (5) startle or start; (6) starve; (7) bright; (8) starlet; (9) starfish; (10) Jesus; (11) star light, star bright; (12) starship.

Dreamy Words Puzzle

Use the words below to fill in the puzzle.

Words to Use

GROOM	LOVE
USHER	MUSIC
GIFTS	PHOTOGRAPHER
TUXEDO	ALTAR
INVITATION	GOWN
RING	HONEYMOON
CHURCH	GUESTS
BRIDE	PUNCH
PASTOR	CAKE
CANDLES	MINTS

Dreamy Words

Answers: Dreamy Words

Songs

"Stars Get in My Eyes"
"Stardust"
"When You Wish upon a Star"
"This Is My Father's World"
"It Took a Miracle"

Devotions
Walk with God

God's Creation

Woman was created from the rib of man.
Not from his head was she created to be above him.
Nor from his feet to be trampled upon.
She was created from his side to be equal to him.
From under his arm to be protected by him,
And close to his heart to be loved by him.

—Author unknown

Some of us can't think of anything more romantic than a moonlit starry summer night, walking hand in hand along an ocean beach with the one we love. It sounds like a good honeymoon spot, doesn't it? Stars, moonlight, and ocean waves are all part of God's creation.

Sometimes the best part of the day is when we ponder the awesome beauty God has created for us to enjoy. At those times we can relate to Genesis 3:8, when God came to walk with Adam in the cool of the day. Some of the most precious times as a couple are the times you will spend walking and talking with God. I'd like to share three ways we can walk or talk with God.

First, we can walk with God by seeing His glory and handiwork in the world. In Psalm 19:1 and 2 David reminded us that the created universe performs a silent but eloquent symphony to the glory of God both day and night. In verses 3 and 4 David wrote that the voice of the heavens is heard throughout the earth so that everyone can recognize God in creation. But it is not enough to know only that there is a Creator. We need to know God as our Savior and trust Him alone for eternal life. He offers eternal life as a free gift. All we have to do is receive that gift, the gift of His Son. *(Read Ephesians 2:8 and 9.)*

Second, we can also walk with God as we read and study His Word. Psalm 19:7–11 shows us how we can see God in His Word. The verses in this passage state His character. *(Read the verses.)*

• God is perfect (without fault).
• God is sure (doesn't vary or move).
• God is right (straight).
• God is pure (without sin).
• God is clean (without impurities).
• God is true (dependable) and righteous.

As we read God's Word, we grow in our walk with Him. His Word tells us about Who He is and what great things He has done for us. As a couple, you and your husband can find many devotional books to help you in your walk with God. Start your walk with Him by spending time together in God's Word.

Third, we can talk with God as we spend time with Him in prayer. Talking with God should be like calling a good friend, but with God you don't get a busy signal. He is always there and always has the right counsel. *(Read Hebrews 4:16 and Philippians 4:6.)* We can come boldly to God's throne and find grace in our time of need. *(Read Luke 11:9 and James 1:5.)* Find the time to pray. Life can get hectic, and it can easily steal away

our time spent with God if we let it. Don't let precious moments with God slip by. Don't get that busy.

We can walk and talk with God in the cool of the day, just as Adam and Eve did. Enjoy your dreamy summer nights together with each other and God.

Nametags

Prizes

• Star-shaped candles
• Chocolate star candy
• Mounds candy bars
• Starburst candy
• Macadamia nuts

Recipes
Coconut Cream Cake
CAKE
  ½ cup shortening
  ½ cup margarine
  2 cups sugar
  5 eggs, room temperature
  1 cup buttermilk
  1 teaspoon baking soda
  2 cups flour
  1 tablespoon vanilla
  1⅔ cups coconut

FROSTING

½ cup margarine, softened
1 (8 oz.) pkg. cream cheese, softened
1 lb. powdered sugar
1 tablespoon vanilla
1 cup coconut
1 cup chopped nuts

1. For cake, cream shortening, margarine, and sugar. Separate eggs; add yolks to shortening mixture. Combine buttermilk and baking soda. Stir buttermilk and flour, alternately, into egg mixture. Beat egg whites until stiff; add vanilla. Fold into cake mixture. Fold in coconut. Spray and flour three 8" or 9" pans. Bake at 350°F for approximately 30 minutes.

2. For frosting, cream margarine and cream cheese. Add powdered sugar and vanilla. Fold in coconut and nuts. Frost cake. Sprinkle additional coconut on top.

Pineapple Torte

½ lb. vanilla wafers, crushed
½ cup butter
1½ cups powdered sugar
2 eggs, beaten
1 (20 oz.) can crushed pineapple, drained
1 pint whipping cream

1. Butter a 9" x 13" glass baking pan. Put vanilla wafer crumbs in the bottom of the pan. Save a few crumbs for the top.

2. Cream together butter and powdered sugar. Add eggs and mix well. Pour mixture over crumbs. Spread crushed pineapple on top of creamed mixture.

3. Whip the cream and spread on top of pineapple. Sprinkle with reserved crumbs. Refrigerate overnight.

Tropical Punch

6 cups water
1 cup sugar
1 (46 oz.) can pineapple juice
1 (12 oz.) can frozen orange juice, thawed
1 (12 oz.) can frozen lemonade, thawed
1 (2 liter) bottle ginger ale

1. Heat water and sugar until sugar is dissolved, about 2 minutes. Add pineapple juice, lemonade, and orange juice. Freeze.

2. Remove from freezer 1 hour before serving. Mash with knife or potato masher. Add ginger ale.

Falling in Love

Theme and Decorations

- Emphasize a fall theme by decorating with autumn flowers, small pumpkins, and Indian corn.
- Drape tables with artificial grape vines that you've entwined with cream tulle; add fall leaves or gold-colored leaves as accents.
- Light pumpkin-scented candles.

Food

- Pumpkin Cheesecake Roll
- Nuts
- Grape Punch

Games

Names You Might Fall For

1. thewraseet _____
2. beba _____
3. ppniumk _____
4. fifmnu _____
5. garsu _____
6. yeonh _____
7. baodrteam _____
8. stbe ifenrd _____
9. stewiee iep _____
10. tebter fhal _____
11. ym ovle _____
12. eoucrisp _____
13. rldaign _____
14. read _____
15. galen _____
16. plngdumi _____
17. bbya ldol _____
18. letordutev _____

Answers

(1) Sweetheart; (2) babe; (3) pumpkin; (4) muffin; (5) sugar; (6) honey; (7) dreamboat; (8) best friend; (9) sweetie pie; (10) better half; (11) my love; (12) precious; (13) darling; (14) dear; (15) angel; (16) dumpling; (17) baby doll; (18) turtledove.

Don't Fall for the White Lie

Ask each guest to write down two true statements and one lie about their own wedding or dating experiences. The lies should sound like something that could be true; the truths should sound a bit outlandish. Put their lists in a bowl, and then let each guest draw one to read. Have the other guests try to figure out which statement is the lie and who wrote the statements.

Songs

"Falling in Love Again"
"Why Do Fools Fall in Love?"
"Sweeter as the Years Go By"
"When Love Shines In"
"L-O-V-E"

Devotions

Falling in Love

Fall is some people's favorite time of year. They love the cool, crisp air. They love the changing colors and leaves falling to the ground. They love the smells and sounds of harvest. On a breezy fall day on the farm, they can hear the cornstalks crackle and smell the corn as it goes through the combine. The trees turn orange and red and golden yellow, and the grass seems to get greener. Even the sunsets in the fall are more beautiful, with the pinks, yellows, purples, and reds on the backdrop of a bright blue sky. And, of course, there are the pumpkin patches and the apple orchards. In the fall a farm kitchen is filled with the smells of apple pie, apple cider, and apple butter.

But even as special as fall is, falling in love is grander. Our bride to be, _____, has fallen for _____. We hear the term "falling in love," and it sounds romantic. Some may picture a leaf slowly floating on a slight breeze to the ground. It falls slowly and naturally.

Falling in love isn't quite that easy, however. First Corinthians 13 gives us some thoughts on love.

First, love is essential. *(Read 1 Corinthians 13:1–3.)* Love is not an option for us. If we don't have love, we are nothing. If we don't show love, our tongues merely make noise, our knowledge and faith amount to nothing, and our good deeds are of no profit to us. When we choose to marry someone, we love him and want to live with him forever. Love is a choice. Sometimes people think after a few years of marriage that they fall out of love with each other. I really think they choose not to love anymore, not to put any effort into their marriage. We need to love unselfishly. God's example to us is how He unselfishly gave His love to us in the gift of His Son. Christ's love for us is undeserved, not expecting us to love Him in return. *(Read 1 John 4:10.)* That is the kind of love we need for each other. God's love is essential.

Second, love is a demonstration. *(Read 1 Corinthians 13:4–7.)* Our love is shown by how we act. Are we patient, kind, unselfish, truthful, hopeful, and enduring to others and to our mates? In ourselves, we can't be all these things because they go against our sin nature. It is through God's working in and through us that we can show love. He is the only One Who can show us how to love, because He is love. Love here is not described as feelings but by acts of doing. God demonstrated His love to us in that while we were yet sinners, Christ died for us (Rom. 5:8). God's love is a demonstration.

Third, love draws us closer and helps us mature. *(Read 1 Corinthians 13:8–13.)* When the church first started, it was immature, so God gave believers extraordinary gifts to help them grow spiritually. After the New Testament was completed and the church began to mature, these gifts were no longer needed. Prophesies were no longer needed, tongues were no longer needed, knowledge vanished away, but love didn't fail. It was greater than the others.

As we grow closer to God, we will grow in our love for Him and for others. Being patient, kind, unselfish, truthful, hopeful, and enduring will be easier as we become more mature in the Lord. Love will help strengthen the relationships in our home and with those around us. God's love draws us together and helps us mature.

Remember how great the fall season is? Well, it is kind of like this: Now there are spring, summer, winter, and fall, but the greatest of these is fall. When it comes to falling in love, there are faith, hope, and love, but the greatest of these is love.

Nametags

Prizes

- Pumpkin-scented votive candles
- Fall kitchen towels

- Bottle of sparkling grape juice
- Small gold picture frame
- Stationery with leaf design

Recipes
Pumpkin Cheesecake Roll
CAKE
>   3 eggs
>   1 cup sugar
> $^2/_3$ cup canned pumpkin
>   1 teaspoon lemon juice
> $^3/_4$ cup flour
>   1 teaspoon baking powder
>   2 teaspoons cinnamon
>   1 teaspoon ginger
> $^1/_2$ teaspoon nutmeg
> $^1/_2$ teaspoon salt
>   1 cup chopped walnuts (opt.)
>   Powdered sugar

FILLING
>   2 (3 oz. each) pkgs. cream cheese,
>   softened
>   1 cup powdered sugar
>   4 tablespoons butter
> $^1/_2$ teaspoon vanilla

1. For cake, beat eggs on high speed for 5 minutes. Slowly beat in sugar. Stir in pumpkin and lemon juice. Combine flour, baking powder, cinnamon, ginger, nutmeg, and salt in a separate bowl. Fold into pumpkin mixture.

2. Spread batter on a greased and floured jelly roll pan (or a cookie sheet with edges). Sprinkle 1 cup chopped walnuts on batter, if desired. Bake at 375°F for 15 minutes. Then turn cake onto a muslin dishtowel (not terry cloth) dusted with powdered sugar. Roll up and refrigerate for 30 minutes.

3. For filling, beat cream cheese, powdered sugar, butter, and vanilla until smooth. Spread on unrolled cake. Roll up cake again and refrigerate. Slice to serve.

Grape Punch

Mix equal amounts of white or purple grape juice with ginger ale.

Hearts Entwined

Theme and Decorations

- Hang red, white, and pink hearts and streamers.
- Decorate tables with heart-shaped balloons, valentine candy, and red doilies on white lacy tablecloths.
- Place small, red heart-shaped boxes of chocolates and red or pink candles on each table.
- Make a poster with two heart shapes entwined; add the groom's picture on the left and the bride's picture on the right.

Food

- Dainty sandwiches
- Chocolate-covered strawberries
- Cherry Cheesecake
- Icy Red Punch

Games

Love Match Icebreaker

Draw a large heart and divide it into several sections. Write the statements below, one to a section. Give a copy of the heart to all your guests. Ask them to find ladies who can initial the various statements. The first guest to get all the sections initialed wins the game. You can use each lady's initials only once.

Suggested Statements

Has received 12 red roses
Cries at romantic stories
Wearing something red
Kissed spouse on first date
Has eaten a candy Kiss today
Wearing heart-shaped jewelry
Has driven a "love bug" (VW)
Can recite a Bible verse with love in it
Had a crush on a teacher
Dated a man named Tom, Dick, or Harry
Has already purchased a Valentine

Heart Word Scramble

Can you find heart-related words in the puzzle below?

Heart Word Scramble

```
L  T  V  C  W  T  H  D  R  A  C
N  C  A  N  D  Y  A  H  T  E  C
F  L  O  W  E  R  S  E  H  N  B
M  N  H  R  I  E  K  A  E  I  K
S  X  R  R  D  D  D  R  A  T  I
C  H  O  C  O  L  A  T  E  N  S
N  U  S  L  P  M  T  C  E  E  S
O  G  E  F  I  W  E  X  V  L  A
F  E  B  R  U  A  R  Y  O  A  T
D  X  Y  S  W  E  E  T  L  V  Z
```

Words to Use

FEBRUARY	DATE
CHOCOLATE	VALENTINE
CANDY	FLOWERS
LOVE	CARD
WIFE	SWEET
KISS	HEART
HUG	RED

Answers: Heart Word Scramble

Bible Hearts

Fill in the blanks with the missing words from these Bible verses that contain the word "heart."

1. "For man looketh on the outward _____, but the LORD looketh on the heart" (1 Sam. 16:7).

2. "Praise ye the LORD. I will _____ the LORD with my whole heart" (Ps. 111:1).

3. "Thy word have I hid in mine heart, that I might not _____ against thee" (Ps. 119:11).

4. "For as he _____ in his heart, so is he" (Prov. 23:7).

5. "For where your _____ is, there will your heart be also" (Matt. 6:21).

6. "Let not your heart be _____: ye believe in God, believe also in me" (John 14:1).

7. "For with the heart man believeth unto righteousness; and with the mouth confession is made unto _____" (Rom. 10:10).

8. "The heart is _____ above all things, and desperately wicked" (Jer. 17:9).

9. "Create in me a _____ heart, O God; and renew a right spirit within me" (Ps. 51:10).

10. "That Christ may _____ in your hearts by faith" (Eph. 3:17).

11. "The sacrifices of God are a broken spirit: a broken and a _____ heart, O God, thou wilt not despise" (Ps. 51:17).

12. "_____ me, O God, and know my heart: try me, and know my thoughts" (Ps. 139:23).

13. "Blessed are the _____ in heart: for they shall see God" (Matt. 5:8).

14. "A _____ heart doeth good like a medicine" (Prov. 17:22).

15. "_____ in the LORD with all thine heart" (Prov. 3:5).

Answers

(1) Appearance; (2) praise; (3) sin; (4) thinketh; (5) treasure; (6) troubled; (7) salvation; (8) deceitful; (9) clean; (10) dwell; (11) contrite; (12) search; (13) pure; (14) merry; (15) trust.

Songs

"Always"
"L-O-V-E"
"Near to the Heart of God"
"Written in Red"
"In My Heart There Rings a Melody"
"Let Jesus Come into Your Heart"

Devotions
Love Is from God

Love is in the air. This is the time of year when we are excited about sending or receiving a special valentine. It may be a heart-shaped construction paper valentine, sprinkled with glitter and signed with Xs and Os from a four-year-old. Or it might be a Hallmark card with a heartfelt "I love you, Mom" from a daughter. Or a dozen red roses with a card signed "To my darling wife." We want the ones we love to know how dear and special they are to us.

Being in love is so much fun. Young, dreamy-eyed couples express their love to each other with flowers, candy or other treats, teddy bears, balloons, or a romantic candlelit dinner. But as those of us who have been married for a while know, true love grows deeper over time. And whether it's romantic love or another kind of love, our love as Christians should reflect God's love. First John 4:7 and 8 remind us that love is from God and that He is love. God is our example of how to love unselfishly.

First, God is love. *(Read 1 John 4:8–10 and 19.)* God courted us and wooed us to Himself. Maybe you were the one who noticed that boy across the classroom, and you went a little out of your way to meet him. Then he asked you out for a soft drink (or pop) after the ball game. The pursuit was on. He wooed you with cards, candy, and flowers. Whoa, maybe I got carried away! Anyway, you wanted to spend time together until you decided he was the one. You chose him to be your husband. Likewise, God chooses us. He chose us before the foundation of the world. *(Read Ephesians 1:4.)* His Holy Spirit woos us to Him, and we choose to accept His gift of eternal life through His Son, Jesus Christ. Only then can we love unselfishly. God's love in us will enable us to love like Him.

Second, God is forgiving. *(Read 1 John 1:9 and Psalm 86:5.)* God is always ready to forgive. We, on the other hand, are self-centered and sinful; we want others to hurt when they hurt us. The quicker we can forgive and forget, the better life will be. Nothing is worth the anger and bitterness that build up when we are unwilling to forgive our mate. Forgiving isn't always easy, but it is the best way. We will be wiser and happier when we follow God's good example to be ready and willing to forgive.

Third, God is good to us. *(Read James 1:17, Psalm 68:19, and Matthew 7:11.)* It is just natural to want to do good things for the ones we love. Maybe it is preparing your husband's favorite dinner of lasagna and apple pie. We daily clean and do laundry and run children to and fro with little thanks, just because we love them. How much more God desires to give us good things in our lives. Sometimes we get too busy; we forget to look around us and see God's goodness. Daily He loads us with benefits. We need to show His goodness to others.

Fourth, God is our God. *(Read Psalm 100:3.)* We need to be devoted to God. He wants us to be His alone. We belong to Him when we accept Christ as our Savior. When we exchange wedding vows, we make a covenant with each other to be faithful and devoted. We choose to love and cherish until death. As Christians, we need to be devoted to the Savior and faithful to Him. In Revelation 21:2 and 9 God talks about believers as the Bride of Christ. We (the church) will be as a bride made ready for her husband to live with him forever. Psalm 100:3 declares that we are God's people, the sheep of His pasture. As our Shepherd, He loves, cares for, and protects us, much like a husband loves, cares for, and protects his wife. What a comfort to know we are God's and He is *our* God.

Fifth, God gave His all. *(Read 1 Timothy 2:6, Galatians 2:20, and Galatians 1:4.)* Anytime a wedding takes place, many people give. The mother and father give away their daughter. The guests give gifts to the couple to help furnish their new home, and the bride and groom give themselves to each other in pledges of undying love. Like the people at a wedding, Jesus Christ gave. He gave Himself so we could have eternal life. He willingly died in our place. He definitely gave His all. God the Father gave His only Son. *(Read or quote John 3:16.)* We need to love the Lord with all our heart (Mark 12:30) and, with the heart, to believe (Rom. 10:9); then we will be saved (Rom. 10:13).

We truly can get our example of love from God. (1) He is love, and we can learn to love unselfishly as He did. (2) He is forgiving, and we need to forgive our mates and others when they hurt us. (3) He is good, and we can learn to do good things for the ones we love. (4) He is our God, and we can show His devotion by being devoted and faithful to our mates. (5) He gave His all by giving His Son. We can have eternal life by confessing with our mouth the Lord Jesus and believing in our hearts that God raised Him from the dead (Rom. 10:9).

Nametags

Prizes

- Balloons
- Box of chocolates
- Conversation heart candies
- Red or pink candles
- Lace doilies
- Hershey's Kisses

Recipes

Icy Red Punch

1 (6 oz.) pkg. red gelatin dessert
2 cups sugar
8 oz. reconstituted lemon juice
1 (46 oz.) can pineapple juice
1 (2 liter) bottle ginger ale

1. Dissolve gelatin in 1 cup hot water. Mix all ingredients except ginger ale. Pour into a 1 gallon container. Add water to make 1 full gallon. Stir well and freeze.

2. Remove from freezer 1–1$^{1}/_{2}$ hours before serving. Chop until slushy with a wooden spoon. Add ginger ale.

Cherry Cheesecake
CRUST
    12 graham crackers, crushed
    4 tablespoons margarine, softened
    $^{1}/_{2}$ cup sugar

FILLING
    1 (8 oz.) pkg. cream cheese, softened
    1 cup powdered sugar
    1 tablespoon milk
    1 teaspoon vanilla
    1 (8 oz.) container frozen whipped topping, thawed
    1 can cherry pie filling

1. For crust, combine graham crackers, margarine, and sugar. Press mixture into a 9" pie pan. Bake at 350°F for 5–7 minutes. Cool.

2. For filling, beat together cream cheese, powdered sugar, milk, and vanilla. Fold whipped topping into cheese mixture. Spread on crust and chill. Top with cherry pie filling and serve.

Love Notes

Theme and Decorations

- Decorate in black and white; use red as an accent color.
- Cut musical notes out of black paper. Display notes on walls and tables.
- Place music boxes of various shapes, single roses in vases, and bowties from men's tuxedos on tables.
- Display violins around the room or on tables.
- Burn white tea lights or candles.

Food

- Symphony Cakes
- Red Rose Mints
- Mixed nuts

Games

Name That Tune

Give each guest a sheet of paper and a pencil. Play a few notes of familiar love songs on a piano or keyboard. The person with the most correct answers wins the game. A variation is to divide the guests into teams.

Love Note Mad Lib

Without telling the story, ask each guest to fill in a blank in the story on page 25 with a noun, adjective, verb, or adverb. Read the story aloud later. Replace Bride and Groom with your honored bride's and groom's names.

Marriage Mix-Ups

The bride packed her suitcase for the honeymoon; the groom dropped it loading it into the car. Everything is mixed up. What did she have in her suitcase? Unscramble these words.

1. hosse _____
2. greniile _____
3. tumwsisi _____
4. ssoblue _____
5. ylwjeer _____
6. eoynpaths _____
7. reesssd _____
8. tlbe _____
9. rteswae _____
10. sskoc _____
11. kcalss _____
12. nesja _____
13. egeglinse _____

Answers

(1) Shoes; (2) lingerie; (3) swimsuit; (4) blouses; (5) jewelry; (6) pantyhose; (7) dresses; (8) belt; (9) sweater; (10) socks; (11) slacks; (12) jeans; (13) negligees.

Songs

"Arise, My Love"
"Lavender Blue, Lavender Green"
"My Wild Irish Rose"
"Why Do I Sing about Jesus?"
"In My Heart There Rings a Melody"
"Love Lifted Me"

A _____ Note
_{noun}

One day (Groom) headed to work at the _____. He was _____ by the beautiful
_{place}   _{adjective}

new girl there. Her name was (Bride). He immediately asked her for a _____. They had a lot in
_{noun}

common. They both loved _____. (Groom) played _____ in school and (Bride)
_{sport/activity}   _{sport/activity}

_____ too. Now things were moving _____. (Groom) wanted her to be his
_{action verb}   _{adverb}

_____. (Bride) knew marriage would take lots of patience and _____, but she was
_{noun}   _{noun}

ready. She loved him and thought, "This will be a piece of _____." (Groom) pulled up to
_{noun}

(Bride's) apartment in his _____, _____ car. (Bride) came out wearing a new
_{adjective}   _{color}

_____ and her _____ shoes. (Groom) whisked her away for a _____ walk
_{clothing}   _{color}   _{adjective}

on the beach, where he asked her to marry him. (Bride) was so _____! She happily smiled and
_{adverb}

said, "Soon we will be married; won't that be _____! (Groom) answered, "On our honeymoon,
_{adjective}

we will fly to _____. We will swim in the _____ and _____ under the palm
_{place}   _{place}   _{verb (present tense)}

trees. When we come home, we will live in a _____ beside the _____. "And the best
_{noun}   _{noun}

thing," (Bride) said, "is we will never be lonely again because I am hoping we will have a dozen

_____ to keep us company."
_{noun (plural)}

Devotions
Love Notes

Oh, to be young and in love! Some of us have been there, and others are there right now. When you and your spouse were dating, did you ever write little love notes for him to find or write long-distance love letters or send love cards? Do you have love letters tucked secretly away somewhere? Why did you like receiving them? Why do we write love letters? I think the reason I liked receiving a love letter was because it showed me I was loved and missed and cared for deeply by someone. It made my day. By sending a love letter, I could verbalize my love for someone, which is sometimes hard to do face-to-face. Maybe you are miles apart, and it is your way of communicating love to your special someone.

The Bible book called the Song of Solomon records some "love notes" of a lover and his beloved. It was probably King Solomon and the Shulamite girl he was going to marry. You don't have to read far to realize he was crazy about her. She had captured his heart. All through the Song of Solomon, we see their love for each other. They spared no words in describing their feelings.

First, their love for each other was romantic. (*Read Song of Solomon 1:9 and 10 and 2:3.*) Solomon described his beloved as the fairest among women. He compared her to a company of horses, praising her for grace and beauty. She described him as an apple tree with sweet-tasting fruit. It is probably true that women are a little more romantic than men, but Solomon had a lot of sweet things to whisper to his beloved.

Second, their love for each other was affectionate. (*Read Song of Solomon 2:10–14.*) The lovers couldn't stand being apart. They delighted in each other's company and longed to be together again. It was only with him that she felt safe and secure.

Third, they declared their love for each other. (*Read Song of Solomon 2:4.*) The Shulamite woman wanted everyone to know they were in love and going to be married. In Bible times military troops were divided, and a banner was put over each group to declare which group a soldier was in. The Shulamite girl wanted all to see that Solomon had a banner over her, and his banner over her was love. It was his love for her that made him willing to protect and care for her. Don't we declare our love to each other when we decide to become engaged? Everyone wants to see the ring (our banner) that declares our love for each other and our desire to be husband and wife.

Fourth, their love for each other was permanent. (*Read the first part of Song of Solomon 8:6.*) The Shulamite woman asked for ownership of her lover's heart. She wanted him to be hers alone. In Bible times a seal stamped on a document indicated possession and gave the document great importance and value. Like the notary stamps of today, once the imprint was on the paper, it was permanent. The Shulamite woman wanted a seal on her lover's heart for his affection and a seal on his arm for his embrace and protection. The seal showed permanence. Our marriages are permanent. That's the way God planned it. Our love needs to be love that lasts a lifetime.

Fifth, their love for each other was strong and unyielding. (*Read the remainder of Song of Solomon 8:6.*) Their love was as final and irreversible as dying. Don't let anyone or anything break down your marriage. Refuse to give up on each other. Love is strong when God is present in our marriages. (*Read Ecclesiastes 4:12.*) We want our marriages to be strong and unyielding.

Sixth, their love for each other was unquenchable. (*Read the first part of Song of Solomon 8:7.*) Love can be as unquenchable as fire. Have you ever been around a fire that is out of control? The love described in Song of Solomon 8:7 between the two lovers was powerful, like a raging fire that even water couldn't put out. We can have that kind of love for our mates, if we choose to. When we first get married, things seem grand. Then life becomes harder. The bills come in. The kids come along. It takes hard work on our part, but we can have unquenchable love with God's help. Don't let many waters put out the flame.

Seventh, their love for each other was priceless. (*Read the second part of Song of Solomon 8:7.*) You can't buy love. The kind of love that we desire in our marriages is priceless. To even think of buying love is foolish. Sometimes we are guilty of buying each other's affections with gifts or flowers, when really what we want the most is time together with the one we love the most. Giving of ourselves is the best gift of love. Love is priceless. Christ showed us how great and priceless when He died on the cross for our sins.

God has given us His love letter in the form of His Word, the Bible. In it He tells of His love for us. *(Read John 15:11–14.)* Love is a choice, and if we love God, we will follow His commands. Love is a choice in our marriages. Solomon and his beloved made choices that made their love strong and enduring. Their love was romantic, affectionate, declared, permanent, unyielding, unquenchable, and priceless. That is the kind of love we need today.

Nametags

Prizes

- Symphony candy bars
- "Note" pads
- Red roses in vases
- Stationery (love letters)

Recipes

Red Rose Mints

1 egg white
1 lb. powdered sugar
½ cup shortening
Red food coloring
3 drops oil of peppermint flavoring

Mix ingredients together and knead until dough is of working consistency. Press into rose-shaped molds.

Symphony Cakes

CAKES
   1 white cake mix
   1 chocolate cake mix

FILLING
   ¾ cup flour
   3 cups milk
   2 cups sugar
   1 cup margarine
   2 teaspoons vanilla
   2 cups powdered sugar
   1 teaspoon salt
   1 cup shortening

1. Prepare cakes as directed on packages. Bake in 9" x 13" pans. Let cool; then remove from pans and slice lengthwise.

2. For filling, combine flour and milk; heat in saucepan until thick, stirring constantly. Remove from stove and cool. In large bowl cream together the sugar, margarine, vanilla, powdered sugar, salt, and shortening. Add to cooled milk mixture. Beat until fluffy, about 2 minutes.

3. Spread filling on a white cake layer and a chocolate layer. Top the white layer with a chocolate layer and vice versa. Cover cakes and store in a cool place overnight. Do not refrigerate. The flavor is better if cakes are made the day ahead.

Love's a Bloomin'

Theme and Decorations

- Place watering cans on the table. Fill with daisies or other springtime flowers.
- Set wooden wheelbarrows around the room. Fill them with gardening supplies and potted plants.
- Accent decorations with the bride's colors.
- If available, have a tandem bicycle in the room to go along with the song "Bicycle Built for Two." (See "Songs.")

Food

- Layered Lemon Dessert
- Lovely Lemon Pie
- Luscious Lemon Cake
- Assorted crackers or pretzels
- Iced tea, water, or lemonade with lemon slices

Games

Flowery Love Story

Name the flower described in each sentence of this love story.

1. What's the bride's name? What's the color of her hair?
2. When her groom looks into her eyes, what color do her cheeks turn?
3. What is the color of her eyes?
4. What part of her eyes have color?
5. What did the groom do when he proposed?
6. What did he lay at her feet?
7. How did he feel when she accepted?
8. His name was Bill, but she called him this name.
9. What did he call her?
10. What time was the wedding?
11. What did they both feel as they were waiting?
12. Who gave the bride away?
13. When the wedding march started, what did the people do?
14. The groom's brother played what musical instrument?
15. Who stood when the wedding march started playing?
16. What were the names of the two bridesmaids?
17. What met when the bride and groom kissed?
18. Overcome with emotion, what did the mom do?
19. Who married them?

Words to Use

aster	iris	rose
balsam	jack in the	rosemary
bleeding	pulpit	sweet pea
heart	marigold	sweet william
four o'clock	mum	trumpet (vine)
glad	pink	tulips
impatiens	poppy	violet

Answers

(1) Marigold; (2) pink(s) or rose; (3) violet; (4) iris; (5) aster; (6) bleeding heart; (7) glad; (8) sweet william; (9) sweet pea; (10) four-o'clock; (11) impatiens; (12) poppy; (13) rose; (14) trumpet (vine); (15) mum; (16) rosemary; (17) tulips; (18) balsam; (19) jack in the pulpit.

Garden Dress-Up

Gather a supply of gardening items for this game: a big floppy hat, a trowel, a basket of seeds, a flower pot, gardening gloves, a watering can, a hoe, a rake, and the like. Ask two friends of the bride-to-be to dress her up so she will be ready to work in the flower garden at her new home. When they are done, have the bride leave the room. Distribute paper and pencils to the guests; tell them to list as many of the gardening items as they can remember.

Songs

"When Love Shines In"
"In the Garden"
"Bicycle Built for Two" ("Daisy, Daisy")
"You Are My Sunshine"
Medley of "In the Good Old Summertime"; "In the Shade of the Old Apple Tree"; "By the Light of the Silvery Moon"; and "Ida, Sweet as Apple Cider"

Devotions

Love's a Bloomin'

Isn't springtime beautiful? The countryside turns green with little patches of life. Soon brightly colored flowers are blooming and sending their warmth and fragrance around us. Brides have traditionally chosen springtime to get married. It is the time of year when love is in the air. A good marriage, like a good flower garden, grows and blooms over the years. And just like a successful flower garden, a successful marriage requires hard work.

The first thing you need to do is start with good soil. If the ground is rocky or has lots of clay, it will be difficult to grow anything beautiful or lasting. Begin your marriage with the good soil of God's Word. First, make sure that both you and your husband-to-be know and love God and desire to serve Him. You can know God's will for your lives by reading, studying, and thinking about His Word. His Word is good soil to be in, so start digging.

Next you need to plant the seeds. The best seeds you can sow are seeds of love (1 Cor. 13). You can show people you love God by loving others. *(Read John 13:34 and 35.)* It is not hard to see that our bride and groom have sown seeds of love. *(Read Mark 12:30 and 31.)* They love God, they love their neighbors, and they definitely love each other.

Third, a good flower garden needs lots of water. If you want a happy home, keep the watering can handy. Water your marriage with words of encouragement, kindness, and forgiveness. Ephesians 4:32 says, "Be ye kind one to another, tenderhearted, forgiving one another, even as God for Christ's sake hath forgiven you."

Fourth, a successful flower garden needs sunshine to make it grow. The sunshine in a marriage is prayer. You have probably been in the sunshine and felt its warmth and rays. Just like it feels good to bask in the sun, you should bask your home and loved ones in prayer. Your husband-to-be needs you to pray for him daily. Philippians 4:6 says, "Be [anxious] for nothing; but in every thing by prayer and supplication with thanksgiving let your requests be made known unto God." First Thessalonians 5:17 says, "Pray without ceasing." Your marriage will blossom and grow as you pray together.

One more thing a good garden needs so it can flourish is weeding and pruning. I always hate that job! It isn't fun. But that's how it is in our lives too. It is not fun when God prunes out the negative things from our lives and has to discipline us. We want to hang on to those feelings of anger or jealousy or whatever it might be that is hindering our spiritual growth. First Corinthians 13:4–6 says that love is not jealous or easily provoked to anger. It is not proud or self-centered or rude. No marriage can survive with these feelings growing. They need to be cut out quickly before they take over. After they are gone, we can grow and mature in the things of God.

A good marriage is like a flower garden. It takes good soil (God's Word), good seed (love), lots of water (kind and forgiving words), plenty of sunshine (prayer), and pruning (discipline). When you decide to have a flower garden in your yard, you make a commitment to yourself that this year it is going to be the best ever. In your marriage, make a lifelong commitment, and over the years your marriage will grow in God and become a sweet-smelling fragrance to those around you. A good marriage, like a good flower garden, is truly a thing of beauty.

Nametags

Prizes

- Gardening gloves
- Flower seeds
- Hand lotion
- Silver picture frame
- Daisies from tables
- Watering can

Recipes

Lemonade

6 cups water
1 cup plus 2 tablespoons sugar
½ cup freshly squeezed lemon juice

Boil the water and add the sugar. Boil for 2 minutes and let cool. Add the lemon juice and ice. Serve with lemon slices.

Layered Lemon Dessert

FIRST LAYER
1 cup cold margarine
2 cups flour
1 cup chopped pecans

SECOND LAYER
2 (8 oz. each) pkgs. cream cheese, softened
1 cup powdered sugar
1 (8 oz.) container frozen whipped topping, thawed

THIRD LAYER
2 (3.4 oz. each) pkgs. instant lemon pudding and pie filling
4½ cups cold water, divided
4 egg yolks

FOURTH LAYER
1 (8 oz.) container frozen whipped topping, thawed

1. For base layer, cut margarine and flour until crumbly. Stir in pecans. Press into a 9" x 13" pan. Bake at 350°F for 12–15 minutes until lightly browned. Cool.

2. For second layer, combine cream cheese and powdered sugar. Beat well. Fold in whipped topping and spread over cooled crust.

3. For third layer, combine pudding mix, 1 cup water, and egg yolks in a sauce pan; blend until smooth. Stir in remaining water; bring to boil over medium heat until thickened. Cool. Spread over cream cheese layer.

4. For fourth layer, spread whipped topping over lemon layer. Refrigerate.

Lovely Lemon Pie

CRUST

$1\frac{1}{2}$ cups lemon cookie crumbs

$\frac{1}{2}$ cup chopped almonds

$\frac{1}{4}$ cup butter, melted

FILLING

1 cup powdered sugar

2 (3 oz. each) pkgs. cream cheese, softened

$\frac{1}{2}$ cup sour cream

$\frac{1}{2}$ cup frozen whipped topping, thawed

TOPPING

1 (3.4 oz.) pkg. instant lemon pudding and pie filling

1 teaspoon fresh lemon juice

$1\frac{3}{4}$ cups milk

1 teaspoon grated lemon rind

$\frac{1}{2}$ cup frozen whipped topping, thawed

Lemon-drop candies

1. For crust, combine cookie crumbs, almonds, and butter. Press into bottom of 9" pie pan. Bake at 300°F for 10 minutes. Cool.

2. For filling, mix together powdered sugar, cream cheese, sour cream, and whipped topping. Pour into cooled crust.

3. For topping, mix together milk, lemon juice, lemon rind, and pudding mix. Spread on cream cheese layer. Add whipped topping and crushed lemon-drop candy. Refrigerate.

Luscious Lemon Cake

CAKE

1 lemon cake mix

FROSTING

1 (3 oz.) pkg. cream cheese, softened

$\frac{1}{2}$ cup butter, softened

4 cups powdered sugar

1 teaspoon vanilla

3 tablespoons lemon juice

3 teaspoons grated lemon peel

1. Prepare lemon cake according to directions on box. Bake in two 9" round pans. Cool.

2. Beat frosting ingredients until fluffy. If needed, add a little more lemon juice, 1 teaspoon at a time. Frost cake.

'Tis the Season for Love

Theme and Decorations

- Decorate with burgundy or white poinsettias on lacy white tablecloths.
- Accent with fresh greenery entwined with clear Christmas lights.
- Float candles in clear jars or vases filled with water and cranberries.
- Use burgundy and dark green ribbon for the bows on the jars or on the ends of the greenery.

Food

- Petite Cucumber Sandwiches
- Crepes
- Cream Puffs
- Wedding Tea Cakes
- Chocolate Orange Slices
- Eggnog

Games

Seasonal Scramble

Unscramble these words that remind us of the holidays.

1. deutliey _____
2. hasiscrmt _____
3. alrngcoi _____
4. awtreh _____
5. lgnae _____
6. burche _____
7. hcruch _____
8. psteresn _____
9. teficuark _____
10. cissgotnk _____
11. ntrmeaons _____
12. brionb _____
13. wosb _____
14. dacnle _____
15. lmtetosie _____
16. areyybrb _____
17. iglhse _____
18. tnlise _____
19. cymnhie _____
20. cseoiok _____
21. seedshprh _____
22. grenam _____
23. veregrnee _____
24. sjeus _____
25. lyhlo _____

Answers

(1) Yuletide; (2) Christmas; (3) caroling; (4) wreath; (5) angel; (6) cherub; (7) church; (8) presents; (9) fruitcake; (10) stockings; (11) ornaments; (12) ribbon; (13) bows; (14) candle; (15) mistletoe; (16) bayberry; (17) sleigh; (18) tinsel; (19) chimney; (20) cookies; (21) shepherds; (22) manger; (23) evergreen; (24) Jesus; (25) holly.

Rolling Pin Advice

Cut out slips of paper in the shape of a rolling pin. Ask the ladies if they have ever heard this old rhyme: "When you get married and your husband is cross, pick up a rolling pin and show him who's boss."

The rhyme does *not* tell the best way to handle an angry husband! Have each lady write the bride a piece of advice on how to calm an angry husband. They should write their advice on the rolling pin–shaped papers. Give the papers to the bride to keep. Have her read aloud some of the advice.

Tips for Married Bliss

Unscramble the following phrases of advice for a newly married couple.

1. vahe a fsot weansr _____
2. veas a nneyp _____
3. evah tecepain _____
4. peke inslmign _____
5. ryael ot dbe, rylea ot esri _____
6. aevh a sseen fo umhor _____
7. voel dna eb odlve _____
8. tciparec sdseknin _____
9. sedpn mtie oehretgt _____
10. ndto og to edb ayrng _____
11. tpu dgo rifst _____
12. eb no meti _____
13. kas frieesogvns _____
14. epek ruoy rmsseiop _____
15. velo si oeervrf _____

Answers

(1) Have a soft answer; (2) save a penny; (3) have patience; (4) keep smiling; (5) early to bed, early to rise; (6) have a sense of humor; (7) love and be loved; (8) practice kindness; (9) spend time together; (10) don't go to bed angry; (11) put God first; (12) be on time; (13) ask forgiveness; (14) keep your promises; (15) love is forever.

Songs

"Mary, Did You Know?"
"What Child Is This?"
"It Came upon a Midnight Clear"
"Joy to the World"
"There's a Song in the Air"
"Silent Night, Holy Night"

Devotions
'Tis the Season

Christmas is such an exciting time! Christmas shopping, decorating the tree, and baking goodies are great, but Christmastime is even more exciting and special when you are planning a wedding. It is neat to see how God works in two people's lives to bring them together.

Mary and Joseph were young and engaged to be married. They had the makings of a perfect couple, yet God had a difficult road for them to travel. I am sure they looked to the future with plans of a family and a carpenter shop, but God had plans to use that couple to fulfill His redemptive plan for mankind. Before they were even married, an angel told them Mary would have a baby boy and that God the Holy Spirit would be the Father. Mary and Joseph had to change their plans.

Then they had to travel to Bethlehem to pay taxes, and Mary ended up having the baby in a cattle stall because all the rooms in the inn were taken. Another change in their plans.

Later they had to relocate because Herod wanted to kill their young son. Wow, another change in their plans. That is a lot of stress on a new marriage. Mary and Joseph showed great courage and commitment. They chose to trust and obey God. They knew He was in control.

We can learn from their example as they started their married life. God had an amazing plan for them, and He does for your marriage too. Every marriage will have unexpected troubles and hardships. Life always seems to have lots of twists and turns, but those changes can bring a couple closer to each other and closer to God.

Through your marriage, you can show the love of God by how you (1) love your mate (Titus 2:4; Eph. 5:25); (2) raise your children (Prov. 22:6; Eph. 6:4); (3) respond to others and forgive (Eph. 4:32; Matt. 6:14); and (4) love God and give Him thanks (Ps. 68:19).

This holiday season as you think about the Christmas story with Mary and Joseph and their love for each other and for God, take time to reflect on your love for your husband-to-be. Thank God for your love for each other, but most importantly, thank Him for His Son, Jesus . . . the reason for the season we celebrate.

Nametags

Prizes

- Christmas ornaments
- Lace doilies
- Cranberry candles
- Mistletoe

Recipes

Petite Cucumber Sandwiches

1 pkg. (3 oz.) cream cheese, softened
1 pkg. Good Seasons Italian salad
     dressing mix
Miracle Whip to taste
1 loaf party rye bread
Cucumbers
Dill weed

Mix together cream cheese and salad dressings. Spread on party rye bread. Place a cucumber slice on top and sprinkle with dill weed. Makes enough for one small loaf.

Crepes

$2/3$ cup flour
$1/2$ teaspoon salt
3 eggs
$1 1/2$ cups milk
$1 1/2$ tablespoons margarine, melted
Melted margarine to coat skillet
Ice cream and toppings
Nuts

1. In medium bowl, with wire whisk or hand beater, beat flour, salt, and eggs until smooth. Gradually beat in milk and $1 1/2$ tablespoons melted margarine until blended. Cover and refrigerate at least 2 hours.

2. Brush bottom and sides of a 7" skillet with margarine. Heat skillet on low. Pour in $1/4$ cup batter, tipping pan to coat bottom. Cook until top is set and underside is lightly browned, about 3 minutes. Turn crepe and cook on other side, about 1 minute. Slip crepe onto waxed paper. Repeat until all batter is used, stacking with waxed paper between crepes.

3. Cool completely; remove waxed paper; fill with ice cream. Roll up and drizzle with hot caramel, chocolate, and nuts. Serve immediately.

Wedding Tea Cakes

1 cup margarine
$1/2$ cup powdered sugar
$2 1/4$ cups sifted flour
$1/4$ teaspoon salt
1 teaspoon vanilla
$3/4$ cup chopped pecans

Cut ingredients together with pastry cutter. Chill dough for 1 hour. Shape into small balls or logs. Place on cookie sheet. Bake at $450°$F for 7–10 minutes. Cakes will be brown on the bottom but not on the top. Roll in powdered sugar. Cool and roll in powdered sugar again.

Cream Puffs

1 cup hot water
½ cup margarine
1 cup flour
4 eggs
1 (3.4 oz) pkg. vanilla instant pudding and
    pie filling
1 (8 oz.) container frozen whipped topping,
    thawed

1. Boil water and margarine. Add flour. Stir until dough comes loose from the sides. Add eggs one at a time. After adding each egg, beat 30 seconds with electric mixer or 5 minutes by hand.

2. Drop by spoonfuls on greased cookie sheet. Bake at 450°F for 10 minutes, then at 325°F for 20 minutes. Let cool. Cut small slit in top of each to let dry.

3. Prepare pudding according to directions on box. Fold in whipped topping and fill each puff. Sprinkle with powdered sugar. Cream puffs freeze well.

Chocolate Orange Slices

Dip store-bought candy orange slices into melted dipping chocolate and then into coconut.

To Have and to Hold

Theme and Decorations

- Decorate with a "hugs and kisses" theme. Stamp imprints of red lips on disposable white tablecloths. Use black and silver for accent colors.
- Place a vase of red tulips (two lips) on each table.
- Sprinkle heart-shaped silver and red confetti on tablecloths.
- Toss Hersey's Hugs and Kisses on tables.

Food

- Chocolate Praline Cake
- Dipped Pretzels
- Fresh strawberries dipped in white chocolate

Games

Packed for the Honeymoon

This game is a relay race. Pack two suitcases with clothes the bride will need for her honeymoon, such as a robe, shoes, a belt, a hat, and a necklace. Divide guests into two teams, and choose two "non-runners" to be the inspectors. Put suitcases on chairs on the opposite side of the room. Have ladies remove their shoes. One lady from each team will run to the suitcase and put all the clothes on over her own clothes, except for shoes. When she gets the okay from the inspector, she repacks the clothes, shuts the suitcase, and runs back to the next person in her line. Keep going until everyone has had the clothes on and the last person puts the clothes back in the suitcase, shuts it, and crosses back over the starting line.

Silly Song

Ask someone to pantomime the song "Hold Me, Hold Me" by Frankie Avalon. Have that person dress up like the groom-to-be in a man's suit.

Envelope Door Prize

Purchase a package of thank-you cards. As each guest arrives, hand her an envelope from the package and have her address it to herself. Before the end of the shower, have the bride draw an envelope out of a bowl and give a door prize to the person whose name is on that envelope. Then give the bride the stack of envelopes and the thank-you cards to send to the guests.

Wedding Words

Write wedding-related words (bride, groom, gift registry, etc.) at the top of index cards—one card for each word. Below each word, write five words you would use to make someone guess the word. Divide the guests into two teams. Have each team take turns giving their own team clues to guess the "wedding" words without saying the clues on the cards. Each team has one minute to guess as many words as they can. Give one point for each correctly guessed word; subtract one point for each time a clue was used. The winning team is the one with the most points.

Songs

"O Love That Will Not Let Me Go"
"Trust and Obey"
"Tiptoe through the Tulips"

Devotions
Leave and Cleave!

What Love Can Do

Love can make a sad heart sing,
A beggar feel just like a king,
A cloudy sky looks bright and blue.
That's what love can do.

Love can ease a broken heart,
Make the common look like art,
Change the winter into spring.
Love can do most anything.

Love can stand the strongest test,
If you spare time to invest.
Find a love that is deep and true.
See for yourself what love can do.

—Author unknown

Few brides-to-be stop to think about all the things they will have to leave behind and what things they will have to hold onto to make their marriage a success. When you are young and in love, life is grand. You are excited to be making a new home of your own. You really don't see a problem in leaving your childhood home. It is a natural part of adulthood. When we meet the person of our dreams and decide to get married, God tells us in Genesis 2:24 that we will need to leave and cleave. (*Read Matthew 19:5.*)

When we hold one thing and reach for something else, we need to completely let go of the first object so we can hold securely to the object we are reaching for. It is that way when we start a new home together as husband and wife. We can't be split between two households. We must let go of one to be able to start another.

First, we must leave our parents physically. This "leaving" is easy to understand. Married couples need a home of their own, a place where the two can develop a bond with each other. Through childhood, parents provided a house to live in and physical protection. Now, as a bride and groom, you will learn to look out for each other's needs and to protect each other. You need a place where you can create a home using the good lessons you each learned from your parents.

Second, we must leave our parents financially. This "leaving" is a little harder sometimes. As a couple you have to budget your hard-earned dollars. The hardest thing is not to run to parents for help. You may need them in an emergency, but if you follow Biblical principles of finances and if you use self-discipline in spending, you will not depend on their financial support.

Third, we need to leave our parents emotionally. This "leaving" can prove the hardest for some people. Maybe your relationship with your parents wasn't the best, and you harbor bitterness toward them. When you have unresolved problems, they will go with you and cause problems between you and your spouse. Emotional ties to our parents can interfere in our desire to cleave to our mate. Ask God to show you areas of conflict and how you can let them go. Only then can you truly depend on your mate and grow closer to each other.

Fourth, we need to leave our parents spiritually. Your husband is the spiritual leader in the home. He is the one you are to look to for spiritual guidance. Your dad may have been the spiritual leader in your home, or you may not be used to having a spiritual leader. Either way, now you must adjust and let your husband be the head of your home. Ephesians 5:21–31 speaks to us about the chain of submission in our homes. First is God. Equal to God but under submission to Him is Jesus Christ. In the home, the husband is under Christ. Equal to the husband but under submission to him is the wife.

Husbands are to love their wives and lead them in spiritual things. Wives are to submit to their husbands' leadership and are to love and respect them. When we follow this chain of submission in our families, we honor God and receive His blessing.

Nametags

Prizes

- Napkin holders
- Lip gloss
- Pot holders
- Tulips

Recipes

Chocolate Praline Cake

CAKE

    $\frac{1}{2}$ cup butter or margarine
    $\frac{1}{4}$ cup whipping cream
    1 cup brown sugar
    $\frac{3}{4}$ cup chopped pecans
    1 devil's food cake mix
    $1\frac{1}{4}$ cups water
    $\frac{1}{3}$ cup oil
    3 eggs

TOPPING

    $1\frac{3}{4}$ cups whipping cream
    $\frac{1}{4}$ cup powdered sugar
    $\frac{1}{4}$ teaspoon vanilla
    Whole pecans and chocolate curls (opt.)

1. In a saucepan, combine butter, $\frac{1}{4}$ cup whipping cream, and brown sugar. Melt over low heat. Add chopped pecans and pour mixture into two 9" round pans.

2. In a large mixing bowl, beat cake mix, water, oil, and eggs for two minutes. Spoon over pecan mixture. Bake at 350°F for 35–45 minutes. Cool 5 minutes and remove from pans.

3. For topping, beat $1\frac{3}{4}$ cups whipping cream until soft peaks form. Add powdered sugar and vanilla. Beat until stiff peaks form.

4. Place first layer on a cake plate, praline side up; frost with half the topping. Add second layer, praline side up; frost with remaining topping. Add pecans and chocolate curls, if desired.

Dipped Pretzels

1 pkg. (14 oz.) caramels
1 tablespoon water
15–20 large crunchy pretzel twists (about 4" wide, $\frac{1}{2}$" thick)
4 (1 oz. each) squares semisweet chocolate, chopped
1 teaspoon shortening
Finely chopped pecans

1. Lightly butter large cookie sheet and set aside. In a small saucepan, combine unwrapped caramels and water. Cook and stir over low heat until caramels are melted. Remove from heat.

2. Dip each pretzel into the caramel mixture about $\frac{3}{4}$ of the way down. Let excess caramel drip off each pretzel and place on the prepared cookie sheet. (If caramel sauce is too thin, let it set for a few minutes; it will thicken.)

3. In another small saucepan, place chocolate and shortening. Cook over low heat until chocolate is melted and smooth. Cool slightly. Spoon chocolate into a small plastic bag. Use scissors to snip a small hole in one corner of the bag. Drizzle chocolate over pretzels. Sprinkle with nuts. Chill in the refrigerator about 20 minutes.

Warm Hearts around the Fire

Theme and Decorations

- Decorate with snowmen of all shapes and sizes.
- Hang glittery snowflakes and red hearts.
- Accent with real or artificial greenery, holly berries, and fake snow.
- Be sure to have candlelight to add warmth to the atmosphere.
- For the skit, make a fake fireplace out of cardboard. Add an electric fire log or wood logs with a light underneath. Throw a rug in front of the fireplace. Set two chairs or a couch on the rug.
- Arrange photos of the honored couple on the fireplace mantel.
- If it is Christmastime, decorate a Christmas tree.

Food

- Three-tiered white cake with snowmen on top
- White Almond Bark Nuggets
- Hot Chocolate
- Red Hot Apple Cider

Games

Who Has My Heart?

Cut out one large paper heart for each guest; write the name of a famous person on each heart. As each lady arrives, hang one of the paper hearts around her neck so that it hangs down her back. Each lady should ask other ladies, "Who has my heart?" and then can ask questions that can be answered only yes or no. Each guest may ask each other person only one question. When a guest guesses "who has her heart," she can move her heart to the front and sit down.

Wedding Warmth

Find the verb that best tells a dating couple or wedding participants what to do.

1. _____ the candles.
2. _____ the cake.
3. _____ the pastor.
4. _____ the question.
5. _____ the engagement.
6. _____ the bride.
7. _____ a tear.
8. _____ the guest book.
9. _____ the vows.
10. _____ a ring.
11. _____ the church.
12. _____ the invitations.
13. _____ the gifts.
14. _____ in prayer.
15. _____ some rice.
16. _____ the car.

Words to Choose From

Decorate	Repeat	Pop
Open	Pay	Address
Announce	Kiss	Choose
Sign	Bake	Reserve
Light	Throw	
Kneel	Shed	

Answers

(1) Light; (2) Bake; (3) Pay; (4) Pop; (5) Announce; (6) Kiss; (7) Shed; (8) Sign; (9) Repeat; (10) Choose; (11) Reserve; (12) Address; (13) Open; (14) Kneel; (15) Throw; (16) Decorate.

Skit

Winter Wonderland Skit

Ask a couple to pantomime "Winter Wonderland" and "Let It Snow, Let It Snow, Let It Snow." Have the couple wear wool scarves and stocking hats. As the music leads into "Let It Snow, Let It Snow, Let It Snow," the couple should head to the fireplace and take off their scarves and hats. At the end of the skit, have everyone join the couple in singing these words to the tune of "We Wish You a Merry Christmas."

We wish you a happy marriage;
We wish you a happy marriage.
We wish you a happy marriage
And a home filled with love.
These presents we bring (point to gifts)
For you and your beau;
We wish you a happy marriage
And a home filled with love.

Songs

"Let It Snow, Let It Snow, Let It Snow"
"Winter Wonderland"
"Whiter Than Snow"
"Give Me Thy Heart"
"Thy Word Have I Hid in My Heart"

Devotions
Warm Hearts around the Fire

It's cold outside, and the snow is falling. You and your sweetheart are cuddled up by the fireplace drinking steamy hot chocolate and eating freshly popped popcorn. You listen as the fire crackles, and you make plans for your future together. Sounds like a wonderful evening, doesn't it? Warm and snuggly inside, as the world becomes a blanket of white outside. Everything is fresh and clean when it is covered with newly fallen snow.

God's Word talks about how our hearts can be whiter than snow. They can be washed clean from sin and its stain. (Read Psalm 51:7 and 10.) We can keep our hearts pure (whiter than snow) before a holy God. (Read Matthew 5:8 and Psalm 119:11.) If we want to have hearts that are pure and clean, we need to spend time reading, studying, and thinking about God's Word. As a couple, especially when starting a new home, it is important to spend time in His Word.

Psalm 19:7–9 describes what God's Word will do for us. (Read Psalm 19:7.) The word "law" in this verse means God's will for us. His perfect will for us is to restore our souls, or to have our souls converted to Him. God's Word in our lives will change us and give us new life. God's Word will show us the way to have eternal life with him.

(Reread Psalm 19:7.) When something is sure, it is secure and does not move. God's testimony, or His truth, does not change or move. We can count on His Word to make us wise. It will help us with decisions for our families. We can count on God and His Word because His Word never changes. In this world, where things change quickly, we need God to be our rock, our anchor, and our hope because we know His Word is sure and steadfast and will be there to guide us in every situation we face as a married couple.

(Read Psalm 19:8.) God's Word gives us direction that leads us to do what is right. When we do right, we are happy. There is nothing better than a rejoicing heart. I love to be around people who are happy and secure. The Word of God will give us that joy.

(Reread Psalm 19:8.) God's authoritative words are pure and without alloy (something that lessens the value, an alien element). When gold or silver has no impurities in it, it is without alloy. That is how God's Word is too. It is pure, so it enlightens us and helps us see things more clearly. If you feel as if you are in the dark about something and don't know what to do, go to the Word.

(Read Psalm 19:9.) When we fear the Lord, we realize He is all-powerful and all-knowing. By studying His Word, we will develop a reverence or trust in Him. The fear of the Lord is the beginning of wisdom. *(Read Proverbs 1:7.)* His Word makes us wise, and His Word is eternal.

(Reread Psalm 19:9.) God is God, and He knows what is best for us. Sometimes His judgments bring us closer to Him. *(Read Psalm 19:10 and 11.)* Success in life and in marriage will be great when we desire God's Word and spend time in it. If you want a heart that is clean and pure before God, keep His commandments. *(Read Romans 10:10.)* God takes away our sin and its stain when we confess our sin to Him. *(Read Isaiah 1:18 and Psalm 51:7.)*

As you sit around the warm fire inside and the new snow has fallen outside, think about how God makes our hearts clean and whiter than snow. Daily be reading and thinking about His Word. Your hearts will grow closer to each other as you grow closer to God.

Nametags

Prizes

- Hot chocolate mixes
- Heart-shaped cookie cutters
- Heart-shaped candy or chocolate
- Glittery snowflakes

Recipes

White Almond Bark Nuggets
1 pkg. almond bark
Salted almonds

Melt almond bark according to directions on package. Stir in salted almonds and pour onto waxed paper. When cool, break into nuggets.

Hot Chocolate Mix
3–4 cups powdered milk
$\frac{1}{2}$ cup cocoa
$\frac{3}{4}$ cup coffee creamer
1 (3.4 oz.) pkg. instant vanilla pudding and pie filling
1 (3.4 oz.) pkg. chocolate pudding and pie filling
$\frac{1}{2}$ teaspoon salt
1 cup powdered sugar
1 cup sugar

Stir ingredients until blended. Store in tight container. For a single serving, mix 2–4 tablespoons in 8 ounces of hot water.

Red Hot Apple Cider
4 cans frozen apple juice concentrate
10–12 cans water
1 orange, cut in fourths
1 pkg. red hot candies
1 teaspoon whole cloves

Put juice and water in coffee percolator. In top, put orange, red hots, and cloves. Perk.

With This Ring

Theme and Decoration

- Decorate in gold and white; use the bride's colors as accents.
- Spray gold paint on two hula hoops. Overlap the hoops with super glue or wire to make two overlapping rings. Accent with flowers, white bells, and gold ribbon. Hang the rings from the ceiling, on a wall, or on a large bulletin board.
- Slip gold craft rings on white tapered candles. (You can find craft rings in the crafts section of discount stores.) Place candles in gold candleholders.
- Tie two of the gold rings together with ribbon in the bride's colors. Toss several sets of gold rings on the tables.
- Sprinkle gold-wrapped Hershey's Kisses among the rings and candles.
- Supply a gold picture frame with a photo of the honored couple.

Food

- Traditional Ring-Shaped Wedding Cakes
- Minty Mints
- Mixed nuts
- Punch (matched to bride's colors)

Games

Drawing Rings

Give each guest a piece of paper and a pencil and ask her to shut her eyes. No peeking allowed! Instruct the group to draw two overlapping rings. Without looking, they are to write Mr. and Mrs. _____ below the rings. Then tell them to write the groom's name in the left ring and the bride's name in the right ring. Give 5 points if the rings overlap nicely, 5 points if the couple's name is centered under the rings, 5 points for the bride's name in the right ring, and 5 points for the groom's name in the left ring. The one with the most points wins.

Ring Story

Ask volunteers to tell the stories of their engagement rings: where the ring came from, where she was when she received it, etc.

A Piece of Cake

Answer the following with a kind of cake.

1. Which cake is flipped? _____
2. Which cake is crazy? _____
3. Which cake is like a piece of paper? _____
4. Which cake is the month of June famous for? _____
5. Which cake weighs a lot? _____
6. Which cake would a mouse like? _____
7. Which cake is full of tiny seeds? _____
8. Which cake is an individual serving? _____
9. Which cake is jiggly? _____
10. Which cake is heavenly? _____
11. Which cake is a vegetable from your garden? _____
12. Which cake is baked in a tube pan? _____

13. Which cake is
    always turned over?   _____
14. Which cake do you
    throw together?   _____
15. Which cake is
    stuffed with filling?   _____
16. Which cake is
    a man's cake?   _____
17. Which cake grows on trees?   _____
18. Which cake is a
    popular breakfast beverage? _____
19. Which cake
    is used to clean?   _____
20. Which cake is velvety?   _____
21. Which cake is
    a cold treat?   _____
22. Which cake is
    a kid's favorite at parties? _____

23. Which cake is
    often jelly-filled?   _____
24. Which cake is religious?   _____

Answers

(1) Pancake; (2) wacky; (3) sheet; (4) wedding; (5) pound; (6) cheese; (7) poppy seed; (8) cup; (9) Jell-O; (10) angel food; (11) carrot; (12) bundt; (13) upside down; (14) dump; (15) Twinkie; (16) groom's; (17) fruit; (18) coffee; (19) sponge; (20) red; (21) ice cream; (22) birthday; (23) rolled; (24) Scripture.

It Rings!

Give each guest a pencil and paper. Have the guests list all the things that ring, buzz, or beep at you each day. Ring a bell to start and when the time is up. Give them about five minutes to make their lists.

Ring Quiz

1. When does a ring bring luck?   When it is _ _ _ _ _ ring.
2. When does a ring bloom?   When it is _ _ _ _ ring.
3. When does a ring pay compliments?   When it is _ _ _ _ _ ring.
4. When does a ring bring good news?   When it is _ _ _ ring.
5. When does a ring seem brave?   When it is _ _ring.
6. When does a ring reply?   When it is _ _ _ _ ring.
7. When is a ring annoying?   When it is _ _ _ _ ring.
8. When does a ring cook slowly?   When it is _ _ _ _ ring.
9. When is a ring pounding?   When it is _ _ _ _ ring.
10. When does a ring give to others?   When it is _ _ _ ring.
11. When does a ring speak softly?   When it is _ _ _ _ _ ring.
12. When does a ring bring things in?   When it is _ _ _ _ ring.
13. When does a ring show affection?   When it is _ _ring.
14. When does a ring rise above all the rest? When it is _ _ _ ring.
15. When does a ring talk a lot?   When it is _ _ _ _ _ ring.
16. When does a ring make you tired?   When it is _ _ _ ring.

Answers

(1) Prospering; (2) flowering; (3) flattering; (4) cheering; (5) daring; (6) answering; (7) bothering; (8) simmering; (9) hammering; (10) sharing; (11) whispering; (12) gathering; (13) caring; (14) towering; (15) chattering; (16) wearing.

Songs

"Ring the Bells of Heaven"
"The Bells Are Ringing for Me and My Gal"
"Circle of Two"

Devotions
With This Ring

Beautiful rings are every woman's delight. From little girls to any age, we all drool over expensive gold or silver, diamond-laden rings. They come in all shapes and sizes and price ranges. It is fun to go to a jewelry store just to look around, isn't it? For a couple in love and planning to get married, shopping for a ring is a dream come true. You find a ring you both like and then patiently wait for your boyfriend to "surprise" you with it! The best part is surprising Mom and Dad and all your friends.

Do you know the origin of the wedding ring? One school of thought says it evolved from the round fetters Anglo-Saxons used to tether their abducted brides as they took the women to their new homes. Another theory is that the Egyptians, who used a circle as a symbol of eternity, first used wedding rings to denote an everlasting, unending union. Personally, I like the second theory best.

As wedding vows are spoken, think about what the ring shows.

First, "With this ring, I thee wed" shows a love that has no end. A ring is in the form of a circle. It is round with no beginning and no end. It symbolizes our unending love and commitment to each other. God has no beginning or end. God's love for us is unending, and no one can separate a Christian from God's love. (*Read Romans 8:38 and 39.*)

Second, "With this ring, I thee wed" shows a love that is valuable. A ring is made of gold or silver, a precious and expensive metal. When we give something that costs us something, it shows that we love and care enough to give our best. (*Read Proverbs 31:10.*) Song of Solomon 8:7 states that love is priceless.

Third, "With this ring, I thee wed" shows a love that belongs to someone else. When we are joined together in marriage, two become one. (*Read Genesis 2:24.*) We belong to each other. Belonging to someone doesn't mean that the person owns you. It means that the two of you work at strengthening each other's weaknesses, delight in each other's strengths, and encourage each other to be the most that God intends you to be. We can find comfort in belonging to someone. As Christians, we belong to Christ. By belonging to Christ, we become heirs!

Fourth, "With this ring, I thee wed" shows a committed love. When you say your vows, you are making a commitment to each other and to God. You are making a legally binding commitment. That means we should take what we say seriously. It is sad today to see how easily vows are broken and marriages fall apart. I am sure it grieves God when we break our promises to Him. "What . . . God hath joined together, let not man put asunder" (Matt. 19:6). God wants to be an active part of your marriage (Eccles. 4:12). The promise of God's presence in your marriage will make your love stronger and be the secret to its success. I hope you will commit your marriage to God.

As you exchange rings, remember how your ring shows an unending love, a valuable love, a love that belongs to someone else, and a committed love. God bless you in your new life together.

Nametags

Prizes

- Small gold picture frames
- Small pretty bell that rings
- Kitchen timer that rings, buzzes, or beeps
- Gummy candy rings

Recipes

Traditional Ring-Shaped Wedding Cakes

Prepare two cake mixes, one white and one chocolate. Decorate to look like double rings. Put the name of the groom on one cake and the name of the bride on the other. If you want to make a special cake, use one of the following recipes.

Applesauce Cake

CAKE

$1/2$ cup butter or margarine
1 cup sugar
$1^1/2$ cups applesauce
2 cups flour
1 teaspoon cinnamon
1 teaspoon ground cloves
2 teaspoons baking soda
1 tablespoon hot water

SAUCE

$1/2$ cup butter or margarine
2 tablespoons flour
$1/2$ cup granulated sugar
$1/2$ cup brown sugar
$1/2$ cup light cream

1. For cake, cream together butter and sugar. Add applesauce, flour, and spices. Mix baking soda and hot water; add to batter. Pour batter into two 9" round greased and floured pans. Sprinkle with granulated sugar on top before you bake. Bake at 350°F for 30–35 minutes.

2. For sauce, combine margarine and flour in a small saucepan over low heat. Add sugars; then stir in cream. Stir sauce constantly until thickened. Serve over warm cake.

Red Waldorf Cake

CAKE

$1/2$ cup shortening
$1^1/2$ cups sugar
2 eggs
2 teaspoons cocoa
2 oz. red food coloring
1 teaspoon salt
$2^1/4$ cups cake flour
1 cup buttermilk
1 teaspoon baking soda
1 tablespoon vinegar

FROSTING

1 cup milk
3 tablespoons flour
1 cup sugar
$1/2$ cup margarine
$1/2$ cup shortening
1 teaspoon vanilla

1. For cake, cream $1/2$ cup shortening and $1^1/2$ cups sugar; add eggs and salt. Mix well. Make a paste of cocoa and coloring; add to creamed mixture. Add cake flour and buttermilk alternately to the creamed mixture. Mix baking soda and vinegar together and fold slowly into batter. Bake at 350°F for 30 minutes in two 9" round pans, greased and floured.

2. For frosting, heat 1 cup milk and 3 tablespoons flour until thickened. Cool. Cream 1 cup sugar, margarine, and shortening together. Add vanilla. Stir in cooled flour and milk mixture and beat until smooth. Frost cake.

Minty Mints

1 egg white
1 lb. powdered sugar
$1/2$ cup shortening
Red food coloring
3 drops oil of peppermint flavoring

Mix together and knead until dough is of working consistency. Mold.

Poppy Seed Cake

CAKE
- 1 yellow cake mix
- 1 (3.4 oz.) pkg. instant butterscotch pudding and pie filling
- 4 eggs
- 1 cup oil
- 1 cup water
- 1 (1.25 oz.) container poppy seeds

SAUCE
- $\frac{1}{2}$ cup margarine
- 2 tablespoons flour
- 1 cup brown sugar
- $\frac{1}{2}$ cup light cream or half-and-half
- 1 teaspoon vanilla

1. For cake, beat with mixer the cake mix, pudding mix, eggs, oil, and water. Stir the poppy seeds in last. Bake in two 9" round pans at 350°F for 25–30 minutes or in a bundt pan for 35–45 minutes.

2. For sauce, combine margarine and flour in a small saucepan over low heat. Add sugar; then stir in cream and vanilla. Stir sauce constantly until thickened. Drizzle sauce over cake.

Better Than Ever Chocolate Cake

- 1 German chocolate cake mix
- 1 (14 oz.) can sweetened condensed milk
- 1 (11.75 oz.) jar caramel ice cream topping
- 1 (8 oz.) container frozen whipped topping, thawed
- 2 Heath candy bars, crushed

1. Prepare cake mix according to directions on box. Bake in two 9" round pans. Cool.

2. Poke holes in each layer with a small wooden handle. Mix together sweetened condensed milk and caramel topping; pour over cake.

3. Spread on whipped topping and sprinkle with Heath candy bars. Refrigerate.

Fancy Cake

CAKE
- 1 yellow pudding cake mix
- 4 eggs
- $\frac{1}{2}$ cup oil
- 1 (11 oz.) can mandarin oranges, with juice

TOPPING
- 1 (3.4 oz.) pkg. instant French vanilla pudding and pie filling
- 1 (5 oz.) can crushed pineapple
- 1 (8 oz.) container frozen whipped topping, thawed

1. For cake, mix together cake mix, oil, eggs, and juice; fold in mandarin oranges. Pour into two 9" round pans, greased and floured. Bake at 350°F for 25–30 minutes. Cool.

2. For topping, combine together pudding mix, pineapple, and whipped topping. Spread over cake.

Luscious Lemon Cake

CAKE
- 1 lemon cake mix

ICING
- 1 (3 oz.) pkg. cream cheese, softened
- $\frac{1}{2}$ cup butter, softened
- 4 cups powdered sugar
- 1 teaspoon vanilla
- 3 tablespoons lemon juice
- 3 teaspoons grated lemon peel

1. Prepare cake mix according to directions on box. Bake in two 9" round pans. Cool.

2. For icing, beat cream cheese, butter, powdered sugar, vanilla, lemon juice, and lemon peel until fluffy. If needed, add a little more lemon juice, 1 teaspoon at a time. Spread on cake.

Baby Showers

A Special Gift from God

(An excellent shower theme for an adopted baby.)

Theme and Decorations

- Wrap empty gift boxes (all shapes and sizes) with baby-theme paper. Place the decorated boxes around the room. (See "Prizes.")
- Accent the room with balloons and baby blocks. Spell the name of the new baby with the baby blocks.
- Fill small, empty baby food jars with water and confetti; add a floating tea candle. Tie a pink or blue ribbon around the ring of each jar.
- Make baby pacifiers with two white LifeSavers, some white decorator's frosting, and a jelly bean. Hold one LifeSaver vertically, and place the other one on top horizontally. Use frosting to hold them together. Add a jelly bean on top, and hold in place with frosting. Scatter pacifiers on tables.
- Tie a pink or blue bow around a Bible to symbolize God's gift of eternal life.

Food

- Pitter Patter Peanut Dessert
- Chubby Cheeks Chocolate Layered Dessert
- Assorted crackers
- Banana Slush Punch

Games

Mom's Gift of Advice

Supply guests with two small pieces of paper. Ask each lady to write an advice question on one piece of paper and the answer to that question on the other piece. Gather all the questions in one basket and all the answers in another basket. Pass the baskets around, and instruct each lady to draw a paper from each basket. Going around the room, ask each lady to read the question she drew and then the answer. The answers will not match the questions, resulting in fun and laughter!

Examples of Questions and Answers

Q: How will you involve the father in the first month?

A: Let him help with feedings, diaper changes, and baths.

Q: How do you calm a just-fed fussy baby?

A: Rock him over your shoulder and gently pat his little bottom.

Mixed-up Questions and Answers

Q: How will you involve the father in the first month?

A: Rock him over your shoulder and gently pat his little bottom.

Q: How do you calm a just-fed fussy baby?

A: Let him help with feedings, diaper changes, and baths.

Guessing the Gifts for Mother

Before the shower, obtain a small baby picture of the mother-to-be without letting her know. Frame the baby picture to protect it during the game.

In a large envelope, put the photograph and

diaper pins, Q-tips, a baby spoon, a baby wash-cloth, a pacifier, a teething ring, or other small baby items.

Each guest will need a sheet of paper and a pencil. Pass the envelope around the room, giving everyone thirty seconds to feel the package. Then ask the guests to write what baby items they think are in the envelope.

When everyone has finished, ask the mother to open the envelope and show everyone what is inside. The picture will be a special surprise, and the baby items will be her gifts to keep. The guest who correctly guesses the most items is also a winner.

Who Is That Baby?

Ask each guest to bring her baby picture to the shower. Make sure each lady puts her name on the back of her picture. Place all the pictures in rows on a table with a number by each picture. Ask guests to number their papers according to how many pictures there are. Give everyone ten minutes to identify the babies. The person with the most correct guesses wins.

Baby Blocks Name Game

Give every guest a piece of paper and a pencil. Instruct the guests to make as many words as they can from the baby's name, which you have spelled out with blocks. If you don't have blocks, write the first, middle, and last names of the baby on a chalkboard or large piece of paper. Give one point for each word that is three letters or fewer. Give two points for each four-letter word, three points for each five-letter word, and so on. The lady who gets the most points wins.

Fussy Babies Puzzle

Choose words from the list below to fill in the puzzle.

Words to Use (do not use spaces)

TEETHING	SHOTS	STUFFY NOSE
CROUP	TEMPERATURE	HICCUPS
HUNGRY	RASH	TUMMY ACHE
COLIC	WET DIAPER	PRICKLY HEAT

Things That Make Babies Fussy

Answers: Things That Make Babies Fussy

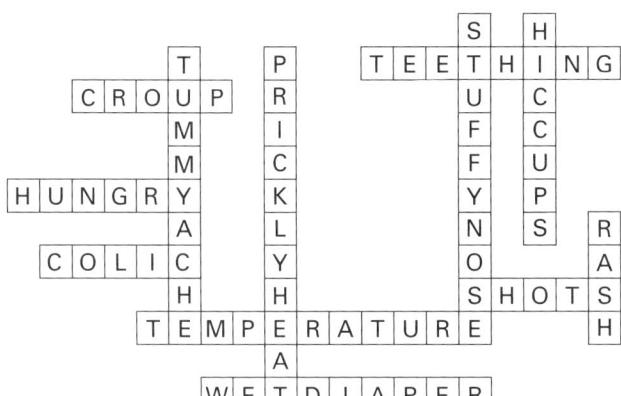

Songs

"You Are a Masterpiece"
"Something Beautiful"
"Saved by Grace"

Devotions
A Gift from God

Boxes with pretty paper and colored ribbon—they excite us, and our hearts skip a beat. "Wow, is that for me?" It doesn't even matter if the box is big or small. It's a gift. It's for us from someone who cared enough to give us something.

> _____ [mother's or parents' names] have been chosen by God to be adoptive parents to a precious new baby. Joseph "adopted" Jesus. He loved and cared for Jesus as his own child. Jesus grew up in the home of Mary and Joseph. He probably took on some of his "adopted" father's characteristics and mannerisms. He learned to work with wood just like His earthly father. Your new baby will learn your ways and actions. You may even have people say to you, "_____ [child's name] is so much like you."

Today we are celebrating the gift of something special: a precious baby. The Bible tells us why a baby is precious. (*Read Psalm 127:3.*)

What a precious gift God gives to a father and mother. (*Read James 1:17 and John 3:27.*) The baby we are honoring today is a bundle from Heaven.

One of the most precious gifts God sent from Heaven was a baby, His Son, Jesus Christ. God sent Him as a gift to bring a gift.

Romans 6:23 tells us that "the gift of God is eternal life through Jesus Christ our Lord."

I cannot imagine the offer of a gift—especially an expensive, priceless gift—and not accepting that gift with a thankful heart. But that is what people do when they don't put their faith in Jesus Christ. They reject God's gift of His Son. God promises something different for those who accept God's gift. (*Read John 1:12.*) Ephesians 2:8 explains it further. (*Read the verse.*)

Baby _____ will receive many nice gifts today. Receiving gifts is fun and exciting. Have you received the gift of eternal life? The best gift you will ever receive is Jesus Christ as your personal Savior. (*Read 2 Corinthians 9:15.*)

First, the gift of salvation in Jesus Christ gives us peace with God and forgiveness of sin. It provides deliverance, or freedom, from sin. (*Read Romans 5:1 and 8:1.*)

Second, the gift of salvation in Jesus Christ gives us freedom from the Old Testament law. (*Read Romans 10:4.*) The law required a human priest to sacrifice bulls and goats and the shedding of blood to receive forgiveness of sin. Christ became our sacrifice to God on the cross. Hebrews 10:10 tells us so. (*Read the verse.*) Christ Himself becomes our great high priest. He has experienced every facet of life and intercedes on behalf of us when we pray. (*Read Hebrews 4:14–16.*) We now come directly to God's throne of grace through Jesus, our High Priest. He gives us freedom from the law.

Third, the gift of salvation in Jesus Christ gives us fellowship with Him. (*Read 1 John 1:3.*) When we receive the gift of God's Son, we receive the gift of abundant life. Jesus said, "I am come that they might have life, and that they might have it more abundantly" (John 10:10). What a wonderful gift! We can enjoy fellowship with Jesus as we read the Bible and go to Him in prayer. Jesus' name "Emmanuel" means "God with us," and through Him we have fellowship with God.

Fourth, the gift of salvation in Jesus Christ gives us authority. Romans 8:17 calls us "children, . . . heirs; heirs of God, and joint-heirs with Christ." John 1:12 describes our authority as the "power to become the sons of God." What a privileged position we can claim with God. We go from condemnation to being joint heirs with Christ.

All these things—peace and forgiveness, freedom from the law, fellowship with God, and joint heirs with Christ—come as a result of God's gracious goodness to us in the person of His Son, Jesus. "Thanks be unto God for his unspeakable gift" (2 Cor. 9:15).

Nametags

Prizes

Wrap the products listed and use them as prizes and decorations. These prizes are designed for the winners to give to the mother (or mother-to-be). If you prefer to have the winners keep their prizes, choose other items.

- Box of cereal
- Box of diapers
- Box of baby wipes
- Box of baby detergent
- Box of Q-tips
- Baby blocks

Recipes
Pitter Patter Peanut Dessert

1½ cups crushed vanilla wafers
¼ cup butter or margarine, melted
2 tablespoons plus ½ cup chunky peanut butter
½ cup chopped peanuts
2 (8 oz. each) pkgs. cream cheese, softened
½ cup sugar
2 teaspoons vanilla
4 eggs
2 (8 oz. each) containers frozen whipped topping, thawed
1 (11.75 oz.) jar hot fudge ice cream topping

1. In a bowl, combine wafers, butter, 2 tablespoons peanut butter, and peanuts. Mix until crumbly. Press one cup of the mixture into the bottom of a 12-cup bundt pan.

2. In a large bowl, combine cream cheese, sugar, ½ cup peanut butter, and vanilla. Beat 3 minutes at high speed. Beat in eggs one at a time. Fold in whipped topping. Spoon half of the cheese mixture over the crumbs in the pan. By spoonfuls drop half of the hot fudge; then add remaining cheese mixture. Marble by cutting through with a table knife. Sprinkle with remaining crumbs; freeze until solid.

3. Remove dessert from freezer 30 minutes before you serve it. Then unmold it onto a serving dish and drizzle with more hot fudge sauce. Sprinkle with peanuts, if desired.

Chubby Cheeks Chocolate Layered Dessert

FIRST LAYER
  1 cup flour
  ½ cup margarine
  ¼ cup chopped pecans

SECOND LAYER
  1 (8 oz.) pkg. cream cheese, softened
  ½ (12 oz. divided) container frozen
      whipped topping, thawed
  1 cup powdered sugar

THIRD LAYER
  2 (3.4 oz. each) pkgs. instant chocolate
  pudding and pie filling
  1 tablespoon vanilla
  3 cups milk

FOURTH LAYER
  ½ (12 oz. divided) container frozen
      whipped topping, thawed
  Chopped pecans (opt.)

1. For first layer, cut flour, margarine, and pecans with a pastry cutter. Press into a 9" x 13" pan and bake at 350°F for 12–15 minutes. Cool.

2. For second layer, beat the cream cheese, 6 oz. whipped topping, and powered sugar until smooth. Spread on first layer.

3. For third layer, stir pudding, vanilla, and milk until thickened, about 1 minute. Place on second layer.

4. Spread remaining whipped topping on top. Sprinkle with pecans, if desired.

Banana Slush Punch

4 cups sugar
6 cups water
1 (46 oz.) can pineapple juice
1 (46 oz.) can orange juice
5 ripe bananas, mashed
2 lemons, squeezed
1 (2 liter) bottle ginger ale

Cook sugar and water about 5 minutes until dissolved. Cool. Combine bananas and lemon juice. Add juices. Mix well and freeze. Thaw 3 hours before serving. Add ginger ale right before serving. Makes 5 quarts.

Baby Farm Animals

Theme and Decorations

- Decorate with all kinds of stuffed farm animals, such as puppies, kittens, ducklings, chicks, and bunnies.
- Set children's barn sets or farm animal sets and children's farm animal books on tables.
- If the baby is a boy, use toy tractors for decorations.
- Hang a pair of baby bib overalls on the corner of a table; use an appropriate shirt to indicate a boy or a girl.
- Set straw bales around the room.

Food

- Sugar Cookies (shaped like farm animals)
- Candy Corn Mix
- Slushy Fruit Cups

Games

Baby Farm Animal Cries

Hide wrapped candies around the room ahead of time. Divide the ladies into groups of three or four. Assign each group a baby animal name, such as baby chicks, puppies, kittens, colts, calves, lambs, or ducklings. Give the leader of each group a bandana, a small bucket, or a new cloth diaper for collecting the candy.

No one starts looking for candy until you shout "Go." When someone finds a piece, she must make the noise of her team's animal to get her leader's attention. Only the leader may collect the candy. Therefore, the guests may need to cry really loud to get their group leader's attention. When all the candy has been found, the teams keep and divide what they have collected in their sacks.

Baby Animal Names

What do you call a baby . . .

1. cat   _____
2. deer   _____
3. goat   _____
4. cow   _____
5. goose   _____
6. donkey   _____
7. fox   _____
8. chicken   _____
9. duck   _____
10. dog   _____
11. sheep   _____
12. pig   _____
13. raccoon   _____
14. rabbit   _____
15. swan   _____

Answers

(1) Kitten; (2) fawn; (3) kid; (4) calf; (5) gosling; (6) foal; (7) kit; (8) chick or chicklet; (9) duckling; (10) puppy; (11) lamb; (12) piglet; (13) kit; (14) kit or bunny; (15) cygnet.

Name Scramble

Unscramble these names for mothers and babies.

1. amma   _____
2. am   _____

3. mmo _____
4. ormeth _____
5. dream _____
6. summ _____
7. amma mai _____
8. mkpupin _____
9. etwse epa _____
10. gumdlnpi _____

Answers

(1) Mama; (2) ma; (3) mom; (4) mother;
(5) madre; (6) mums; (7) mamma mia;
(8) pumpkin; (9) sweet pea; (10) dumpling.

Songs

"New Life in Christ"
"Because He Lives" (stanza 2)
"Old McDonald Had a Farm"
"The Farmer in the Dell"
"Just as I Am"
"Look to the Lamb"

Devotions
New Life

Tiny yawns and sleepy sighs.
Nursery rhymes and lullabies.
Ticklish tummies, sweet, toothless smiles.
Precious little baby styles.
A brand new life has just begun.
Thank You, God, for this little one.
—Author unknown

Babies are so precious, new little lives. We are thankful for our new baby, _____ _____. Most of us marvel at the birth of a baby. If you have ever visited a farm or seen a TV program about farm life, you may have seen a newborn colt struggle to stand on wobbly legs. Or you may have seen newborn puppies blindly search for a place to nurse on their mother. Have you ever seen someone help pull a calf? Being born in early spring, the baby calf comes from a warm womb into a

chilly world. Its big, wide-open eyes take in its new surroundings. Or how about baby chicks? Maybe you even owned one. Chicks are soft, and they make the cutest little cheeping sounds. You've probably seen an orphaned lamb, being fed milk from a baby bottle. Or how about kittens? On a farm they can be found tucked away between bales of hay. You might want to sit and watch mother and babies for hours. New life on the farm is exciting!

It's even more exciting to think about the new life that Christ offers to us. (*Read 2 Corinthians 5:17.*) We all like new things. Even if it is a small item, it is always fresh and clean. That is how our lives can be when we put our faith in Jesus Christ and in what He did for us on the cross. We can receive forgiveness for our sins through His shed blood. Then God gives us a clean slate.

What we need to do is simple.

First, we must realize we are sinners. (*Read or quote Romans 3:23.*)

Second, we must confess that because we are sinners, we need a Savior. (*Read or quote Romans 10:9.*)

Third, we must trust in Christ for eternal life. (*Read 1 John 5:12.*) How do we receive eternal life? It is a gift. Romans 6:23 reads, "For the wages of sin is death; but the gift of God is eternal life through Jesus Christ our Lord." John 1:12 tells us that when we believe in Christ and receive Him, He gives us "power to become the sons of God." And Romans 6:4 says that "like as Christ was raised up from the dead by the glory of the Father, even so we also should walk in newness of life."

I hope you have put your faith in Jesus Christ and that today you are "[walking] in newness of life." As we open gifts today for the baby and see new outfits and clean bibs and blankets, think about how we, too, can have clean hearts and brand-new lives as we trust in Christ.

Nametags

Prizes

These prizes are designed for the winners to give to the mother (or mother-to-be). If you prefer to have the winners keep their prizes, choose other items.

- Boxes of frosted animal crackers
- Rubber duckies
- Stuffed animals
- Bib with an animal on it

Recipes

Sugar Cookies

1 cup margarine
1 cup sugar
3 eggs
3¾ cups flour
½ teaspoon salt
1 teaspoon baking soda
2 teaspoons cream of tartar
1½ teaspoons vanilla

1. Cream together margarine and sugar. Add eggs and blend well.

2. Sift together flour, salt, soda, and cream of tartar. Gradually add flour mixture to creamed mixture. Add vanilla; chill dough thoroughly (at least 1 hour).

3. Roll chilled dough on floured surface and cut with cookie cutters. (Use farm animal shapes if available.) Bake on ungreased cookie sheet at 375°F for 6–8 minutes. Frost.

Decorator's Frosting

½ cup shortening
¼ cup milk
¼ teaspoon vanilla
4 cups powdered sugar

Mix together, adding sugar one cup at a time. Beat on high for 4–5 minutes.

Candy Corn Mix

1 bag candy corn
1 jar salted peanuts
1 bag candy-coated chocolate pieces

Mix together the bags of candy and peanuts.

Slushy Fruit Cups

1 (6 oz.) can frozen orange juice, thawed
1 (6 oz.) can frozen lemon juice, thawed
1 (10 oz.) pkg. frozen strawberries or 1 pint fresh strawberries, sliced
2 (20 oz. each) cans crushed pineapple (do not drain)
5 bananas, sliced
1 (15 oz.) can sliced peaches
4 cups water
2 cups sugar

Combine juices, water, and sugar. Add fruit. Freeze in 9 oz. clear plastic cups. Thaw 30–60 minutes before serving.

Jesus Loves Me

Theme and Decorations

- Decorate room with pink and blue hearts.
- Set a small toy lamb and small Bible by a vase filled with fresh flowers tied with pink or blue ribbons.
- Use pink, blue, and white candles on white doilies.
- Make cutout paper chain boys or girls and string them across the front of the gift table. Fold paper accordion style; start cutting on the left. Do not cut the fold. Dolls should be joined at the hands.

- Make sock flowers by rolling baby socks, starting at the toe. Turn back the cuffs and attach green floral wire and tape for stems. Use baby bottles filled with candy for vases. Tie ribbons around the bottles and hang the nipples and covers down the sides.
- Fold napkins into triangles, points down. Fold up the bottoms and two sides; pin with small safety pins. Fill the "diapers" with pastel M&M's that are held together with tulle.

Food

- Patty-Cakes
- Heart-shaped candies
- Mixed nuts

Games

Mothers and Babies

Draw a line connecting the mother to her baby.

1. Hagar	Obed
2. Bathsheba	Jacob
3. Jochebed	Jesus
4. Hannah	Solomon
5. Eve	Timothy
6. Sarah	Moses
7. Ruth	John the Baptist
8. Eunice	Ishmael
9. Lois	Boaz
10. Rebekah	Cain
11. Naomi	Isaac
12. Rahab	Samuel
13. Mary	Eunice
14. Elisabeth	Mahlon

Answers

(1) Ishmael; (2) Solomon; (3) Moses; (4) Samuel; (5) Cain; (6) Isaac; (7) Obed; (8) Timothy; (9) Eunice; (10) Jacob; (11) Mahlon; (12) Boaz; (13) Jesus; (14) John the Baptist.

Scrambled Baby Words

1. sitbenas _____
2. irnbhigt orom _____
3. edairps _____

4. ybba wings　　　_____

5. gapar sett　　　_____

6. ditmgtnh diegefn　_____

7. licoc　　　　　_____

8. rupb　　　　　_____

9. gcoion　　　　_____

10. kirgonc hicar　_____

11. cirifepa　　　_____

12. wdpero　　　_____

13. soibtoe　　　_____

14. rca etsa　　　_____

15. nseeios　　　_____

Answers

(1) Bassinet; (2) birthing room; (3) diapers; (4) baby swing; (5) Apgar test; (6) midnight feeding; (7) colic; (8) burp; (9) cooing; (10) rocking chair; (11) pacifier; (12) powder; (13) booties; (14) car seat; (15) onesies.

Diapering Baby

Divide the ladies into pairs. Give each pair a baby doll, a cloth diaper, and two diaper pins. Ask each pair to stand side by side at a table. The one on the left can use only her left hand. The one on the right can use only her right hand. Instruct each team to work together to fold the diaper and pin it onto the baby doll. The first pair to diaper their doll properly wins. The diaper cannot fall off when the baby is picked up!

Songs

"Jesus Loves Me"

"Jesus Loves the Little Children"

"I Am So Glad That Jesus Loves Me"

Devotions

Jesus Loves Me

(Use pictures from Sunday School materials or children's Bible story books to illustrate this devotional.)

The arrival of a new baby in the family is excit-ing. Remember how you felt the first time you saw a new member of your family? It's amazing how each little bundle steals your heart away the moment you see him or her.

God loves us even more than we can love our sweet little babies. With songs such as "Jesus Loves Me" and "Jesus Loves the Little Children," we teach our young ones that God loves them. *(Show picture of Jesus and the children.)* A favorite story to teach children is the one of Jesus and the children. The disciples told the children to go away, but Jesus rebuked the disciples. Matthew 19:13 and 14 record what He said. *(Read the verses.)* Jesus took the children into His arms and blessed them. Jesus loves and cares for each of us as well.

Another favorite story is the one about the Good Shepherd. *(Show appropriate picture.)* The Good Shepherd looked and looked until he found the missing lamb. Just as Jesus took the children into His arms, He also gathers His lambs, or children, to Himself. *(Read Isaiah 40:11.)* What a picture of love!

An even greater love is when Jesus became the lamb for us. In the Old Testament, people had to sacrifice a lamb for the forgiveness of sin. When John the Baptist saw Jesus coming toward him, he announced, "Behold the Lamb of God, which taketh away the sins of the world" (John 1:29). *(Show a picture of the Crucifixion.)* Jesus was the ultimate sacrificial lamb. "For God so loved the world, that he gave his only begotten Son, that whosoever believeth in him should not perish, but have everlasting life" (John 3:16). "We love him, because he first loved us" (1 John 4:19).

We need to become childlike and put our trust in Jesus to save us from our sins and give us eternal life. Have you done that? There is no other way. *(Read Mark 10:15.)*

Give God your sincere, simple trust for eternal life. Become like a little child and believe. It's as simple as "Jesus loves me, this I know, for the Bible tells me so."

A new baby in the family and a new baby in the family of Christ—both are exciting!

Nametags

Prizes

These prizes are designed for the winners to give to the mother (or mother-to-be). If you prefer to have the winners keep their prizes, choose other items.

- Teething rings
- Baby socks
- Stuffed lamb
- Candy hearts

Recipes

Patty-Cakes

1 white cake mix
1 (3 oz.) pkg. pink gelatin dessert
1 (3 oz.) pkg. blue gelatin dessert
2 cups boiling water
1 (12 oz.) container frozen whipped topping, thawed

1. Make a white cake according to directions on box, and bake in two 9" pans or in two heart-shaped pans. Remove cakes from oven and pierce with large fork at $\frac{1}{2}$ inch intervals.

2. In separate bowls, stir 1 cup boiling water into each flavor of gelatin. Stir 2 minutes or until dissolved. Pour pink mixture over first cake. Pour blue mixture over the other one. Refrigerate the cakes 3 hours.

3. Dip pans into warm water 10 seconds to remove cakes from pans. Spread first layer with 1 cup whipped topping. Remove second cake from pan and place on top of first cake. Frost with more whipped topping. Refrigerate 1 hour.

If you know the gender of the honored baby, use all one color, if desired.

Love My Teddy Bear

Theme and Decorations

- Set a teddy bear in a small rocking chair. Dress several other teddy bears in diapers and/or baby outfits, and set them around the room.
- Place little red wagons filled with teddy bears around the room.
- Use soft-colored, snuggly blankets on the rocking chair and in the wagons.
- Display books with bear themes, such as *Goldilocks and the Three Bears* and *Corduroy*.
- Purchase helium-filled balloons for added color. Sometimes you can find balloons in the shape of a bear face.

Food

- Baby Bear Cake
- Cuddly Cupcakes
- Beary Juice Punch

Games

Same as Baby Game

The object is to see who is the same as the baby in these categories:

1. Same first name as baby
2. Same middle name as baby
3. Same initials as baby
4. Same birthday (or due date) as baby
5. Same name as the baby's mother

Whose Name Is It?

Write down the name for a boy or girl described in the phrases.

1. Used to lift a car _____
2. A soft reassuring tap with the hand _____
3. To steal _____
4. Comes at sunrise _____
5. Sung at Christmas _____
6. Something you hang curtains on _____
7. Honestly outspoken or blunt _____
8. A month of the year _____
9. A small nail _____
10. Someone who custom sews clothing _____
11. A red gem _____
12. Vegetable or beef soup _____
13. A beautiful flower with thorns _____
14. Christmas greenery _____
15. A beam of sunshine _____
16. Child's favorite cuddly bear _____
17. Amplifies voices _____
18. To wed _____
19. A colored length of yarn _____
20. The male turkey _____

Answers

(1) Jack; (2) Pat; (3) Rob; (4) Dawn; (5) Carol; (6) Rod; (7) Frank; (8) April, May, or June; (9) Brad or Penny; (10) Taylor (tailor); (11) Ruby; (12) Stu (stew); (13) Rose; (14) Holly; (15) Ray; (16) Teddy; (17) Mike; (18) Mary; (19) Hank; (20) Tom.

Songs

"A Teddy Bear Parade" (background music)
"I Love My Teddy Bear"
"Fuzzy Wuzzy Was a Bear"
"Leaning on the Everlasting Arms"
"Under His Wings"

Devotions
Secure in Our Savior

What makes you feel safe and secure? It is part of our human nature to want to be protected and loved. As parents, we also want our children to feel loved and secure. It is fun to note some of the things babies adopt to help them feel secure. Maybe it is a blanket, a thumb, or a special teddy bear. Many a mother has gone into a panic when Teddy can't be found anywhere.

For babies the safest and most secure place is Mother's arms. The warmth of her body and her soft lullabies are soothing. As children grow, they climb into Daddy's lap to snuggle. Daddy is strong yet tender and loving. As adults, we feel loved and secure in the embrace of our loved ones. Sometimes the best comfort is just being held close.

God is our Heavenly Father. He wants to put His arms around us to give us security and protection. Listen to the words of Matthew 23:37: "O Jerusalem, Jerusalem, . . . how often would I have gathered thy children together, even as a hen gathereth her chickens under her wings, and ye would not."

The book of Psalms is full of verses about hiding in the shadow of God's wings. *(Ask volunteers to read the following verses as you say the references.)*

(Volunteer reads Psalm 17:8.) The psalmist asked to be hidden in the shadow of God's wings.

(Volunteer reads Psalm 36:7.) The writer said that he took refuge in the shadow of God's wings.

(Volunteer reads Psalm 61:4.) The psalmist took refuge in the shelter of God's wings.

(Volunteer reads Psalm 63:7.) In the shadow of God's wings, the psalmist was able to rejoice.

The idea of God's "wings" is used as a symbol of protection. This is the safest place in the world to be. Psalm 91:4 says, "He shall cover thee with his feathers, and under his wings shalt thou trust."

The Holy of Holies in the tabernacle and temple contained the ark of the covenant. The wings of the two cherubim on the ark of the covenant touched. Beneath their wings was the mercy seat, the place of God's presence and glory. The high priest went into the Holy of Holies once a year to make atonement for the sins of the people and to meet with God.

We can go to God any time and pray because of what Christ did on the cross. He shed His blood for us. Under His wings we find guidance, safety, and protection.

God is available to us all the time. As our children grow, we need to show them that God is there for them and that they, too, can find comfort under His wings. Through life and all its trials and ups and downs, be secure in knowing God is there for you. He is always there for those who trust in Christ, and in that we can be secure. *(Read Matthew 28:20.)*

Nametags

Prizes

These prizes are designed for the winners to give to the mother (or mother-to-be). If you prefer to have the winners keep their prizes, choose other items.

- Bit O' Honey candy bars
- Box of Teddy Grahams
- *Goldilocks and the Three Bears* storybook
- Package of gummy bears
- A teddy bear

Recipes

Baby Bear Cake

1 yellow or chocolate fudge cake mix
1 container pink, blue, or chocolate frosting
Oreo cookies
1 stick red licorice

1. Prepare cake according to directions on the box. Bake in two round 9" cake pans or in a bear-shaped pan. Remove from oven and cool.

2. To make the round cakes into a bear face, place one cake on a plate or round platter. Then cut a large oval section out of the second cake and place on top of the first cake (bottom of the oval should match the bottom of the first cake). Cut two round ears out of the remaining cake.

3. Frost the cake with pink, blue, or brown icing. Use Oreo cookies for the eyes and nose and red licorice to make the mouth.

Cuddly Cupcakes

1 German chocolate cake mix
1 (8 oz.) pkg. cream cheese, softened
1 egg
⅓ cup sugar
1 (6 oz.) pkg. chocolate chips
Teddy Grahams (opt.)

1. Prepare cake according to directions on box. Fill paper baking cups in muffin pan ⅔ full.

2. Beat the cream cheese, sugar, and egg until smooth. Stir in chocolate chips. Drop 1 rounded teaspoon of the cheese mixture into each cupcake.

3. Bake at 350°F for 15–20 minutes.

4. Decorate with Teddy Grahams (opt.).

Beary Juice Punch

1 (128 oz.) bottle cranberry juice
1 (2 liter) bottle 7-Up
Pour together and enjoy!

Noah's Zoo

Theme and Decorations

- Decorate with Noah's ark sets and all kinds of animals. Find several large stuffed animals to set around the room.
- Use the seven colors of the rainbow in balloons, napkins, place settings, and tablecloths. The seven colors are red, orange, yellow, green, blue, indigo, and violet.
- Make a soft-colored rainbow from strips of tulle. Attach tulle onto a backdrop in the shape of a rainbow.
- Hang a yellow raincoat and hat. Place umbrellas around the room or hang umbrellas and clouds from the ceiling.

Food

- Banana-Split Boats
- Soft drinks in all the colors of the rainbow

Games

Animals in Nursery Rhymes

Fill in the blanks with names of animals.

1. Lost by Little Bo Peep _____
2. Made a visit to London _____
3. Ridden to Banbury Cross _____
4. Seen in the meadow _____
5. Was out in the corn _____
6. Stolen by Tom _____
7. Owned by Mary _____
8. Lived with Old Mother Hubbard _____
9. Frightened Miss Muffett _____
10. Went to the market _____
11. Seen with the fiddle _____
12. Was big and bad _____
13. Were blind _____
14. Lost their mittens _____
15. Laughed to see such sport _____

Answers

(1) Sheep; (2) pussycat; (3) horse; (4) sheep; (5) cow; (6) pig; (7) lamb; (8) dog; (9) spider; (10) pig; (11) cat; (12) wolf; (13) mice; (14) kittens; (15) dog.

Animals That Entered Noah's Ark

Give each lady this list of animal names. Have the ladies list the male, female, and baby names of the animals.

Animals in the Ark

ANIMAL	MALE	FEMALE	BABY
deer	_____	_____	_____
goat	_____	_____	_____
donkey	_____	_____	_____
fox	_____	_____	_____
hog	_____	_____	_____
duck	_____	_____	_____
seal	_____	_____	_____
goose	_____	_____	_____
horse	_____	_____	_____
lion	_____	_____	_____
kangaroo	_____	_____	_____

Answers

ANIMAL	MALE	FEMALE	BABY
deer	buck	doe	fawn
goat	billy	nanny	kid
donkey	jack	jenny	foal
fox	dog, reynard	vixen	kit
hog	boar	sow	shoat
duck	drake	hen	duckling
seal	bull	cow	calf
goose	gander	goose	gosling
horse	stallion	mare	foal, colt, filly
lion	lion	lioness	cub
kangaroo	boomer, buck, jack	flyer	joey

Skit

Noah and the Promises of God

The play begins with Noah and his wife walking onto the stage, both rocking back and forth as though they are on a boat. Mrs. Noah looks quite ill.

WIFE: (*groaning*) Ohhhhhhhhhhhhhhhh!

NOAH: What seems to be the trouble, my dear?

WIFE: I don't feel so good.

NOAH: You don't look so good, either. You aren't pregnant again, are you?

WIFE: No! It smells in here! These animals smell worse than a dead skunk in a heat wave.

NOAH: Oh, come now, it can't be all that bad—just because we have two of every animal on this ark.

WIFE: Well, that's not all. This boat goes back and forth and back and forth. We've been in here 278 days, 12 hours, 3 minutes, and 17 seconds. We have been floating in this water so long that I am beginning to feel like a teabag.

NOAH: Don't worry, dear. I don't think God is going to keep us in here much longer. Have patience.

WIFE: Well . . . maybe for a little while longer.

NOAH: Is it still raining outside?

WIFE: Does it ever rain inside?

NOAH: No respect, no respect.

WIFE: Take a peek and see.

NOAH: Well, it's not raining cats and dogs!

WIFE: Oh, good! There isn't room for one more animal!

NOAH: It was only a figure of speech.

WIFE: Noah, do boats sink often?

NOAH: Only once!

WIFE: What if we get a hole in the ark and it sinks?

NOAH: Impossible. For one thing, God wouldn't let us sink. That would ruin the whole plan. Besides, I can't swim.

WIFE: What if we do sink? We don't have any life preservers big enough to fit the elephants.

NOAH: Very funny. Trust God. He's holding this boat together.

WIFE: But it is so dull around here. I wake up in the morning to the rooster's crow, the pigs' oink, and the zebras' . . . whatever noise they make. Have you ever tried to get a 600-pound Siberian tiger to use the litter box? Well, don't!! And you have to do something about those woodpeckers. They are driving me crazy! I don't know how much more of this I can handle.

NOAH: Like I said before, you must have patience.

WIFE: Oh, I have patience. I've always had patience. I was born with patience! What's patience?

NOAH: Patience is the suffering of affliction with a calm, unruffled temper. When you stay patient through times of trial and tribulation, God will shape and mold you into a new and better you.

WIFE: But Noah, I am so bored. This whole place is boring. I want off this ark.

NOAH: But don't you want to grow?

WIFE: I finished growing when I was a teenager.

NOAH: I don't mean that kind of growth. I am talking about growing in the Lord. You see, dear, through each trial, we should praise God because we can grow to be a stronger servant for Him. So just be patient.

WIFE: I'll try. I am going to cook dinner.

NOAH: What are we having?

WIFE: What do you want?

NOAH: Barbecued barley with cheese sauce.

WIFE: Want a side order of fries with that?

NOAH: No, thanks, but maybe some alfalfa sprouts.

WIFE: By the way, have you seen dry land yet?

NOAH: I sent a raven out earlier this morning to find dry land, but that poor bird had aquatic phobia. With water all around him, he totally freaked out.

WIFE: Why don't we try it again, only with a smaller bird? Maybe a dove?

NOAH: Nah, that wouldn't work. (*pauses*) I know, we'll use a dove!

WIFE: Why didn't I think of that?

NOAH: Here, pretty bird. Now listen carefully. I want you to fly out and find dry ground. If you do, bring back something as proof. God be with you! Fly and be free! (*flaps arms*) That's it! Go, go, go!

NOAH: (*pauses*) Look!

WIFE: Where?

NOAH: Up there! The dove is coming back, and it has something in its beak. Look, the dove has found land. I knew God would not let us down. You just have to have . . .

WIFE: I know, I know, patience. And trust in God.

NOAH: You've got it, dear; you've got it! Uh oh.

WIFE: What?

NOAH: I hope we can find a hotel with a vacant room. Just kidding, just kidding. It won't be long now, dear, until we are off this ark. Just like God promised.

Noah puts his arm around his wife, and they exit.

Songs

"Standing on the Promises"
"Arky, Arky"
"Great Is Thy Faithfulness"
"Never Alone"

Devotions
God Keeps His Promises

Noah must have loved animals! I know he loved God, because he obeyed God even when it was unpopular. What made Noah believe God and build an ark when all the people except his family continually did evil? The world was corrupt and full of violence. In the midst of all this, the Bible tells us, Noah was a righteous, blameless man. Noah walked with God and knew God was faithful.

Can you imagine the responsibility Noah must have felt when God told him to build an ark? Thinking about the world's being destroyed by a flood would have been scary and overwhelming, but Noah trusted God and His promise to protect and guide him.

Parenting can be overwhelming too. The responsibility of training and guiding a precious child to love and follow God has been given to you as a new parent. We parents can trust God to help us because just as He was faithful to Noah, He promises to be faithful to us. (*Read Lamentations 3:22 and 23.*)

In Psalm 92:2 the psalmist declared God's loving-kindness in the morning and His faithfulness every night. What does it mean to be faithful? The word describes someone who is honest, loyal, and true. We can rely on God to keep His Word.

After Noah trusted God, God gave him a promise in the form of a rainbow and said that He would never again destroy the earth with a flood (Gen. 9:11–13).

When we place our trust in Jesus Christ for salvation, we, too, can rejoice in His promises.

(*Read or ask a volunteer to read John 14:2.*) What a great promise to look forward to someday—a home in Heaven with God.

(Read or ask a volunteer to read 1 John 5:14.) When we pray in God's will, He will hear and answer our prayers.

(Read or ask a volunteer to read 1 John 1:9.) If we confess our sins, God will forgive us.

(Read or ask a volunteer to read Hebrews 13:5.) God will never leave or forsake us.

(Read or ask a volunteer to read John 16:7.) He gives us the Holy Spirit as our Helper.

(Read or ask a volunteer to read Romans 5:1.) We have peace with God.

(Read or ask a volunteer to read Philippians 4:19.) He will supply all our needs.

(Read or ask a volunteer to read Romans 8:38 and 39.) Nothing can separate us from God's love.

What great promises these are for parents to teach to their children! *(Read 2 Peter 1:3 and 4.)* These promises should encourage us to know that we can rely upon God in these challenging times of training our children to know and love Him. We can trust God today to be faithful to the promises in His Word, just as He promised Noah many years ago. God always keeps His promises.

Nametags

Prizes

These prizes are designed for the winners to give to the mother (or mother-to-be). If you prefer to have the winners keep their prizes, choose other items.

- Rattle
- Bib
- Baby lotion
- Baby wash
- Baby sheet
- Stuffed animals

Recipes

Banana-Split Boats
Bananas
Ice cream
Hot fudge, caramel, pineapple, and
   strawberry toppings
Whipped cream topping
Nuts

Homemade Ice Cream
6 eggs
2 cups sugar
1 quart half-and-half
1 tablespoon vanilla
1 teaspoon salt
Milk to fill freezer container

Beat eggs until light and fluffy. Gradually add sugar and blend until thick. Add the half-and-half and vanilla. Add milk to fill line on freezer container. Mix well and freeze.

Caramel Topping
1 cup butter or margarine
2$\frac{1}{4}$ cups brown sugar
Dash salt
1 cup light corn syrup
1 (14 oz.) can sweetened condensed milk
1 teaspoon vanilla

Melt butter in heavy 3-quart saucepan. Add sugar and salt. Stir thoroughly. Stir in corn syrup; mix well. Gradually add milk, stirring constantly. Cook and stir over medium heat 12–15 minutes. Add vanilla.

Hot Fudge Topping

4 (1 oz. each) squares semisweet baking
    chocolate
1$\frac{1}{2}$ cups sugar
1$\frac{1}{2}$ cups evaporated milk
Salt
1 tablespoon vanilla (opt.)

Melt baking chocolate. Stir in sugar, evaporated milk, and pinch of salt. Cook until thickened. Add vanilla, if desired. Keeps well in refrigerator.

O Baby, Beautiful Baby Mine!

Theme and Decorations

- Decorate with clocks that have a baby theme. Our babies are from God to be ours for a time.
- Drape a soft-colored blanket over the edge of a baby buggy or bassinet. Fill the buggy or bassinet with baby dolls from times past.
- Decorate with items that a mom might save to remind her of this special time with her new baby; baby shoes that have been worn over time; sentimental baby clothes, such as a take-home-from-hospital outfit or a first dress; baby's first fork, spoon, and cup.

Food

- Peekaboo Pastry Puffs
- Chicken Salad
- Sugar 'n' Spice Muffins
- Watermelon Buggy

Games

Babies over Time Game

Ask each guest bring a baby picture. Tape all the pictures onto a poster board and number them. Give guests five minutes to write down whose baby picture they think each photo is. The lady with the most correct guesses wins.

"Timed" Memory Test

Place fifteen to twenty small baby items on a tray and cover them with a baby blanket. These items could include teething toys, pacifiers, Q-tips, a disposable diaper, nail clippers, baby soap, washcloth, bottle, rattles, toys, and the like. When you play the game, remove the blanket and give the guests two to three minutes to look over the items on the tray. They are not allowed to take notes. Cover the tray and ask the guests to write down as many items as they can remember. The person who remembers the most items wins.

Shopping for Baby with No Time to Spare

Match the brand names to the items in three minutes.

1. Zwieback _____
2. Orajel _____
3. Pampers _____
4. Desitin _____
5. Similac _____
6. Pedialyte _____
7. Chubs _____
8. Evenflow _____
9. Swimmers _____
10. Banana Boat Kids _____
11. Nuk _____
12. Gerber _____
13. Snuggle _____
14. Isomil _____
15. Tylenol _____
16. Johnson's _____
17. Dreft _____

18. Q-tips   _____
19. Cosco   _____
20. Shout   _____

Words to Select From

pacifier	fabric softener
stain remover	cotton swabs
swimming diapers	baby wipes
formula (used twice)	high chair
diaper rash ointment	shampoo
disposable diapers	bottle
maintenance water	sunscreen
baby food	teething toast
teething medicine	laundry detergent
pain reliever	

Answers

(1) Teething toast; (2) teething medicine; (3) disposable diapers; (4) diaper rash ointment; (5) formula; (6) maintenance water; (7) baby wipes; (8) bottle; (9) swimming diapers; (10) sunscreen; (11) pacifier; (12) baby food; (13) fabric softener; (14) formula; (15) pain reliever; (16) shampoo; (17) laundry detergent; (18) cotton swabs; (19) high chair; (20) stain remover.

Songs

"Water Colored Ponies"
"Arrow and the Bow"
"Goodnight Kiss"
"Sweet Hour of Prayer"
"What a Friend We Have in Jesus"

Devotions

Ours for a Time

Time Is of the Essence
Now is the time to get things done . . .
Wade in the water,
Sit in the sun,
Squish my toes in the mud by the door,

Explore the world in a boy just four.
Now is the time to study books,
Flowers,
Snails,
How a cloud looks;
To ponder "up,"
Where God sleeps nights,
Why mosquitoes take such big bites.
Later there'll be time,
To sew and clean,
Paint the hall
That soft new green,
To make new drapes,
Refinish the floor—
Later on . . . when he's not just four.

—Irene Foster

Babies are gifts from God. (*Read Psalm 127:3.*) Babies are ours for a time: to love, train, and teach about God. God has commanded Christian parents to do just that. (*Ask volunteers to read Proverbs 22:6, Ephesians 6:4, and Deuteronomy 6:7.*)

Being a parent is a blessing, but it is also a big responsibility. God gives children to us for a time, but they are still His. Our children belong to God from birth. A good example from God's Word is Hannah. She was a humble, determined woman who loved God and believed He could give her the desire of her heart . . . to have a child.

As women and mothers, we can note four examples Hannah provides for us that resulted in the blessing of God.

First, Hannah prayed to God. (*Read 1 Samuel 1:10 and 11.*) Hannah was troubled, disappointed, and hurting. She had a good husband who loved her and wanted to make her happy. She had his affection, companionship, and security *but no children.* She also had to endure his second wife's anger and taunting.

Hannah longed to find comfort, so she poured her heart out to God in prayer. In her pain and anguish Hannah went to the only One truly capable of providing help. God was there to answer her prayers, not only for a child, but for comfort in her misery. As soon as she had finished praying, "her countenance was no more sad" (1 Sam. 1:18).

Hannah didn't yet know that God would give her a son, but she did know the grace and comfort of God that no husband, friend, or parent could give her. Whatever the situation, God is ready and willing to give grace and comfort in our time of need when we look to Him and pray. From Hannah's example we mothers can learn the power that prayer can have in our lives. God is eager to hear our prayers and to help us train our children to honor and glorify Him.

Second, Hannah obeyed God. Hannah was devoted to God. First Samuel 1:27 and 28 record her words. *(Read the verses.)* Hannah was determined to obey no matter what the cost. She had made a vow to God, and she was going to keep it.

Samuel was just a small boy. Can you imagine the strength and faith it took to leave him at the tabernacle? Maybe Hannah understood that Samuel truly was a gift from God and was hers only for a time. Children really belong to God, and we need to be ready to let God use them for Himself. We can learn from Hannah's example to obey willingly whatever God asks us to do in regard to our children. We need to do whatever it takes to see them grow, mature, and come to trust Jesus as their Savior.

Third, Hannah praised God. Hannah's response to God was to glorify Him and to praise His name. Hannah's prayer of praise and thanksgiving to God was probably recited in the tabernacle right after she had given Samuel to Eli to raise. She was thankful to God. She praised Him for four reasons: (1) God is holy. *(Ask a volunteer to read 1 Samuel 2:2.)* (2) He is a God of knowledge. The last part of verse 3 reads, "For the LORD is a God of knowledge, and by him actions are weighed." (3) He is a God of power. Verses 4–8 remind us that God gives strength to the feeble, bread to the hungry, and life to the barren woman, and that He kills and makes alive, exalts the poor and makes them rich.

(4) God is a judging God. Verses 9 and 10 tell us that one day He will judge the earth.

As women, we have so much to praise God for, yet we get so busy with our families and schedules that we forget to give God the praise and honor He deserves. We should follow Hannah's example of praise.

Fourth, Hannah was devoted to her family. We learn from 1 Samuel 2:19 that from "year to year" Hannah made Samuel a little robe and took it to him when she went with her husband "to offer the yearly sacrifice."

Hannah is an example of a mother who took care of the needs of her family. I am sure a lot of love and many tears went into every stitch of Samuel's coat. Hannah went with her husband every year to offer sacrifices to God. We can learn from her example to be concerned about our family's physical and spiritual needs. As mothers, we have an awesome responsibility to teach our children about God's love and their need for a Savior. Many times it is with Mother that a child will see his or her need to trust in Jesus for eternal life.

As a faithful mother, Hannah prayed to God, obeyed God, praised God, and led her family in God's way. May we be women of faith who seek God and desire to train our children to honor and serve Him.

Nametags

Prizes

These prizes are designed for the winners to give to the mother (or mother-to-be). If you prefer to have the winners keep their prizes, choose other items.

- Baby spoon and fork
- Small decorative clock
- Booties
- Pacifier
- CD of lullabies

Recipes
Watermelon Buggy

1 watermelon
1 pint (2 cups) fresh strawberries
2 cups grapes
1 pineapple
1 cantaloupe
3 bananas, if desired
2 cans peach pie filling
1 large orange
Pink or blue ribbon
Toothpicks

1. Cut watermelon halfway down from the top and halfway in from the side to take out a quarter section. Remove the inside of watermelon; cut into bite-size chunks.

2. Cut fresh fruit (except orange) into bite-size chunks; add pie filling. Put mixture into the watermelon buggy.

3. Slice thick slices of an orange to make wheels for the buggy. Attach with toothpicks. Using toothpicks, attach pink or blue ribbon bows to hood of buggy.

Sugar 'n' Spice Muffins

$1/4$ cup margarine
$1/2$ cup sugar
$1/2$ cup milk
1 egg, beaten
$1/4$ tablespoon butter flavoring
$1 1/2$ cups flour
$1/2$ teaspoon salt
1 tablespoon baking powder
$1/2$ teaspoon cinnamon
1 cup raw chopped apple

TOPPING
$1/3$ cup brown sugar
$1/3$ cup chopped pecans
$1/2$ teaspoon cinnamon

1. Cream margarine and sugar together. Add milk, beaten egg, and butter flavoring. Combine flour, salt, baking power, and $1/2$ teaspoon cinnamon; add to mixture. Stir in apples; spoon into greased muffin tins.

2. In small bowl, combine the brown sugar, $1/2$ teaspoon cinnamon, and pecans. Mix well and sprinkle on unbaked muffins.

3. Bake muffins at $350°$F for 20–25 minutes.

Peekaboo Pastry Puffs

$1/2$ cup margarine
1 cup hot water
1 cup flour
4 eggs

1. Boil water and add flour. Stir dough until it pulls away from sides of mixing bowl. Add eggs, one at a time. Beat 5 minutes after each egg. (If using electric mixer, beat 30 seconds after each egg.)

2. Drop by spoonfuls or small ice cream scoop onto greased cookie sheet. Bake at $450°$F for 10 minutes, then at $325°$F for 20 minutes. Let cool. Cut slits in top to let dry. Fill with chicken salad.

Chicken Salad

2 cups diced apples
2 tablespoons lemon juice
2 cups diced cooked chicken
$1/2$ cup finely chopped celery
$1/2$ cup grapes, halved
Miracle Whip to taste

Toss apples in lemon juice. Combine with other ingredients and add Miracle Whip. Refrigerate before serving.

Precious Moments and Sweet Dreams

Theme and Decorations

- Decorate with Precious Moments dolls or figurines.
- Use blue, yellow, gold, and white as theme colors. Accent with moons, stars, and clouds. Hang at various heights from ceiling.
- Drape clear Christmas lights in tulle across the fronts of tables.

Food

- Heavenly Lemon Bars
- Baby Blueberry Dessert
- Soft Pretzels (teething rings)

Games

Nursery Rhyme Match

Match the person on the left to his or her belonging or associated item on the right.

1. Little Kittens	tarts
2. Jack Horner	sheep
3. Jack	bone
4. Jack Sprat	garden
5. Jack and Jill	pipe
6. Little Bo Peep	peppers
7. Pussy Cat	crying girls
8. Blind Mice	wall
9. Mother Hubbard	pumpkin
10. Black sheep	pig
11. Cat	bread and butter
12. Cow	fat
13. Tom	carving knife
14. King Cole	kettle
15. Baby Bunting	haystack
16. Mary	moon
17. Peter	pail
18. Boy Blue	spider
19. Georgie Porgie	mittens
20. Simple Simon	plum
21. Humpty Dumpty	candlestick
22. Miss Muffet	wool
23. Tom Tucker	fair
24. Peter Piper	fiddle
25. Polly	broken cradle
26. Queen of Hearts	hunting
27. Hot Cross Buns	stockings
28. Wee Willy Winkle	queen
29. John	penny
30. Contrary Mary	nightgown
31. Rockabye	lamb

Answers

(1) Mittens; (2) plum; (3) candlestick; (4) fat; (5) pail; (6) sheep; (7) queen; (8) carving knife; (9) bone; (10) wool; (11) fiddle; (12) moon; (13) pig; (14) pipe; (15) hunting; (16) lamb; (17) pumpkin; (18) haystack; (19) crying girls; (20) fair; (21) wall; (22) spider; (23) bread and butter; (24) peppers; (25) kettle; (26) tarts; (27) penny; (28) nightgown; (29) stockings; (30) garden; (31) broken cradle.

Baby Name Word Scramble

For months we dream about a name for our baby. What will that name be? See who can find the most names in this word scramble.

Baby Name Word Scramble

```
A  X  C  D  E  M  L  R  J  A  M  I  E  N  J  A  B  S
M  E  I  L  E  E  N  U  F  R  E  E  I  T  A  K  U  P
A  Z  N  T  V  G  I  J  A  Z  E  B  O  Z  A  S  I  L
T  O  K  A  F  A  C  N  Z  P  O  K  Y  G  A  I  S  A
T  S  H  D  J  N  H  B  A  R  A  S  U  N  S  D  G  D
H  Y  B  O  B  I  O  S  X  M  C  B  T  C  E  O  X  A
E  R  O  A  J  Y  L  S  A  M  O  H  T  G  B  M  I  M
W  V  J  O  H  N  O  P  M  N  I  D  I  B  H  X  A  S
W  L  K  T  R  I  S  T  A  N  I  W  F  E  L  K  G  U
R  A  C  H  A  E  L  V  Q  R  Y  T  O  Z  I  A  H  J
N  J  D  M  X  A  H  Z  O  L  F  U  A  T  O  R  I  K
L  A  I  U  M  E  Y  T  A  M  M  Y  N  Y  Y  G  Z  R
L  K  Y  T  V  L  W  E  C  K  E  A  A  D  N  A  M  A
M  E  A  E  G  P  N  F  A  T  R  I  A  B  A  R  X  T
A  E  T  K  X  A  M  I  C  H  A  E  L  K  T  Y  Y  M
L  S  N  A  I  T  C  N  L  E  A  N  N  A  T  S  G  A
L  C  S  R  Z  K  D  N  I  N  J  H  N  Q  I  V  A  D
O  F  B  X  Y  Z  E  E  N  R  W  I  G  Y  R  P  Z  I
R  P  A  R  B  C  P  J  T  Y  T  E  Z  E  B  A  S  S
Y  N  E  R  A  K  J  H  E  A  M  N  I  Z  U  U  A  O
Y  E  S  R  T  N  P  Y  C  P  G  K  Y  T  V  L  U  N
E  R  H  V  Z  E  D  A  V  I  D  A  R  K  A  E  X  T
I  U  G  P  S  M  X  O  G  X  X  S  A  B  R  U  C  E
U  A  T  O  E  L  E  I  N  A  D  R  M  W  I  A  F  G
J  L  J  R  W  D  O  Y  K  Q  J  Y  Y  E  S  L  E  K
```

Names in Puzzle

ADAM	HENRY	MALLORY	THOMAS
AMANDA	JAKE	MARY	TINA
ANITA	JAMIE	MATTHEW	TRISTAN
ANN	JANE	MICHAEL	
BLAIR	JEN	MEGAN	
BOB	JOHN	NICHOLAS	
BRANDON	JOSEPH	PAM	
BRIAN	KAREN	PAUL	
BRITTANY	KATIE	RACHAEL	
BRUCE	KELSEY	ROBIN	
CLINT	KIM	SARA	
DANIEL	LAUREN	STEVE	
DAVID	LEANN	SUSAN	
EILEEN	LISA	TAMMY	
GARY	MADISON	TED	

Answers: Baby Name Word Scramble

Skit

What's Best for Baby?

BARBIE: Good evening and welcome to *20/20*. I am Barbie Waters. Tonight we have an exclusive interview with a new mother at Greenwood Hospital. Can you tell me your name?

PEG: *(young mom)* Peg Cravis.

BARBIE: And you, ma'am?

LEANN: *(the grandmother)* Leann Cravis. This is my daughter-in-law. She is married to my boy James.

BARBIE: I see. Well, I would like to congratulate you on the birth of your son. After coming home from the hospital, you'll have many new responsibilities. I'd like to ask you a few questions on the methods you will be using. First . . . about bathing. How frequently will you give your son a bath?

PEG: The doctor recommended I bathe him just once a week.

LEANN: Once a week? But won't he smell? That baby needs to be washed at least once a day and rubbed down with baby oil, lots of baby oil!

PEG: Won't he be slick? What if I drop him?

LEANN: *(paying no attention to Peg)* I just love that baby oil smell. Just makes you want to kiss him all over.

BARBIE: *(wanting to change the subject quickly)* Okay. Now what type of diapers do you recommend for the new baby?

LEANN: Why, cloth diapers, of course. They are so much softer and cleaner than those plastic things.

PEG: I was planning on using disposable. Cloth diapers are gross!

LEANN: Oh, but honey, there is nothing better than the smell of fresh diapers on the clothesline. All clean—

PEG: *(interrupts Leann)* It's not the smell of the clean ones I'm worried about!

LEANN: And those plastic diapers are expensive.

Cloth diapers are so much more economical. If you use those plastic diapers, when he gets a diaper rash—like babies get from those terrible things—you will need lots of cornstarch on his little red bottom. *(pulls out a box of cornstarch)* It's the best and most natural. Everybody knows that.

PEG: Actually, now that you mention diaper rash, I got this improved-formula Desitin. It says here that it cures diaper rash 63 percent faster than other remedies.

LEANN: But look how little that tube is! That won't last two days. *(talks to baby)* Don't you worry, Puddin'. Grandma has been stocking up. I have four new boxes at home.

BARBIE: Excuse me, ladies—moving on to the next question. Mommy, how will you be feeding the baby? Will you be nursing or using formula?

PEG: Oh, definitely nursing. I have already adapted the baby to a strict three-hour schedule.

LEANN: What?

PEG: Yes, Dr. Izzo says this baby is a part of the family, not the center of it.

LEANN: But if that baby is hungry, he definitely needs to be fed. I have even heard of babies starving because you don't know how much milk they are getting when nursing. Do you really think you will have enough?

PEG: Well, in a few days—

LEANN: And I know his daddy wants to be involved. And when you bottle feed, it gives someone else a chance to bond with this sweet little baby.

PEG: Well, actually, Leann, nursing is more natural and more economical, things we are both concerned about. *(baby fusses)* Don't cry honey—only 23 more minutes until supper.

LEANN: *(takes baby in her arms)* You come see your grandma. Don't you worry. We will have you eating cereal in two weeks. That will fill up your tummy.

PEG: Two weeks! The box advises starting cereal at four months, and all the mommies in my chat room confirm that.

LEANN: How do you expect him to ever sleep through the night?

PEG: Well, after his last feeding at 8:00 P.M., he will have his 20-minute daddy time and diaper change. So that will be about 9:10 or 9:15. I'll put him in his crib—on his back, of course.

LEANN: On his back?

PEG: Oh, yes, studies have shown that the chance of SIDS increases significantly by laying babies on their tummies.

LEANN: Well, I put all my babies on their tummies. Little ones can startle so easily and wake up. On their tummies, their little hands are all tucked in and snuggly.

PEG: Back to sleep, back to sleep . . .

LEANN: On their backs, if they spit up they will choke to death! *(Grandma starts talking baby talk to baby)*

PEG: *(talking under her breath)* I'd throw up, too, if someone talked to me like that.

LEANN: *(still talking to baby)* Your grandma would never just put you in that cold, old crib. Here, get your little thumby.

PEG: No, no, no. I will not have a thumb sucker! These pacifiers are the latest on the market. They are antibacterial and dishwasher safe so we can sterilize them daily.

LEANN: Well, his dad sucked his thumb.

PEG: 'Til the third grade.

(nurse enters)

NURSE: Time to take baby for his final check. If you have a special outfit for the baby to wear home, go ahead and get it ready. I will be right back.

(Each lady reaches down and picks up a sack and holds up the "perfect" outfit. They stare at the other one's "awful" outfit in disbelief. Peg's outfit: a contemporary outfit with matching hat; Leann's outfit: crocheted sweater, bonnet, and booties.)

BARBIE: Well, it sounds like you are about ready to go home. You ladies sure seem to have a lot of knowledge about taking care of a baby. I am curious where you have gotten all this information.

PEG: Well, I have done a lot of reading and research, especially on the Internet. I have a weekly chat at mommies.com and found a plethora of information on the Web.

BARBIE: And you, Grandma?

LEANN: Well, I have always said experience is the best teacher. When I was starting my family, I relied solely on the wisdom of my mother and my dear mother-in-law.

PEG: *(rolls her eyes)*

BARBIE: Well, the things I have seen from you two today are so different. Is there anything you both agree is important in raising this child?

PEG: Oh, yes! All opinions and methods aside, our one true goal is to teach this child to love and serve the Lord.

LEANN: Absolutely! Third John 4 says, "I have no greater joy than to hear that my children walk in truth."

PEG: Yes, and I love Proverbs 22:6, which reminds us to train a child in the way he should go, and when he is old, he will not depart from it.

LEANN: I guess we did get a little carried away before. I know you are going to be a great mommy, Peg.

PEG: And James and I are so glad to have such a godly grandmother to teach our son spiritually. *(Peg and Leann hug)* But he's not wearing that bonnet.

Songs

"Sweet Hour of Prayer"
"Moment by Moment"
"Jesus Loves Even Me"

Devotions
Precious Moments in Prayer

So many precious moments come with motherhood. Even before the baby is born, you'll have precious moments that you will always remember. Like when you knew for certain that you were pregnant and you told your husband. How about when you felt the baby move for the first time? Or when you heard the baby's heartbeat? Or the first time you saw a picture of him or her with all ten toes and fingers on the ultrasound monitor. And then there was that precious moment when you heard your baby's little cry as the doctor placed your new baby in your arms. Babies are precious gifts from God.

Precious moments in prayer are important for new mothers. I am sure before your baby was born, you prayed for it to be healthy and for it to arrive here safely. You started having those precious moments with God concerning the new life you were carrying. Busy days and nights as a mom can be stressful. Prayer enables us to accomplish things that we can't do on our own.

In Psalm 61 David felt overwhelmed. However, he instinctively turned to God in prayer. Praying was as natural as breathing to him.

First, prayer enables us to talk to God anywhere, anytime. *(Read Psalm 61:1 and 2.)* David prayed from what seemed like the ends of the earth. He was away from his home, Jerusalem, but he was not away from God. We can come boldly before God's throne in prayer wherever we are, no matter what we are doing. Maybe it is in the middle of the night and the baby has fallen back asleep and you are counting sheep. Don't count sheep; talk to the Shepherd. Use those precious moments to spend time with Him in prayer.

Second, prayer enables us to go higher. *(Read Psalm 61:2 and 3.)* David pleaded, "Lead me to the rock that is higher than I." God was his tower and strength. When we pray, God lifts us up. We can see things much clearer when we are on the mountaintop.

Third, prayer enables us to stay close to God. When we go to God in prayer, we pour out our thoughts and fears to Him. David said he dwelt in God's tent and took refuge in the shelter of His wings. The wings David talked about were the wings of the two cherubim in the Holy of Holies. That is

where God dwelt in the tabernacle. Through Jesus and what He did for us on the cross, we can enter the presence of God in prayer and dwell close under His wings. Those are very precious moments when we feel His protective, loving wings around us.

Fourth, prayer enables us to live a fuller and happier life. *(Read Psalm 61:5–8.)*

According to verse 5, God gives us an inheritance. That inheritance is in Jesus Christ. *(Read Ephesians 1:11 and 1 Peter 1:4.)*

With prayer, praise comes naturally. David started by crying out to God and ended by praising God. Prayer gives a richer, fuller depth to our lives. When we pray to God, He lifts us up, draws us close, gives us good things, and makes us happy. God made a promise in Matthew 7:7. *(Read the verse.)* That's a precious promise!

Nametags

Prizes

These prizes are designed for the winners to give to the mother (or mother-to-be). If you prefer to have the winners keep their prizes, choose other items.

- Baby powder
- Booties
- Pacifier
- Rattle
- Comb and brush

Recipes

Heavenly Lemon Bars

3 cups crushed Ritz crackers
$^1/_2$ cup sugar
$^1/_2$ cup margarine, melted
1 (12 oz.) can frozen lemonade, thawed
2 (14 oz. each) cans sweetened
    condensed milk
2 (8 oz. each) containers frozen whipped
    topping, thawed

1. Combine crushed crackers, sugar, and margarine. Save $^3/_4$ cup for topping. Press remaining mixture into a 9" x 13" pan.

2. Combine sweetened condensed milk and lemonade. Fold in whipped topping. Pour over crust. Sprinkle reserved crumbs on top.

3. Freeze overnight. Serves 12.

Baby Blueberry Dessert

GRAHAM CRACKER CRUST
20 graham crackers, crushed
6 tablespoons margarine, melted
$^1/_4$ cup powdered sugar

FILLING
1 (8 oz.) pkg. cream cheese, softened
1 (12 oz.) container frozen whipped
    topping, thawed
2 cans blueberry pie filling

1. In a 9" x 13" pan, combine crushed graham crackers, melted margarine, and powdered sugar. Mix well and press evenly in bottom of pan.

2. For filling, mix together cream cheese and whipped topping. Spread on crust.

3. Top with blueberry pie filling. Chill and serve.

Soft Pretzels (Bread Machine)

DOUGH
1 cup plus 2 tablespoons water
1 tablespoon vegetable oil
3 cups flour
1 teaspoon salt
1 tablespoon sugar
$2^1/_2$ teaspoons active dry yeast

TOPPING
3 tablespoons salt
1 tablespoon water
1 egg white
Coarse salt or sesame seeds

1. Place all dough ingredients in bread machine. Choose the dough cycle and start machine.

2. Cut dough into 15 pieces. Cover with towel to prevent drying. Roll each piece into 15" rope. Twist each rope into pretzel shape. Cover; let rise in warm place for 20–25 minutes or until almost double in size.

3. Heat oven to 375°F. Generously spray cookie sheet with nonstick cooking spray.

4. Dissolve 3 tablespoons salt in 2 quarts boiling water. Lower 3 or 4 pretzels at a time into boiling water; top sides down. Boil 2 minutes, turning pretzels once. Remove pretzels from water with slotted spoon; drain on paper towels. Let stand a few seconds, then place $^1/_2$ inch apart on cookie sheet.

5. Beat 1 tablespoon water and the egg white; brush over pretzels. Sprinkle lightly with coarse salt or sesame seeds. Bake 20–24 minutes or until light golden brown. Remove from cookie sheet. Cool on wire rack.

Rock-a-Bye

Theme and Decorations

- Decorate a rocking chair for the honored mother to use when she opens the gifts. Drape a baby afghan or blanket over the rocker and set a large-size Mother Goose or lullaby book on it. Place a rocking horse beside the rocker.
- String a clothesline with baby clothing (T-shirts, bibs, hat or bonnet, onesies, headband with bow, booties or socks). Use the items on the clothesline as gifts for the new mom.
- Hang a wicker laundry basket or a cradle from the ceiling. Drape with garlands or ivy to make it look like it is hanging from a tree.
- Place containers of wet wipes on the table to use for napkins. (Give the unused wet wipes to the new mom.)
- Play background music of lullabies.
- Decorate in greens, blues, yellows, and pinks.

Food

- Messy Baby Bars
- Chocolate Crumble Bars
- Apple Bars
- Lemon Bars

Games

Snatch the Clothespin

Give a clothespin to each guest as she comes in the door. Ask each guest to pin a clothespin onto her clothes. Each time she hears someone say the word "baby," she can steal a pin from that person. The lady with the most pins at the end of the game's allotted time wins.

What Babies Do

Unscramble the following words.

1. tew _____
2. pcuich _____
3. elsep _____
4. rajbeb _____
5. ycr _____
6. prbu _____
7. itps _____
8. lorl _____
9. glnusge _____
10. wclar _____
11. kscu _____
12. ckki _____
13. ceahr _____
14. uglah _____
15. ecrpe _____
16. cweh _____
17. oco _____
18. ilmse _____
19. enseez _____
20. veol _____

Answers

(1) Wet; (2) hiccup; (3) sleep; (4) jabber; (5) cry; (6) burp; (7) spit; (8) roll; (9) snuggle; (10) crawl; (11) suck; (12) kick; (13) reach; (14) laugh; (15) creep; (16) chew; (17) coo; (18) smile; (19) sneeze; (20) love.

Name That Lullaby

Play a few notes of a lullaby, and ask guests to write down what song they think it is. A variation would be to let the ladies call out the name when they recognize the lullaby. Examples of lullabies: "Lullaby and Good Night"; "Rock-a-Bye Baby"; "Hush, Little Baby"; "Twinkle, Twinkle, Little Star"; "Sleep, Baby, Sleep"; "Bye, Baby Bunting."

Baby Food Connoisseurs

Select a panel of four or five ladies. Choose panelists by criteria such as the mom with the most children, the oldest mom, the youngest mom, and the mom with the youngest baby. Put a blindfold and a bib on each lady and give them baby spoons. Ask the honored mother to approach each lady and, using that lady's spoon, put a taste of baby food into her mouth. Each panelist must guess what kind of baby food she is tasting. The panelist with the most correct guesses wins.

Songs

"Blessed Quietness"
"A Quiet Place"
"Rock-a-Bye Baby" and other lullabies

Devotions

Christ Is Our Comfort

Being a new mother is an exciting and wonderful time. Emotions flow freely for a new mother. First of all, it is hard to imagine that this little miracle, so perfect and sweet, is yours. It is a part of you and your husband. You have many new events and feelings to experience.

A favorite time may be rocking your baby to sleep. A new mother enjoys the warmth of her baby's little body and soft little sighs. A sleeping baby can melt your heart. Most new mothers are thankful for sleep—for the baby and for themselves. Being a new mom is very tiring. Nighttime feedings, diapers, colic, the first tooth, and earaches quickly wear a mother down physically and emotionally. New moms would give anything for some much needed rest!

Jesus issued a wonderful invitation in Matthew 11:28. *(Read the verse.)* He invites us to "come." We can go to the Lord and rely on Him to give us strength and comfort for our souls. We can go to Him in prayer anytime. We need to find a quiet place to sit, read, and reflect on His Word.

Isaiah 40:31 is a good verse to meditate on when your children are little and you feel overwhelmed. *(Read the verse.)* Doesn't that verse give you a feeling of strength just by hearing it?

Another Scripture that gives great comfort is Psalm 23:1–3. *(Read the verses.)* Verse 2 mentions rest. *(Reread the first part of verse 2.)* Can you find a quiet spot, a green pasture, where you can talk to God? Maybe you can find a place outside where you can enjoy God's creation, or maybe you can just imagine the scene in your mind. There is something about God's creation that brings calmness and quietness to the heart.

Verse 2 also alludes to refreshment. *(Reread the second part of verse 2.)* Is there anything more relaxing than the sound of a cool, flowing stream of water? Find refreshment in God's Word. Take your shoes off, put your bare feet in, and relax in the Lord.

Verse 3 promises restoration. By spending time with God, we will find restoration. It's like eating food when we are hungry or drinking water when we are thirsty. God restores our soul and mind and prepares us to face the job of motherhood for another day.

As women and mothers, we can find restoration, refreshment, and rest in the Lord.

Nametags

Prizes

Use items from the clothesline. (See "Theme and Decorations.") These prizes are designed for the winners to give to the mother (or mother-to-be). If you prefer to have the winners keep their prizes, choose other items.

Recipes

Messy Baby Bars

1 German chocolate cake mix
$^1\!/_2$ cup plus $^1\!/_3$ cup evaporated milk
$^3\!/_4$ cup butter, melted
$1^1\!/_2$ cups chopped pecans
$^3\!/_4$ cup milk chocolate chips
1 (14 oz.) pkg. caramels, melted

1. Preheat oven to 350°F. Spray and flour a 9" x 13" pan. Combine cake mix, $^1\!/_2$ cup evaporated milk, and melted butter in a large mixing bowl. Pour half of the batter into baking pan. Bake for 5 minutes

2. While first layer is baking, combine caramels and $^1\!/_3$ cup evaporated milk in a double boiler or microwave. Dribble mixture over first layer, which will look puffy and doughy when you remove it from the oven.

3. Spread chocolate chips and chopped pecans onto the caramel layer. Drop spoonfuls of remaining batter on top.

4. Bake 18–20 minutes. Do not overbake.

Chocolate Crumble Bars

OATMEAL BASE

1 cup margarine
2 cups brown sugar
2 eggs
$2^1\!/_2$ cups flour
1 teaspoon baking soda
1 teaspoon salt
2 teaspoons vanilla
3 cups quick oatmeal

FILLING

1 (12 oz.) pkg. chocolate chips
1 (14 oz.) can sweetened condensed milk
2 teaspoons vanilla
2 tablespoons margarine
$^1\!/_2$ teaspoon salt

1. For oatmeal base, cream 1 cup margarine and brown sugar. Beat in eggs. Add flour, baking soda, 1 teaspoon salt, vanilla, and oatmeal. Mix well and spread $^2\!/_3$ of the mixture in a jelly roll pan.

2. For filling, melt chocolate chips in a double boiler with 2 tablespoons margarine, sweetened condensed milk, and $^1\!/_2$ teaspoon salt. Add vanilla and mix well. Spread mixture over first layer.

3. Spread or dot remaining oatmeal mixture on top of filling. Bake 20–25 minutes at 350°F.

Apple Bars

FILLING

6 apples, peeled and sliced
1 cup sugar
2 teaspoons cinnamon
3 tablespoons flour
3 tablespoons margarine

CRUST

2 cups butter-flavored shortening
4 cups flour, heaping
1 teaspoon salt
1 cup cold milk

1. Mix together apples, sugar, cinnamon, and 3 tablespoons flour. Set aside.

2. For crust, cut shortening into 4 cups flour and 1 teaspoon salt with pastry cutter. Add cold milk. Roll out half of dough to fit a deep cookie sheet. Fill with apple mixture and dot with margarine. Add top crust; seal the edges. Sprinkle with sugar and bake at 375°F for 40–45 minutes.

3. Drizzle with Powered Sugar Glaze.

Powdered Sugar Glaze

1$\frac{1}{2}$ cups powdered sugar
2 tablespoons cold milk

Stir together. Add more milk if needed for right consistency.

Lemon Bars

CRUST
  2 cups flour
  $\frac{1}{2}$ cup powdered sugar
  1 cup margarine
  $\frac{1}{4}$ teaspoon salt

FILLING
  2 lemons, juiced (or $\frac{1}{3}$ cup reconstituted lemon juice)
  2 cups sugar
  4 eggs
  3 tablespoons flour
  $\frac{1}{4}$ teaspoon salt

1. For crust, cut together until crumbly 2 cups flour, powdered sugar, margarine, and $\frac{1}{4}$ teaspoon salt. Press mixture on the bottom and sides of a 9" x 13" pan. Bake 12–15 minutes at 350°F.

2. For filling, mix together lemon juice, sugar, eggs, 3 tablespoons flour, and $\frac{1}{4}$ teaspoon salt. Pour onto baked crust. Bake at 350°F for 20 minutes. Remove from oven and sprinkle with powdered sugar.

Tiny Hands to Hold

Theme and Decorations

- Enlist the help of young children to make hand-prints on disposable tablecloths. Trace around their hands. Or dip childrens' hands in paint and "stamp" on the tablecloths. Use pink and blue markers to make Xs and Os for kisses and hugs.
- Scatter Hershey's Hugs on the tables.
- Display baby items that a tiny hand could hold, such as rattles or teething rings.
- Tie a bow on clear baby bottles and fill all of them with the same number of Hershey's Kisses. Use to decorate and to play a game. (See "Games.")
- Prepare a three-tiered "diaper cake" with disposable diapers. Make the first layer by tightly rolling a diaper and then adding diapers until you have a circle that is ten to twelve inches in diameter. Secure diapers with tape or rubber bands. Tie the roll of diapers with curly ribbon the way you would a package. Repeat for two more layers, making each layer smaller. Hang curly ribbon, pacifiers, combs, brushes, rattles, or teething rings down the sides. Top with a toy, stuffed animal, or baby blocks. (Variation: Use receiving blankets, washcloths, and towels for the middle layer.)

Food

- Baby Shrimp Salad or Baby Shrimp Dip
- Baby carrots
- Assortment of crackers
- Baby Bunting Cake

Games

Baby Bottle Guess Icebreaker

Ask guests to guess the number of candies in the baby bottles, which are part of your decorations. The winner gets to keep the candy.

What's in the Bag?

Pack a diaper bag with ten to fifteen items. Tell the guests how many items there are, and have them guess what is inside. If you have ten items, they may write only ten items. The winner is the one with the most correct answers. Give the winner a prize, and present the honored mom with the diaper bag and items as your gift to her.

Nursery Rhyme Quiz

See how many of the following questions you can answer.
1. How much wool did the black sheep have?
2. What letter of the alphabet did the baker put on his cake?
3. What grew in a row in Mary's garden?
4. What did Jack jump over?
5. Who put the kettle on?
6. Where was the cow when Little Boy Blue blew his horn?
7. What happened when the clock struck one?
8. Where does the muffin man live?
9. What couldn't Jack Sprat eat?
10. How old do some like their porridge?
11. What was pussycat doing in London?
12. What did Yankee Doodle have in his hat?

13. What did Georgie Porgie do to make the girls cry?
14. What was Little Jack Horner eating in the corner?
15. Who were the three blind mice chasing?
16. What did Mother Hubbard go to the cupboard for?
17. What did Bo Peep lose?
18. What do the stars twinkle like?
19. When riding a white horse to Banbury Cross, what did the fine lady have on her toes?
20. What time was it when Wee Willie Winkie ran through town?
21. What three things did Old King Cole call for?
22. Who did Simple Simon meet going to the fair?
23. What were the professions of the three men in the tub?
24. What did the itsy bitsy spider climb on?

25. What was the cat playing when the dish and the spoon ran away?

Answers
(1) Three bags full; (2) the letter "B"; (3) silver bells, cockle shells, and pretty maids; (4) candlestick; (5) Polly; (6) in the corn; (7) the mouse ran down; (8) Drury Lane; (9) fat; (10) nine days old; (11) visiting the queen; (12) a feather; (13) kissed them; (14) Christmas pie; (15) the farmer's wife; (16) a bone; (17) her sheep; (18) a diamond; (19) bells; (20) eight o'clock; (21) pipe, bowl, and three fiddlers; (22) pieman; (23) butcher, baker, and candlestick maker; (24) waterspout; (25) the fiddle.

Sweet Names Puzzle
Choose from the names on the next page to complete the puzzle.

Sweet Names We Call Babies

Names to Use (do not use spaces)

SWEET PEA   DUMPLING   LITTLE MAN
BUNDLE OF JOY   BABE   BUDDY
DOLLY   PRECIOUS   MUNCHKIN
BABY CAKES   ANGEL   PUMPKIN
CUDDLE BUG   SWEETIE PIE   MUFFIN
SUGARPLUM   BUBBA

Answers: Sweet Names We Call Babies

Songs

"Jesus Loves Me"

"Praise Him, Praise Him"

"In the Hollow of His Hand"

"The Touch of His Hand on Mine"

"He Leadeth Me"

Devotions

Tiny Hands to Hold

Isn't it amazing? Your new baby is here, and you and your family are thrilled.

Every mother looks at her new baby in awe as she checks the baby's feet for ten toes and hands for ten tiny fingers. Then those little fingers curl around Mommy's little finger and take her breath away.

We choose to hold hands for many reasons. We hold hands with our children when we cross the street or when we are in a crowded place to protect them. When people are in love, they like to hold hands. Their hand-holding shows us they belong to each other. It is also comforting to hold someone's hand when they are hurting or sick. Holding someone's hand is a good way of showing we care.

God wants to show us His love, His care, His direction, and His protection by holding on to our hand with His strong, almighty hand.

Protection and strength are from God's hands. (*Read Isaiah 41:10.*) Having a baby can make you fearful and anxious. What is labor like? Am I that strong? What if the baby won't stop crying? Then there are sleepless nights that make us tired and grouchy. (*Read Psalm 18:35.*) God will hold you up and give you strength with His strong hands.

God's hands give us direction along the right path, as Psalm 139:10 points out, "Even there shall thy hand lead me, and thy right hand shall hold me." God's hands will lead you and show you the way to go. Many times as a parent you will feel overwhelmed and need God's directions in decisions for your family. God promises to lead you when you take hold of His guiding hand.

According to Psalm 16:11, we can find comfort and pleasure in God's hands. (*Read the verse.*) If we want joy, we can find it by trusting God to supply all our needs. He knows when we are down and discouraged, and He cares. First Peter 5:7 tells us to cast all our anxiety upon Him, because He cares for us. God cares when we are discouraged, and He will give us joy when we hold on to His comforting hand.

God's hands also show possession and love for His children. (*Read Psalm 31:14 and 15.*)

We belong to God when we trust Him as our personal Savior. Nothing can take that salvation away from us. (*Read John 10:28.*) God loves us, and we choose to love Him back. He holds our hands, and nothing can separate us from His love. Listen to this list from Romans 8:37–39. (*Read the verses.*)

Moms need to hold on to God's almighty hand for protection, direction, comfort, and love. You are in good hands with God.

Nametags

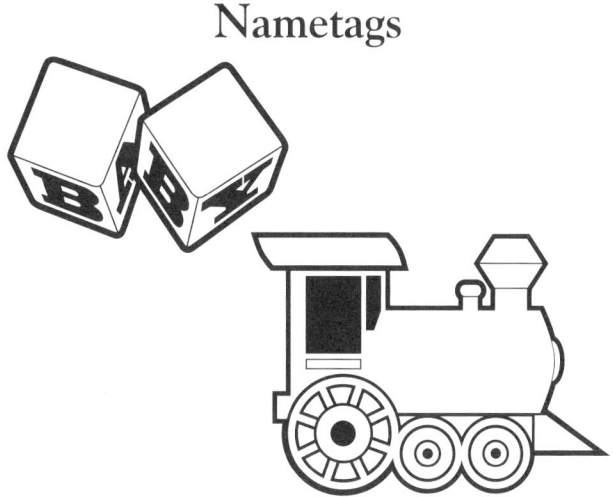

Prizes

These prizes are designed for the winners to give to the mother (or mother-to-be). If you prefer to have the winners keep their prizes, choose other items.

- Baby bottles with candy
- Hershey's Hugs and Kisses
- Baby rattles and teething toys

Recipes

Baby Shrimp Dip

1 (8 oz.) pkg. cream cheese, softened
1 cup catsup
1 teaspoon creamy horseradish
1 small can baby shrimp

1. Spread cream cheese on serving dish. Mix catsup and horseradish together and spread on top of cream cheese. Cover with baby shrimp.

2. Serve dip with crackers.

3. Easy variation: Substitute catsup and horseradish sauce with a store-bought shrimp cocktail sauce.

Baby Shrimp Salad

8 oz. baby shrimp
8 oz. rotini pasta, cooked
¹/₂ cup Miracle Whip
1 cup ranch dressing
Black olives, sliced (opt.)
Cucumbers, peeled and chopped (opt.)
Celery, chopped (opt.)
Carrots, sliced (opt.)
Cherry tomatoes (opt.)
Broccoli or cauliflower (opt.)

1. Combine shrimp, pasta, and dressings.

2. Add black olives, cucumbers, celery, carrots, tomatoes, broccoli, or cauliflower as desired. Season with salt and pepper.

3. Chill in refrigerator. (Make this salad a day ahead of time so the flavors blend.)

Baby Bunting Cake

1 devil's food cake mix
1 (3.4 oz.) pkg. instant chocolate fudge
    pudding and pie filling
1 cup sour cream (fat free or light)
4 egg whites
¹/₂ cup warm water
¹/₂ cup light margarine
1 teaspoon vanilla
2 cups semisweet chocolate chips

1. Stir dry ingredients together in a large mixing bowl. Add sour cream, egg whites, water, margarine, and vanilla. Beat with mixer. Stir in chocolate chips. Pour into bundt cake pan that has been sprayed with cooking spray. Bake at 350°F for 40–45 minutes. Cool.

2. Invert cooled cake on serving plate and drizzle with Powdered Sugar Glaze. (See page 81.)

3. Fill baby bottle with candy; place in center of cake. Place extra candy around cake base and bottle.

Toy Chest

Theme and Decorations

- Fill a toy chest with toys, dolls, balls, tops, and stuffed animals. Drape a soft baby blanket out of the corner of the toy box. If available, put a train set on the table or around the toy chest.
- On the table with the train set and toy chest, set up children's Bible story books or train-related books (e.g., *The Little Engine That Could*).
- Put teething toys and baby rattles in the cars of the train set.
- Add color with balloons to identify a baby boy or a baby girl.

Food

- Fruit Pizza
- Honey roasted peanuts
- Chocolate candies

Games

Toy Chest Bingo

Give each guest a copy of the Bingo card. Have the guests fill in the blanks with toy names, such as dolls, tractors, balls, cars, whistles, puzzles, crayons, and marbles. Going around the room, ask each lady to call out one item from her own card. For example, she could call out "puzzles under O," and any player who has that item under "O," including the lady who calls it out, can cross it out on her card. The first one to get a row or column crossed out should yell, "TOYS!"

Toy Chest Scramble

Unscramble these words to find the names of toys.

1. tho ehlwse   _____
2. fstfude maslnia   _____

T	O	Y	S

3. megas _____

4. lalb _____

5. rbbiae _____

6. rplieana _____

7. ypal enpoh _____

8. oksbo _____

9. inubgldi clobsk _____

10. oty ritan _____

11. yapl shides _____

12. lsodl _____

13. trocdo tik _____

14. cutrks _____

15. rrotstac _____

Answers

(1) Hot Wheels; (2) stuffed animals; (3) games; (4) ball; (5) Barbie; (6) airplane; (7) play phone; (8) books; (9) building blocks; (10) toy train; (11) play dishes; (12) dolls; (13) doctor kit; (14) trucks; (15) tractors.

Songs

"Toyland, Toyland"
"Babes in Toyland"
"Tell Me the Story of Jesus"
"Train Up a Child in the Way He Should Go"

Devotions
Train Up a Child

Trains, wheels, and whistles! Who doesn't love to watch toy trains as they speed around the track and toot their whistles? Many children enjoy the story *The Little Engine That Could.* Remember how the engine kept saying, "I think I can, I think I can, I think I can"? I'm sure you recall your mom or dad telling you, "You can do it if you set your mind to it!"

One of our responsibilities as parents is to encourage and "train" up our children in the ways of rightness. Proverbs 22:6 reads, "Train up a child in the way he should go: and when he is old, he will not depart from it."

The word "train" in Hebrew comes from the root meaning "to put something into the mouth." To help her newborn baby learn to suck, a mother dipped her finger into date syrup and put it into her baby's mouth. This ritual encouraged the baby to do what he or she should.

We, as parents, can encourage and motivate our children in positive ways. We need to fill up their lives with positive things and godly influences. Just as we fill a toy chest full of toys, we can fill our children's lives with the things of God.

Read them Bible stories as soon as they are born. Tell them about Jonah and the big fish, Noah and the ark, and David and Goliath. There are many good books and videos to choose from.

Learn Bible verses. It is amazing how easily a young child can learn verses from God's Word. Short portions such as Ephesians 6:1, "Children, obey your parents"; Ephesians 4:32, "Be ye kind"; and 1 John 4:8, "God is love" are examples.

Teach your children that church and Sunday School are important to your family. They will learn to praise God in songs, and even little ones like to fellowship with one another. Well, actually, they probably fight over toys and chairs or something, but this way they can learn to share too. Make every Sunday God's day to worship Him and praise Him.

Next, tell and show your children what genuine love is. We need to model godliness in what we do and say. God loves us so much that He sent His Son to die in our place so we can have eternal life. John 3:16 is familiar: "For God so loved the world, that he gave his only begotten Son, that whosoever believeth in him should not perish, but have everlasting life." We can't even begin to love as God does, but we can teach our children about His love.

We can fill our children's lives with godly things and train them to walk in His ways.

Nametags

Prizes

These prizes are designed for the winners to give to the mother (or mother-to-be). If you prefer to have the winners keep their prizes, choose other items.

- Toys used as decorations
- Rattles and teething toys
- Snap beads
- Small children's books

Recipes
Fruit Pizza

CRUST

　1 cup margarine
　1½ cups powdered sugar
　1 egg
　¼ teaspoon almond extract
　1 teaspoon vanilla
　2½ cups flour
　1 teaspoon salt
　1 teaspoon cream of tartar

PIZZA TOPPING

　1 (8 oz.) pkg. cream cheese, softened
　⅓ cup powdered sugar
　Canned or fresh fruit (mandarin oranges, peaches, pears, pineapple tidbits, strawberries, grapes, kiwis, bananas)
　1 (18 oz.) jar apricot or peach jam

1. For crust, blend together the margarine, powdered sugar, egg, almond extract, and vanilla. Stir in dry ingredients. Chill several hours.

2. Pat chilled dough into 14" pizza pan and bake at 375°F for 15 minutes until lightly brown. Cool.

3. For filling, blend softened cream cheese with powdered sugar. Spread on cool crust. Drain canned fruit. Slice fruit and arrange on cream cheese layer.

4. Melt jam in microwave (30–40 seconds) and drizzle over fruit.

Father and Son Events

Back on the Farm

Theme and Decorations

- Decorate tables with small toy tractors, wagons, and barn sets with farm animals.
- Have the men in charge wear farmer hats, such as seed-corn caps or big straw hats, and overalls with red bandanas in their back pockets.
- Serve water and milk in pitchers with red bandanas tied to the handles.
- Place bags of seed corn or seed beans around the room; stack bales of straw in the corner.
- Bring in a wheelbarrow and a pitchfork.

Food

- French Dip Sandwiches
- Hearty Potato Casserole
- Cherry Fluff Salad
- Chocolate Chip Cow Pies
- Pitchers of water and milk

Games

Farm Animal Sounds Puzzle

Fill in the puzzle with the sounds of the animals listed below.

ACROSS
1. Sheep
2. Duck
5. Goat
6. Horse
7. Cow
8. Rooster
10. Mouse
11. Goose

DOWN
1. Mule
3. Cricket
4. Chicken
5. Cat
6. Dog
9. Pig
11. Coyote

Farm Animal Sounds

Answers: Farm Animal Sounds

```
            B A A
Q U A C K   R     C       M A A
      H     A     L       E
    W H I N N Y   U       O
M O O           C R O W   W
      F   S Q U E A K   I N
              K       I N
          H O N K
          O
          W
          L
          S
```

Tin Time

Take the labels off a dozen cans of different kinds and sizes. Have the men guess what is in each can by its shape and size or by shaking the can. Open the cans to see who made the largest number of correct guesses.

The Farmyard

Hide wrapped candies around the room. Divide attendees into small groups. Give each group a farm animal name, such as cows, pigs, horses, dogs, sheep, chickens, or mules. Have each group choose a leader. When someone says go, everyone runs to find the hidden candy. When someone finds a piece, he has to make the noise of his team's animal to notify the leader. Only the leader can pick up the candy. When all the candy is found, the teams keep and divide what they have collected in their sacks. You could use red bandanas or small buckets for collecting the candy.

Skit

A Letter from the Farm

(Ahead of time, ask a man with a great sense of humor and a good sense of timing to read this letter. He will need to practice it a few times. It should be read with either lots of vibrancy or deadpan.)

Howdy Y' All,

As I have time, 'cause I ain't busy, I thought I would write you a few lines, about eight or ten pages, to let you know the up-to-date news of about six months ago. We ain't sick; we just don't feel good. I'm fine, Aunt Martha is dead, and I hope this letter finds you the same.

I suppose you would like to hear about us moving from Pennsylvania to Collywood, Halifornia. We never started until we left, and we never turned off 'til we came to a road that went there. The trip was the best part of it. If you ever come out here, don't miss that.

They didn't expect to see us until we arrived, and most of the people we were acquainted with we knew. Those we didn't know looked like strangers to us. We are still at the same place we moved to last, which is beside our nearest neighbor and across the road from the other side. John said he thinks we should stay here until we move someplace else.

We are very busy farming. We have three cows, but we are going to sell one because we can't milk him. Eggs are a good price; that's why they're so high. I sure hope we get plenty of them. We just bought twenty-five roosters and one old hen.

Most of the ground is so poor you can't raise an umbrella on it, but we have a fine crop of potatoes. Some are the size of peas, and some are the size of hickory nuts, and a whole lot of them are little.

The dog died last week. John said he swallowed the tape measure and died by inches. But Mary said he went up the alley and died by the yard. Aunt June said he crawled up on the bed and died by the foot.

I would have sent the money I owe you, but I already had this letter in the mail before I thought of it. I did send you that overcoat, but I cut off the buttons so it wouldn't be so heavy. You'll find them in the left-hand pocket.

June fell off the back porch and bruised her somewhat and skinned her elsewhere. Alice got the mumps and is having a swell time. The baby swallowed a roll of camera film, but so far nothing has developed.

I must close for now. If you don't get this in time to read it, let me know and I will mail you a copy. If you can't read my writing, make a copy and read your own.

Signed,

Cuzin Billie

P.S. I wanted to describe our new house where everything is so modern. We have this big house, and there is this little room that we found just last week. It's got a long white trough in it that looks like what we use to water horses in. Then there is a little white thing about three feet tall with hot and cold water. It isn't any good because it has a hole in the bottom of it and all the water runs out. That was to wash your face in. Then there is this other thing over in the corner. It's the handiest thing in the house. You can put one foot in and wash it all over and then push a lever and get clean water for the other foot.

Grandpa tried to drink out of it, but the lid fell and hit him on the head. It has two lids on it. Ma took the solid one to roll pie dough on; the other one has a hole in it, so we framed Grandpa's picture. Everyone says it looks natural—just as if he were sitting there.

Songs

"Since I Have Been Redeemed"

"Lord, I'm Coming Home"

"He Owns the Cattle on a Thousand Hills"

"Wonderful Grace of Jesus"

Devotions

Back on the Farm

Life on the farm is sometimes called the good life. Early mornings and doing chores. Revving up the John Deere and heading out across the field. Watching a newborn calf trying to stand on long, wobbly legs. The smell of fresh black dirt in the spring. Crisp fall days during harvest. The smell of fresh-cut hay on a warm summer day. A good place to raise a family. A good life. With each new day, something happens on the farm: work to be done; animals to be fed and cared for; crops to be planted, cultivated, sprayed, and combined; hay to be cut and baled and put into the barn for winter; machinery to repair and maintain; a fence to replace. If you are a farm kid, you can count on hard work. Everyone is tired at the end of the day, but it is a good kind of tired.

Luke 15:11–32 is a parable that Jesus told of a father and his two sons. One of his sons must have been tired of working hard, because he asked for his inheritance, left his home, and went to a faraway country. There he wasted all his money on loose living. The son was rebellious toward his father and wanted to go his own way. Can you think of a time when you have been like that son? I can think of four ways that we are like him.

First, we are like the prodigal son when we rebel against the Heavenly Father. We were born with a sin nature, and we want to go our own way. *(Read Romans 3:10 and 11 and John 6:44.)*

Second, we, like the prodigal son, are reluctant to go to our Heavenly Father because of our sin. The prodigal experienced a time of sin and pleasure, but his money ran out, and so did his friends. A severe famine dried up everything, and he became destitute. No money, no food. His pride probably kept him from running back to his father, so he found a job feeding green pods to swine. He would have eaten the hogs' food if he could have.

Maybe it's our pride that keeps us from going to God. Sometimes God will use trials like hunger to bring us to a point that we humble ourselves and acknowledge Him and turn to Him.

This son had reached that point and was willing to go back to his father and even to work for him as one of his servants or hired men. Many people today think they can work their way into

God's good graces. They are willing to give money, go to church, or do good deeds to please God to make up for their sin and lifestyle. That is not what God requires.

Third, we can be like the prodigal son and repent to our Heavenly Father. *(Read Luke 15:21.)* The first step is to acknowledge that we have sinned and that we need a Savior. Romans 3:23 says, "For all have sinned, and come short of the glory of God."

We need to go humbly to God and ask Him to save us. We can't do it ourselves (by works). It is only through Jesus Christ His Son.

Fourth, we can, like the son, rejoice with our Father. When something precious to you is lost, you feel happy and joyful when it is found. The father of the prodigal son was so happy when his son returned that he ordered the best robe, ring, and sandals for him to wear. He killed a fatted calf and told everyone to be merry and to rejoice. When we come to our Heavenly Father, it gives God great joy to forgive us. *(Read Luke 15:10.)*

Sadly, the older brother wasn't too happy that his father had so readily forgiven his brother. His attitude must have needed an adjustment. He should have been happy his brother was alive and back at home. Instead he was jealous and proud that he was not the wandering son. He wondered why his father hadn't given him a party for being so good. He sounds like the self-righteous Pharisees of Jesus' day. If he had repented of his jealousy and pride, his father would have rejoiced over him too.

The relationship between the prodigal son and the father was restored. What is your relationship with your Heavenly Father?

Nametags

Prizes

- Farm hats
- Pocket knives
- Pliers
- Red bandanas

Recipes

French Dip Sandwiches

1 pkg. onion soup mix
1 teaspoon garlic
½ cup soy sauce
1 pkg. au jus seasoning
4 cups water
4 lbs. roast beef

Slice meat into thin slices. Combine all ingredients in a slow cooker and cook all day or all night. Serve on hoagie buns; dip in juice.

Hearty Potato Casserole

1 (32 oz.) bag frozen hash browns
1 (16 oz.) sour cream
1 can cream of chicken soup
1 stick margarine
8–12 oz. shredded Colby cheese
1 small onion, chopped

Mix ingredients together and bake at 350°F for 1–1½ hours.

Cherry Fluff Salad

1 can cherry pie filling
1 (14 oz.) can sweetened condensed milk
1 (20 oz.) can crushed pineapple, drained
1 (12 oz.) container frozen whipped top-
    ping, thawed
1/2 cup chopped pecans (opt.)
2–3 bananas, sliced (opt.)

Mix ingredients together and chill.

Chocolate Chip Cow Pies

1 cup flour
1/2 teaspoon baking powder
1/2 teaspoon salt
1/8 teaspoon baking soda
1 (12 oz.) pkg. semisweet chocolate mini
    morsels
1/2 cup chopped pecans
1/3 cup margarine
1 cup brown sugar
1 egg, beaten
1 teaspoon vanilla

1. Mix together first 6 ingredients and set aside.

2. Melt margarine. Add brown sugar; mix and cool. Add egg and vanilla; then add flour mixture. Spread on a greased 10"–12" pizza pan. Sprinkle with mini morsels. Bake at 350°F for 20 minutes.

3. Drizzle with Powdered Sugar Glaze.

Powdered Sugar Glaze

1 1/2 cups powdered sugar
2 tablespoons cold milk

Stir together. Add more milk if needed for right consistency.

Blazing a Trail

Theme and Decorations

- Decorate tables with red checkered tablecloths. Fill red handkerchiefs with candy, tie with twine, and place on each table. Set horseshoes around the handkerchiefs.
- For table centerpieces, make covered wagons, using small candy bars for the bodies. Shape natural or white raffia over the candy bar for a wagon cover (large marshmallows under the raffia will help keep its shape). Use pretzel sticks for the hitch pole and round macaroni for the wheels.
- Stack bales of hay or straw around the room; arrange saddles, bridles, lariats, cowboy hats, and boots on and around the bales.
- Fill an aluminum bucket with ice and water. Use pint Mason jars for beverages and aluminum pie tins for plates. Place carrot and celery sticks in jars.
- Have everyone come dressed in western attire, such as cowboy boots, hats, chaps, vests, play guns, and holsters. Have extra handkerchiefs available for those who don't dress up.

Food

- Cowpoke Stew
- Ranch Hand Chili
- Trailblazer Biscuits
- Carrot and celery sticks
- Ranch dressing
- Cowboy Trail Mix
- Rise and Shine Biscuits
- Branded Brownies
- Rocking T Apple Bars

Games

Horseshoes

Set up a game of horseshoes. Use a pole that is about two feet tall. Locate a farrier or a horse owner to borrow horseshoes from for the game. Each person throws five times, earning five points for a ringer or one point if the shoe is within a foot of the pole. The player with the most points wins.

Trail Rides

Give horseback rides if they're available.

Bible/Western Bingo

Write each Bible word on a piece of paper, and place the papers in a cowboy hat. In another cowboy hat, place strips of paper with the letters B-I-N-G-O written on them. For the western game, place the western words in the hat.

Give a game sheet to each person. Using the words provided, each player should write one word in each available space on his game board. Choose someone to draw one word and one letter at a time from the cowboy hats and call them out. Each player with a space that matches the correct letter and word should circle the word. For example, if a "B" is drawn from the first cowboy hat and the word "law" from the second cowboy hat, then every player with the word "law" in the B column should circle the word. Continue drawing letters and words until someone has circled five words in a row horizontally or diagonally. The first player with five words in a row shouts, "Yahoo!" and is the winner.

B	I	N	G	O
		Free		

Bible Words to Choose From

Law	Rest	Truth	Praise	Confess
Believe	Heaven	Serve	Gift	Joy
Comfort	Peace	God	Fall	Prayer
Light	Man	Love	Repent	Creator
Hope	Heart	Sacred	Savior	Sin
Son	Holy	Cross	Follow	Forgive

Western Version
Words to Choose From

Hat	Corral	Chaps	Cowboy	Tie
Canteen	Rope	Tie	Lariat	Coyotes
Pony	Bridle	Horse	Saddles	Ranches
Wagon	Cow	Straw	Cattle	Boot
Range	Prairie	Trails	Vest	Holster
Bit	Trot	Wheel	Spur	Gun

Songs

"Find Us Faithful"
"Go On"
"Faith of Our Fathers"
"Faith Is the Victory"
"My Faith Looks Up to Thee"
"Home on the Range"
"Git Along, Little Doggie"

Devotions

Blazing a Trail of Faith

Cowboys and pioneers in wagon trains blazed trails across many miles in search of land and a new life. It was a slow, difficult journey by covered wagon and horseback. Pioneers had rivers to forge, broken equipment, and enemies in the hills. Cowboys slept under the stars and ate their meals over campfires. They led the way in opening the western frontier. We have all seen Western movies and wondered what it would have been like to experience those times in history.

Trailblazers found the way, and many followed. As dads, we are blazing a trail for our sons and the generations to follow. Our lives need to be good examples for them. We should be living lives of faith that please God.

Hebrews 11 names some Old Testament examples of men who blazed a trail of faith for us. (Read Hebrews 11:1.) Those Old Testament saints had the assurance of things hoped for, such as the promise of a coming Messiah and the promise of a home in Heaven. They also had the evidence or conviction of things not seen. They lived by faith, certain that God would do what He said He would do. God commended them for their faith (Heb. 11:2).

(Read Hebrews 11:6.) This verse tells us today that if we want to please God, we need to have faith. So what is faith? Biblical faith is confident obedience to God in spite of circumstances or consequences. That means we are assured that we can trust God no matter what happens.

Hebrews 11:6 gives us the basic elements of faith: we must believe that God is God and that He will reward those who seek Him. (Read John 1:12.) This truth should motivate us to live by faith.

The men of faith in Hebrews 11 had four things in common that helped them blaze a trail for us to follow.

First, God spoke to them through His words. God doesn't speak audibly to us today, but He has given us His Word, the Bible, and His Holy Spirit to guide us. We need to read His Word daily.

Second, they believed God. When God spoke to them, they didn't doubt. Faith in God does not require a leap into the dark; it is a decision to trust Someone in Whom you have total confidence. Those men of faith knew the God Who spoke to them, and they believed what He said. They had experienced His faithfulness and provision. They trusted Him completely even when they had no idea what lay ahead.

Third, they obeyed God. Noah obeyed God and built an ark even though he had never seen rain or a flood (Heb. 11:7). When God told Abraham to leave the land he was living in, he obeyed, not even knowing where he was headed. He also offered up Isaac, his only son, as a sacrifice when God told him to, not knowing what would happen. He believed God would raise Isaac from the dead (Heb. 11:8–12). These men of faith knew God and had complete trust and confidence in Him.

Fourth, they had victory and received a reward. They all received a reward of a heavenly Home. (Read Hebrews 11:16.)

They all lived by faith. God counted their faith in Him as righteousness. Therefore, God rewarded them with eternal life. They looked to the future when the once-for-all sacrifice of Christ would be made for their sins.

We look back to the cross and the shed blood of our Savior and put our faith in Him alone for our eternal life. (Read Hebrews 12:1 and 2.)

We can glance back at the Old Testament

heroes, but the One we need to fix our eyes on is Jesus. He is the author and perfecter of our faith. It is because of what He did on the cross that we can be righteous before God. (*Read Romans 5:1.*)

We can be men of faith and blaze a trail for those who follow after us. Are we leaving them a godly heritage? We need to listen when God speaks through His Word, believe that He will do what He has said, obey His leading, and claim the victory.

Nametags

Prizes

- Horseshoes
- Candy in handkerchiefs
- Candy-covered wagons
- Cowboy spurs
- Pint jars with jellies
- Rope licorice

Recipes

Branded Brownies

BROWNIES

  1 cup sugar
  $\frac{1}{2}$ cup margarine
  4 eggs
  1 can chocolate syrup
  $\frac{1}{4}$ teaspoon baking soda
  1 cup flour

FROSTING

  $\frac{1}{2}$ cup margarine
  $1\frac{1}{2}$ cups sugar
  $\frac{1}{3}$ cup milk
  $\frac{1}{2}$ cup chocolate chips

1. To make brownies, cream sugar and margarine. Stir in eggs and syrup. Combine baking soda and flour; add to cream mixture gradually. Bake in a jelly roll pan at 350°F for 20–25 minutes.

2. For frosting, combine margarine, sugar, and milk. Boil 1 minute. Remove from heat. Add chocolate chips; beat with wooden spoon until the frosting loses its shine. Frost warm brownies.

3. To brand the brownies, use a toothpick or knife to carve a brand in each brownie. For a Rocking T brand, make a capital T with a curved line, like a smile, under the T. For a Lazy L brand, lay the L on its side. For a Double B brand, trace two Bs, making one B facing left and one facing right. For a Diamond D brand, make a diamond shape with a D inside it.

Cowpoke Stew

  3 lbs. stew beef
  5 large potatoes, peeled
  5–6 carrots
  1 large onion
  1 stalk celery
  1 tablespoon sugar
  2 tablespoons tapioca
  1 (46 oz.) can V8 vegetable juice
  Salt and pepper to taste

Cut up vegetables into bite-size pieces. Place all ingredients in a large roasting pan with lid. Bake at 275°F for 5 hours.

Ranch Hand Chili

2 lbs. ground beef
Salt and pepper to taste
1 (46 oz.) can tomato juice
1 pkg. chili seasoning
1 jar picante sauce
$^1/_2$ cup brown sugar
Sour cream (opt.)
Grated cheddar cheese (opt.)

Brown ground beef. Season with salt and pepper. Add tomato juice, seasoning, picante sauce, and brown sugar. Simmer on the stove for 1 hour or longer (or use a slow cooker). Top with sour cream and grated cheddar cheese.

Trailblazer Biscuits

3 cups flour
$^1/_4$ cup sugar
4 teaspoons baking powder
$^1/_2$ teaspoon cream of tartar
$^3/_4$ teaspoon salt
$^1/_2$ cup shortening
1 egg
$1^1/_8$ cups milk

1. Combine dry ingredients. Cut in shortening until coarse. Add egg and milk. Mix until dough forms ball. Turn dough out on lightly floured board. Knead 10–12 times. Roll out $^3/_4$ inch thick.

2. Cut out biscuits and place on an ungreased cookie sheet. Freeze. Store frozen biscuits in a plastic bag.

3. Bake frozen biscuits on greased cookie sheet at 450°F for 12–15 minutes. If biscuits are thawed, bake for 8–10 minutes.

Cowboy Trail Mix

1 cup brown sugar
$^1/_2$ cup margarine
$^1/_4$ cup white corn syrup
$^1/_4$ teaspoon baking soda
$^3/_4$ box Crispix cereal (about 10 oz.)
1 bag plain M&M's
1 (9 oz.) can cashews
$1^1/_2$ cups raisins

Combine brown sugar, margarine, and corn syrup in a large microwave-safe bowl. Bring to boil in microwave (about 3 minutes). Stir in baking soda. Add cereal and stir. Microwave 4 minutes, stirring after every minute. Pour on waxed paper to cool. Add M&M's, cashews, and raisins.

Rise and Shine Biscuits

2 cups flour
2 teaspoons baking powder
1 teaspoon salt
1 teaspoon cream of tartar
$^1/_2$ teaspoon baking soda
4 teaspoons sugar
1 teaspoon cinnamon
$^1/_3$ cup shortening
$^3/_4$ cup buttermilk
$^3/_4$ cup soft raisins

1. Combine dry ingredients. Cut in shortening until coarse. Add buttermilk and raisins. Mix until dough forms ball. Turn dough out on lightly floured board. Knead 10–12 times. Roll out $^3/_4$ inch thick.

2. Cut out biscuits. Place on greased cookie sheet. Bake between 425°F and 450°F for 10–12 minutes.

3. Drizzle with Powdered Sugar Glaze.

Powdered Sugar Glaze

$1^1/_2$ cups powdered sugar
2 tablespoons cold milk

Stir together. Add more milk if needed for right consistency.

Rocking T Apple Bars

6 cups apples, peeled and sliced

1 cup sugar

2 teaspoons cinnamon

3 tablespoons flour

4 cups flour, heaping

1 teaspoon salt

2 cups butter-flavored Crisco

1 cup cold milk

1. Sprinkle sugar, cinnamon, and 3 tablespoons flour on sliced apples. Mix well and set aside.

2. Using a pastry cutter, cut 4 heaping cups flour, salt, and shortening together until coarse. Add cold milk.

3. Roll out half the dough to fit a large cookie sheet with sides. Fill with apple mixture and dot with margarine. Add top crust; seal edges. Sprinkle with sugar. Bake 40–50 minutes at 375°F.

4. Drizzle with Powdered Sugar Glaze.

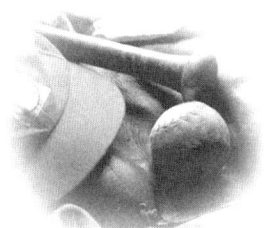

Camping with Dad

Theme and Decorations

- If you can go camping as a father-son outing, that would be best.
- If you can't, gather items you would need for an outdoor camping theme.
- For atmosphere start with setting up a tent in the room, or set up a tent outside to greet the men and boys as they come in.
- Place artificial trees, such as Christmas trees, by the tent.
- Use firewood logs, lawn chairs, flashlights, sleeping bags, and pillows.
- Remember bottles of bug spray and Bactine.
- Put camping lanterns, canteens, containers of hot chocolate mixes, and bags of marshmallows on the tables.
- Set up a table with a cookstove, iron skillets, matches, and other camping cookery. You could also put these items on a picnic table outside the tent.
- Put two or three marshmallows on a tree branch ready for roasting, and lean the branch against the tent or picnic table.
- Place on each table napkins and silverware in empty coffee cans.

Food

- Roasted Food in Foil
- Pumpkin Bars
- Cherry Bars
- Pineapple Bars
- S'mores
- Kick the Can Ice Cream

Games

Longest Potato Peel

Make a game of peeling the potatoes for the roasted foil packets. Have the potatoes washed and ready to peel. Let each fellow pick out the potato he wants to peel. The goal is to see who can cut the longest potato peel without breaking the peel. Wash the potatoes again and use for supper!

Kick the Can

After your meal, make use of the coffee cans you used for napkins and silverware. Make a relay race of kicking the cans to the other end of the room and back. The first team to complete the relay wins.

Name These States

People who go camping might travel to different states to camp. Can you name these states?

State Names to Choose From

Maine	Michigan	Louisiana
Utah	South Carolina	West Virginia
Florida	Mississippi	Missouri
Tennessee	New Hampshire	New York
Wisconsin	Indiana	Montana
Kentucky	Ohio	North Carolina
Illinois	Idaho	

Names These States

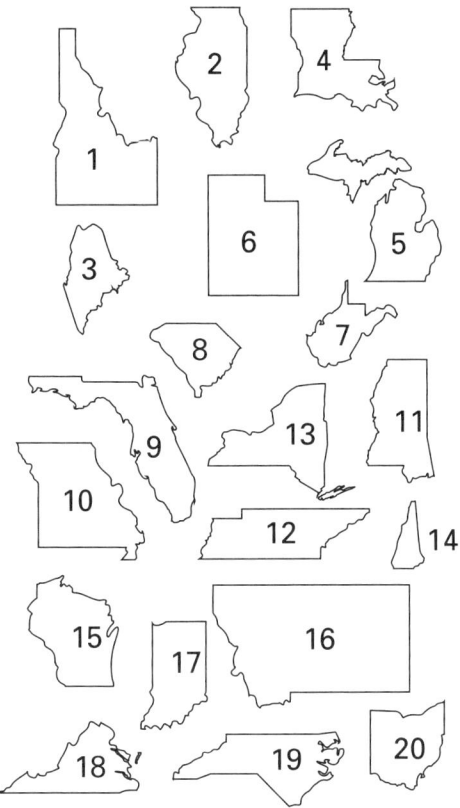

Answers

(1) Idaho; (2) Illinois; (3) Maine; (4) Louisiana; (5) Michigan; (6) Utah; (7) West Virginia; (8) South Carolina; (9) Florida; (10) Missouri; (11) Mississippi; (12) Tennessee; (13) New York; (14) New Hampshire; (15) Wisconsin; (16) Montana; (17) Indiana; (18) Kentucky; (19) North Carolina; (20) Ohio.

Kick the Can Ice Cream

Making your own dessert is a fun activity. See "Recipes" (page 105).

Songs

"Pass It On"
"Thank You, Lord"
"God Is So Good"
"Give of Your Best to the Master"
"Trust and Obey"
"All for Jesus"

Devotions
Camping with Dad

One of the best experiences for a father and son is time spent together camping. Packing up your gear, your tent, your sleeping bag, the firewood, food, and fishing poles adds to the anticipation and excitement of a night or two spent under the stars. Can't you just smell the campfire, see the sun setting on the horizon, taste the toasted marshmallows, hear the crickets chirping, and feel the mosquitoes biting? Spending time together outside in God's great creation can bring you close to each other and to God.

One day God commanded Abraham to take his son Isaac to the hills of Moriah. I am sure they camped as they went on their three-day journey. Abraham and Isaac had to get themselves ready for their journey. They rose early, then split wood and loaded it for the burnt offering (Gen. 22:1–14).

At the end of their journey, God asked Abraham to give Him Isaac as a sacrifice. He wanted to see if Abraham loved Him more than he loved Isaac. God also wanted to test Abraham's faith in Him concerning His promise to give Abraham descendants as numerous as the stars.

You probably know the end of the story. Abraham trusted God and feared Him, even to the point of offering his son as a sacrifice. God spared Isaac and provided a ram for the burnt offering.

What kind of sacrifices does God ask of us today?

First, God wants the sacrifice of a contrite, or repentant, heart. *(Read Psalm 51:17.)* We need to come humbly before God, confessing our sins to Him. When we do, "he is faithful and just to forgive us our sins, and to cleanse us from all unrighteousness" (1 John 1:9).

Second, God wants the sacrifice of our bodies. *(Read Romans 12:1.)* God wants to use our bodies to bring honor to Him. We should be willing to give of ourselves to serve Him through everything we do, everything we say, and everywhere we go.

After all, our bodies are a temple of the Holy Spirit (1 Cor. 6:19, 20).

Third, God wants the sacrifice of our witnessing for Him. God wants us to be willing to share our faith with others. We have good news: the death of Jesus Christ paid our sin debt. Anyone who trusts in Christ alone is forgiven and granted eternal life in Heaven. Sometimes living a godly life isn't easy, but a sacrifice isn't anything if it costs us nothing. Abraham looked to God and trusted His leading in the sacrifice that was asked of him, and we can too.

Fourth, God also wants a sacrifice, or offerings, of our finances, as we see in 2 Corinthians 9:7 and Philippians 4:18. *(Read the verses.)* Everything we have is from God and belongs to Him. We should gratefully give back to Him even when it is hard. God will always supply our needs when we honor Him first with our offerings.

Fifth, God wants a sacrifice of our time and devotion. We need to give God time in prayer and Bible study. Sometimes it is hard to find time alone with God; but remember, if it doesn't cost us something, it isn't really a sacrifice. Put God first, and honor Him by doing what is right and good. *(Read Hebrews 13:16.)*

Sixth, God wants the sacrifice of our giving thanks and praise to Him. *(Read Hebrews 13:15.)* God is worthy of our praise. Praise should be continually on our lips!

How willing are we when it comes to giving sacrifices to God? We need to be like Abraham and Isaac: willing to obey and willing to offer sacrifices such as repentant hearts, our bodies, our witness, our money, our time, and our praise. Offer your best to Him.

Nametags

Prizes

- Small flashlights
- Bactine
- Bug spray
- Bags of marshmallows
- Chocolate bars
- Hot chocolate mixes

Recipes
Roasted Food in Foil

Wrap hamburger patties or minute steaks and raw carrots, potatoes, and onions in heavy foil. Sprinkle with salt and pepper. Put in a pat of butter. Seal foil shut, and set the packets in the campfire, or cook them on a low or medium grill for at least 45 minutes.

Pumpkin Bars

BARS
　4 eggs
　2 cups sugar
　2 cups pumpkin
　$^3/_4$ cup margarine, melted
　2 cups flour
　1 teaspoon baking soda
　2 teaspoons baking powder
　1 teaspoon cinnamon

FROSTING
6 tablespoons margarine, melted
1 tablespoon milk
3 cups powdered sugar
1 teaspoon vanilla
3–4 oz. cream cheese, softened

1. To make pumpkin bars, blend the first four ingredients. Add dry ingredients. Pour batter into a greased jelly roll pan. Bake at 350°F for 30 minutes.

2. Beat frosting ingredients until fluffy; spread on cooled bars.

Cherry Bars

1 cup margarine
1³/₄ cups sugar
4 eggs
1 teaspoon vanilla
3 cups flour
1¹/₂ teaspoons baking powder
1 or 2 cans cherry pie filling

1. Cream margarine and sugar. Add eggs; beat. Add vanilla, flour, and baking powder; mix well. Pour ²/₃ batter into a greased jelly roll pan. Spoon cherry pie filling over batter. Drop remainder of batter by spoonfuls on top.

2. Bake at 350°F for 20 minutes or until top is set and browned.

3. Frost with Powered Sugar Glaze.

Powdered Sugar Glaze

1¹/₂ cups powdered sugar
2 tablespoons cold milk

Stir together. Add more milk if needed for right consistency.

Pineapple Bars

BARS
2 eggs
1 (20 oz.) can crushed pineapple
1³/₄ cups brown sugar
1³/₄ cups flour
1 teaspoon soda
1 teaspoon vanilla

FROSTING
1 (8 oz.) pkg. cream cheese, softened
1 stick margarine, softened
2 cups powdered sugar
1 teaspoon vanilla

1. Blend the ingredients for bars and bake at 350°F for 25 minutes.

2. Beat frosting ingredients until fluffy; spread on cooled bars.

Kick the Can Ice Cream

1 cup whipping cream
1 cup milk
1 beaten egg
¹/₂ cup sugar
1 teaspoon vanilla

1. You will need a 1-lb. empty, clean coffee can and a 3-lb. empty, clean coffee can. In the small coffee can, combine all ingredients. Cover can and seal with duct tape; put it into the large coffee can. Layer ice and rock salt around the small can. When filled, cover large can.

2. Roll the can back and forth for 10 minutes. Open outer can; empty ice and water. Lift out the small can, wipe clean, and open. Scrape the sides and stir the ice cream. Replace cover and reassemble the cans with fresh ice and salt. Roll 5 more minutes. Open and enjoy!

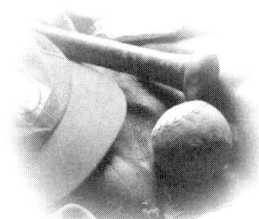

Cars, Trucks, and Chariots

Theme and Decorations

- Decorate the room with jumper cables, gas cans, tires, cleaners, clean oil cans, and new rags.
- Display various types of wheels, such as car tires, wagon wheels, and bicycle tires.
- On the tables place car wax, car air fresheners, hand cleaners, tools, chamois, ice scrapers, etc.
- Have a display table for men and boys to bring in their model cars or trucks or their pinewood derby cars.

Food

- Hot Wheels (grilled hamburgers)
- Rev Your Engine Calico Beans
- Pinewood Derby Potato Salad
- Fast-Fruit Pizza
- Turtle Wax Ice Cream Sundaes

Games

Stop, Get to Know, and Go!

Find a person who fits a description and ask him to sign on the blank. Hurry! Traffic control will signal you to stop after five minutes.

1. Someone who drives a red truck. _____
2. Someone whose birthday is the same month as yours. _____
3. Someone who is wearing orange. _____
4. Someone who can say the first ten books of the Bible. _____
5. Someone who has the same first name or initials as you. _____
6. Someone who has a younger brother or sister. _____
7. A person who has green eyes. _____
8. Someone who has gray hair. _____
9. Someone who does not like chocolate. _____
10. Someone who has a black or white spotted dog. _____
11. Someone who is currently in a Bible study group. _____
12. Someone who has lived in four or more states. _____

Car Races

Have the men and boys make a simple race-track or borrow a pinewood derby track from a Scout or other group. Each man or boy can bring any car he wants to race against others. The one with the fastest car wins. You could also have prizes for the most creative, the slowest, the biggest, or the smallest car.

Brand Names

For each letter of the alphabet, write the brand name of an item related to cars or trucks. For example, you could write "Zip Wax" for Z.

A _____

B _____

C _____

D _____

E _____

F _____

G _____

H _____

I _____

J _____

K _____

L _____

M _____

N _____

O _____

P _____

Q _____

R _____

S _____

T _____

U _____

V _____

W _____

X _____

Y _____

Z _____

Possible Answers

Armor All	Heet	Raindance
Buick	Hummer	STP
Bosch	Interstate	Sunex
Craftsman	Jeep	Turtle Wax
Champion	Kendall	Ultra
Conoco	Kraco	Uniroyal
Delco	Lincoln	Valvoline
DieHard	Mobil	Volkswagen
Everstart	Nissan	Volvo
Eveready	O'Reilly	Wearever
Ford	Prestone	WD-40
Ferrari	Penzoil	X-tend
Goodyear	Quaker State	Xterra
Goop	Rally	Yugo
Halvoline	Rain-X	Z-28

Songs

"We Trust in the Name of the Lord Our God"

"Trust and Obey"

"Trusting Jesus"

"It's Not an Easy Road"

Devotions

Trust in the Lord

We males are fascinated by anything with a motor and wheels. As toddlers, we start making motor sounds as we push our cars and trucks around the house or yard. Next come bicycles and four-wheelers, and then we are finally behind the wheel of a car! We not only like the power and excitement we feel driving a car or truck, but we also like to work on fixing them. As soon as we get a driver's license, most of us are looking for a vehicle of our own. Most of the time, our finances lead us to an old beater that we can't wait to start working on. When it is ready to go, we hit the road, and it feels great! For the most part, we take pride in the vehicles we drive. We trust they will get us where we need to go.

In Bible times some nations used horses in battle. Having horses and chariots gave them an edge over enemies who didn't. However, God didn't allow Israel to have horses because He wanted His people to trust in Him, not in their cavalry (Ps. 20:7; 33:17).

Proverbs 3:1–10 tells us about trusting God and honoring Him. Solomon and his son were having a father-son talk. Solomon wanted to teach his son to trust and honor God. Proverbs 1:7 states, "The fear of the LORD is the beginning of knowledge." As fathers, we can teach this truth to our sons. We can encourage them to get knowledge by fearing the Lord. Each verse that has a command in Proverbs 3:1–10 also has a promise of reward.

(Ask a volunteer to read Proverbs 3:1 and 2.) God promises long life and peace as a reward for obedience.

(*Ask a volunteer to read Proverbs 3:3 and 4.*) We need to show kindness and speak truth all the time. The Israelites would bind Scripture to themselves so they continually had it with them. When we continually practice truth and kindness, our reward will be having favor with God and with man.

(*Ask a volunteer to read Proverbs 3:5 and 6.*) To trust God means to believe what God says He will do. So we trust Him for our salvation and for eternal life. But we can also trust Him to care for us day to day. When we "acknowledge" Him, we know Him personally and have fellowship with Him. Our reward for trusting and acknowledging Him is His leading in our lives. He will show us His will for our lives through His Word and prayer, through other Christians, through circumstances, or maybe through all three. When we trust and acknowledge Him, He will show us the way.

(*Ask a volunteer to read Proverbs 3:7 and 8.*) Sometimes we try to "go it alone." We forget to ask God which way is best. We become wise in our own eyes, thinking we know what is good. Instead we need to have a healthy fear of, or respect for, the Lord and turn to Him. We will feel much better when we do. We will feel healthy and refreshed.

(*Ask a volunteer to read Proverbs 3:9 and 10.*) We can't "outgive" God. Everything belongs to Him. We should cheerfully offer gifts to Him because of all the blessings He gives us. When we honor God by giving, He will reward us with prosperity.

Solomon wanted his son to know these truths. He wanted him to trust and honor God in everything. So many people have trusted in the things they could see, like horses and chariots. Solomon wanted his son to trust in the name of the Lord. That should be the desire of every father. When we obey each of these commands, God promises great rewards. Let's teach our sons to trust and honor God.

Nametags

Prizes

- Car fresheners
- Cleaners
- Car oil
- Armor All
- Car wax
- Ice scrapers
- Chamois

Recipes

Rev Your Engine Calico Beans

1 lb. ground beef
1 small onion, chopped
1 lb. bacon, cut up bite-size
1 (28 oz.) can pork and beans
1 (15 oz.) can butter beans
1 (15 oz.) can kidney beans
1 (15 oz.) can great northern beans
$\frac{1}{2}$ cup brown sugar
$\frac{1}{2}$ cup sugar
$\frac{1}{4}$ cup catsup
2 tablespoons molasses
$\frac{1}{2}$ teaspoon dry mustard

In a skillet, brown ground beef, onion, and chopped bacon; drain. Put in slow cooker and add remaining ingredients (do not drain beans). Cook at least 1 hour on high.

Pinewood Derby Potato Salad

DRESSING

2 cups Miracle Whip

$1/4$ cup pickle juice or vinegar

2 teaspoons apple cider vinegar or pickle juice

$2^{1}/_{2}$ tablespoons mustard

2 tablespoons sugar

4 tablespoons milk

1 tablespoon salt

$1/2$ teaspoon pepper

1 teaspoon celery seed

SALAD

4 lbs. red potatoes

1 small onion, chopped

1 small jar bread and butter pickles

1. Whisk together ingredients for dressing. Set aside.

2. Boil red potatoes with skins on; then peel and cut in bit-size pieces. Add onion, pickles, and dressing. Chill overnight.

Fast Fruit Pizza

CRUST

$1/2$ cup margarine

$1/2$ cup shortening

1 cup sugar

1 egg

$1/2$ teaspoon vanilla

2 cups flour

$1/2$ teaspoon cream of tartar

$1/2$ teaspoon baking soda

$1/4$ teaspoon salt

FILLING

2 (8 oz. each) pkgs. cream cheese, softened

1 (8 oz.) container frozen whipped topping, thawed

1 cup powdered sugar

GLAZE

1 cup pineapple juice

1 cup orange juice

2 tablespoons cornstarch

FRUIT

Raspberries, strawberries, kiwi, grapes, mandarin oranges, pineapple chunks, banana slices

1. For crust, cream together margarine, shortening, and sugar. Add egg and vanilla. Combine dry ingredients and add to creamed mixture. Press dough into cookie sheet with sides. Bake at 350°F for 8–10 minutes until slightly brown. Cool.

2. For filling, mix cream cheese until smooth. Add sugar and whipped topping. Spread over crust.

3. In a large pan, combine pineapple juice, orange juice, and corn starch; cook and stir until thickened. Reserve $1/2$ cup of glaze. Cool glaze and spread over cream cheese filling.

4. Add fruit pieces. Drizzle or brush remaining glaze over fruit; chill.

Turtle Wax Ice Cream Sundaes

Drizzle chocolate or hot fudge and caramel syrup over vanilla ice cream. Top with nuts.

Hot Fudge Topping

3 (1 oz. each) squares semisweet baking chocolate

1 stick margarine

3 cups sugar

1 (12 oz.) can evaporated milk

Melt the baking chocolate and margarine. Stir in the sugar until dissolved. Slowly add the evaporated milk. Cook on low for 30 minutes.

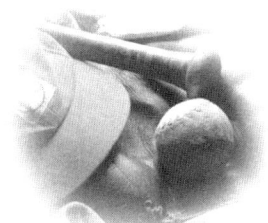

Goals for Life

Theme and Decorations

- Emphasize sports with goals, such as football, hockey, and soccer. Decorate the room with hockey sticks, uniforms, helmets, and jerseys.
- Make football goalposts at one end of the room, and have a soccer or hockey goal at the other end.
- Use footballs, hockey pucks, and soccer balls for centerpieces.
- Celebrate the game with cheer cards on the tables. These could have sayings on them such as "Make That Goal!" "When We Fail to Set Goals, We Are Set to Fail."
- Spread stadium blankets on the floor or drape them over the tables. Place Gatorade bottles on the tables as decorations and as beverages.

Food

- Pasta bar with spaghetti, lasagna, and ravioli
- Lettuce salad
- Hot rolls
- Banana-Split Cake
- Chocolate Cream Puff Dessert
- Gatorade or other sports drinks

Games

Father-Son Game

Plan a father-son football or soccer game.

Books of the Bible

Your goal is to find the answer, which is a book of the Bible.

1. Different stages in a play _____
2. A famous Biblical warrior _____
3. Royal rulers _____
4. One who makes legal decisions _____
5. One of the pair who made up an old radio program _____
6. Residents of Italy _____
7. 759; 28; 1,324; 101,652 _____
8. A widow _____
9. Poems of love _____
10. The beginning _____
11. Songs of praise _____
12. A mineral deposit _____
13. God's chosen people _____
14. A chauffeur _____
15. A career _____
16. Wise sayings _____
17. To have something revealed _____
18. Historical record of events _____
19. Mourning out loud _____
20. Check _ _ _ _ _____
21. _ _ _ _ warm _____
22. To leave or depart _____
23. Pumpkin eater _____
24. Outdoor bathroom _____
25. Grass used for making hay _____

Answers

(1) Acts; (2) Joshua; (3) Kings; (4) Judges; (5) Amos; (6) Romans; (7) Numbers; (8) Ruth; (9) Song of Solomon; (10) Genesis; (11) Psalms; (12) Micah; (13) Hebrews; (14) James; (15) Job; (16) Proverbs; (17) Revelation; (18) Chron-

icles; (19) Lamentations; (20) Mark; (21) Luke;
(22) Exodus; (23) Peter; (24) John; (25) Timothy.

Your goal is to figure out as many "wordles" as
you can in five minutes.

Wordles

ICE	PITCH	PAR 2	FAIR ☐	HEADER HEADER	BASEBALL (in diamond)
D N A H	DECI SION	PLAY PLAY	4 HAND	O / PHD / BA / MS	C C C C C
F I E L D	He ad ac he	MIND ——— MATTER	**I'M** YOU	EZ I I I I I I	B A N · A N A
GROUND FEET FEET FEET FEET FEET FEET	○ ○ ○ CIRCUS	CYCLE CYCLE CYCLE	WEAR LONG	R E D (staggered)	CHAIR
STAND I	ECNALG	J U YOU ME S T	K C U T S	OFF OFF F F STOP	
SEARCH AND	T O U C H	**RED**	LE VEL	R|E|A|D	P E T E P E T E
STROKES *STROKES* strokes	KNEE LIGHTS	LIGHT FEET	R O ROADS D S	B A L L	WORKING ——— TIME

Answers

Row 1: thin ice, low pitch, 2 under par, fair and square, double header, baseball diamond. *Row 2:* backhand, split decision, double play, forehand, three degrees below zero, high seas. *Row 3:* left field, splitting headache, mind over matter, I'm over you, easy on the eyes, banana split. *Row 4:* six feet underground, three-ring circus, tricycle, long underwear, red cross, high chair. *Row 5:* I understand, backward glance, just between you and me, stuck up, off sides, short stop. *Row 6:* search high and low, touch down, Big Red, bi-level or split level, read between the lines, repeat. *Row 7:* different strokes, neon lights, light on your feet, crossroads, low ball, working overtime.

Songs

"Victory in Jesus"
"Who Is on the Lord's Side?"
"When We All Get to Heaven"

Devotions
Goals for Life

It is time for the big game. The whole team is ready. You have pumped yourselves up, and you really want to win this one. Everyone's wearing his team jersey, and his pads and equipment are in place. For weeks you have trained and practiced for this day. You have one thing on your mind, and it is to get the ball to the goal and score. As Christians, we are like athletes. We, too, need to live with one goal in mind: to glorify God.

Every day athletes have to work hard in practice and self-discipline. It would be easy to become discouraged if they didn't have the goal of winning games as their reward. Paul wrote about controlling his body. (*Read 1 Corinthians 9:27.*) We need to discipline our bodies and bring them under control so we can honor and glorify God.

Athletes have to obey rules. If competitors didn't follow the rulebook, any competition would be chaos. We have God's rulebook, the Bible, to help us find our way in a confusing, stressful world. When we read God's Word and follow His directions, we will glorify Him.

Athletes need to wear the right equipment for protection. Playing in a game without pads and a helmet would probably end up with us in the doctor's office—or worse. As Christians, we need to put on God's equipment and wear it as we fight against our foe. Our battle is against the Devil and the spiritual forces of wickedness. We need to put on God's full armor and stand firm when the Devil comes at us.

Let's looks the each piece of God's equipment for us.

First, the girdle of truth. (*Read the first part of Ephesians 6:14.*) Jesus said, "Sanctify them through thy truth: thy word is truth" (John 17:17). We learn the truth from the Word of God.

Second, the breastplate of righteousness. (*Read the second part of Ephesians 6:14.*) When we trust Christ for our eternal salvation, we are made right with God. We can't fight our foe if we are not right before God. God made us right before Him through what Christ did on the cross. (*Read 2 Corinthians 5:21.*) Listen to Paul's testimony in Philippians 3:8 and 9. (*Read the verses.*)

Third, the shoes of the gospel of peace. (*Read Ephesians 6:15.*) We have peace *with* God when we become His children (Rom. 5:1). We have the peace *of* God as we commit our way to the Lord with prayer and thanksgiving (Phil. 4:6, 7). In addition, the Bible tells us to "be at peace among yourselves" (1 Thess. 5:13) and "as much as lieth in you, live peaceably with all men" (Rom. 12:18).

Fourth, the shield of faith. (*Read Ephesians 6:16.*) Our faith should be in God, and we can trust Him for any situation we might face. If can trust Him for our eternal salvation—and we can!—then we can trust Him in all things. Faith in the Christian's life protects him from Satan's fiery attacks. "And this is the victory that over-cometh the world, even our faith" (1 John 5:4).

Fifth, the helmet of salvation. (*Read the first part of Ephesians 6:17.*) God has delivered us from sin through His Son; He will provide deliverance for us from Satan's attacks. (*Read 1 Thessalonians 5:8 and 9.*)

Finally, the sword of the Spirit. (*Read the last part of Ephesians 6:17.*) Jesus used the Word of God against Satan when Satan tempted Him. God's Word is sharp and powerful. It will help us stand fast against the Devil. (*Read Hebrews 4:12.*)

After we have our equipment on, we need to pray. (*Read Ephesians 6:18 and Philippians 4:6.*)

The protection God gives us to wear will make us strong and able as we press toward our goal. In Philippians 3:14 Paul talked about his goal: "I press toward the mark for the prize of the high calling of God in Christ Jesus."

We need to live our lives with the goal of glorifying God in everything we do. As athletes, we need to work hard, obey the rules, and put on the right equipment. As Christians, we need to do the same thing. Then we can say with Paul, who had the goal of Heaven before him, "I have fought a good fight, I have finished my course, I have kept the faith" (2 Tim. 4:7).

Nametags

Prizes

- Notepads and pens
- Small footballs
- Football, soccer, or hockey cards
- Candy bars

Recipes

Spaghetti Sauce

3 (12 oz. each) cans tomato paste
1 qt. tomatoes or tomato juice
4 (15 oz. each) cans tomato sauce
2 pkgs. spaghetti sauce mix
1 teaspoon garlic powder
$1/8$ cup soy sauce
1 teaspoon Italian seasoning
$1/4$ cup sugar
$1/2$ teaspoon oregano
2 lbs. ground beef
Onion, if desired
Mushrooms, if desired

Cook ground beef; drain. Combine all ingredients and cook slowly for several hours.

Lasagna

1 (16 oz.) pkg. lasagna noodles, cooked
   and drained
2 (26 oz. each) jars spaghetti sauce
1 lb. ground beef, cooked and drained
1 (8 oz.) carton cottage cheese
6–8 cups shredded mozzarella cheese

Add ground beef to spaghetti sauce. In a 9" x 13" pan, start with sauce on the bottom. Then layer the noodles, cottage cheese, sauce, and mozzarella cheese twice, ending with mozzarella cheese on top. Bake at 350°F for 40–50 minutes.

Ravioli

1 pkg. frozen cheese ravioli
1 (26 oz.) jar pasta sauce
1 lb. ground beef, cooked and drained
2–3 cups shredded mozzarella cheese

1. Preheat oven to 425°F. Brown ground beef. Layer ingredients in a 9" x 13" baking pan.

2. For first layer, use half the ravioli, half the ground beef, 1 cup of sauce, and half the cheese.

3. For second layer, use half the ravioli and half the ground beef. Spread on sauce. (Do not add cheese.)

4. Cover with foil and bake for 35 minutes. Uncover, add rest of cheese, and bake uncovered until cheese is bubbly, about 9 minutes.

Banana-Split Cake

CRUMB BASE
1½–2 cups vanilla wafers, crushed
½ cup margarine, melted

FILLING
1 (8 oz.) pkg. cream cheese, softened
1 cup powdered sugar
2 tablespoons milk
1 (20 oz.) can crushed pineapple, drained
2 or 3 bananas, sliced
1 (12 oz.) container frozen whipped topping, thawed

1. Combine wafers and margarine. Press into a 9" x 13" baking dish. Bake at 350°F for 5–7 minutes.

2. For filling, combine cream cheese, sugar, and milk. Spread over cooled crumbs. Add a layer of bananas; then add pineapple. Top with whipped topping. Refrigerate.

Chocolate Cream Puff Dessert

CRUST
1 cup water
½ cup butter (no substitutes)
1 cup flour
4 eggs

FILLING
1 (8 oz.) pkg. cream cheese, softened
3½ cups cold milk
2 (3.4 oz.) pkgs. instant chocolate pudding and pie filling

TOPPING
1 (8 oz.) container frozen whipped topping, thawed
¼ cup chocolate ice cream topping
¼ cup caramel ice cream topping
⅓ cup chopped almonds

1. In a saucepan over medium heat, bring the water and butter to a boil. Add flour all at once. Stir until a smooth ball forms. Remove from heat. Let stand for 5 minutes. Add eggs, one at a time, beating well after each one. Beat until smooth. Spread into a greased 9" x 13" baking dish. Bake at 400°F for 30–35 minutes until puffed and golden brown. Cool.

2. For filling, beat cream cheese, milk, and pudding until smooth. Spread over crust. Refrigerate for 20 minutes.

3. Add whipped topping. Refrigerate. Before serving, drizzle with chocolate topping, caramel topping, and almonds.

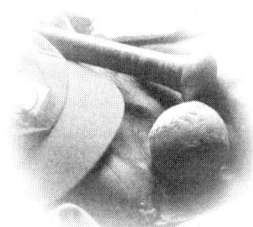

Harvest of Souls

Theme and Decorations

- Decorate for the harvest season. Fill wheelbarrows with pumpkins, Indian corn, and gourds. Stuff a big basket with field corn; fill buckets with oats or beans.
- Make a scarecrow to lean in the corner of the room, or set him in a chair to greet everyone.
- Bring bales of straw to sit on.
- Sprinkle candy corn, pumpkin candy, and autumn-colored M&M's on the tables.
- Tie miniature Indian corn husks together with twine and arrange with small pumpkins on the table.
- Make a shock of corn with dried stalks; tie with twine.

Food

- Baked ham
- Mashed potatoes and gravy
- Corn Casserole
- Apple Salad
- Overnight Rolls
- Pecan Pie
- Pumpkin Pie
- Apple cider

Games

A Corny Game

Answer these questions about corn.

1. When is corn like sugar? _____
2. When is corn musical? _____
3. When is corn sticky? _____
4. What is formed by alternate thawing and freezing? _____
5. What corn goes good with honey? _____
6. What corn creeps up on something? _____
7. How is a simple bad joke described? _____
8. When does corn bark? _____
9. What state is called the Cornhusker State? _____
10. What corn is part of the eye? _____
11. What corn is a fancy part of a building? _____
12. What corn is part of a room or street? _____
13. What corn would a baby curl up in? _____
14. What corn is explosive? _____
15. What corn grows into a majestic timber? _____
16. Which corn was a famous English general? _____
17. What corn is the symbol for plenty? _____
18. What corn is stiff or stuck up? _____
19. What "corn" should be most important in your life? _____

Words to Choose From

cornet   sweet corn   cornucopia
cornstalk   corn syrup   acorn
cornea   corn bread   crib
Cornwallis   corny   cornice
popcorn   Nebraska   corn snow
corner   cornstarch   corn dog
Cornerstone

Answers

(1) Sweet corn; (2) cornet; (3) corn syrup; (4) corn snow; (5) cornbread; (6) cornstalk; (7) corny; (8) corn dog; (9) Nebraska; (10) cornea; (11) cornice; (12) corner; (13) crib; (14) popcorn; (15) acorn; (16) Cornwallis; (17) cornucopia; (18) cornstarch; (19) Cornerstone (Jesus).

Harvest Some Palindromes

A palindrome is a word, verse, sentence, or number that reads the same backward and forward. Choose a three- or four-letter palindrome to "harvest" these words or phrases.

1. To amaze   _____
2. Middle of the day   _____
3. A small child   _____
4. Mother   _____
5. A young dog   _____
6. A joke   _____
7. A short haircut   _____
8. Worn around a child's neck   _____
9. A female sheep   _____
10. Full of energy   _____
11. Father   _____
12. The first wife   _____
13. A soda   _____
14. Something you have done   _____
15. A flower   _____
16. A good act   _____
17. A quick look   _____
18. A train whistle   _____
19. Not your brother   _____
20. Someone who acts silly   _____
21. A woman who belongs to a religious order   _____
22. Dynamite   _____

Bonus: Name a seven-letter palindrome for a fast vehicle.   _____

Words to Choose From

bob   bib   dad
mom   mum   Eve
gag   ewe   did
wow   nun   TNT
pop   sis   deed
noon   pep   toot
tot   kook
pup   peep

Answers

(1) Wow; (2) noon; (3) tot; (4) mom; (5) pup; (6) gag; (7) bob; (8) bib; (9) ewe; (10) pep; (11) dad; (12) Eve; (13) pop; (14) did; (15) mum; (16) deed; (17) peep; (18) toot; (19) sis; (20) kook; (21) nun; (22) TNT; (bonus) race car.

Songs

"Bring Them In"
"A Passion for Souls"
"Work for the Night Is Coming"
"I Will Go Where You Want Me to Go"

Devotions
Harvest of Souls

Fall is a great time of year. It is a time of bounty. Farmers harvest grain. Tractors and wagons bring the grain from the fields to store for winter. There is a crispness in the air and a feeling of anticipation because winter is coming and there is much to be done. Farmers work long, hard days during harvest. They know the crops are ready and need to be brought in before the snows come and it is too late.

As Christians, we are to bring lost souls to Christ before it is too late. (*Read John 4:35 and Luke 10:2.*) The fields of people who need the Lord are ready for us to harvest. They need someone to tell them about the free gift of eternal life that God offers. God loves us so much that He sent His Son to die on the cross for our sins. (*Read or quote John 3:16.*)

We each have a field around us; and, like the farmer, we need to be ready to work in that field. As Christians, we have a great responsibility. Harvesting souls in the Christian life requires hard work. We can look at the example of the hardworking farmer in God's Word. (*Read 2 Timothy 2:6*).

First, the farmer is not afraid of work. No one accomplishes anything by being lazy. Works, or the good things we do, will not grant us salvation. We have to trust Christ for that. But after we're saved, we can show God our love by being rich in good works. (*Read 1 Timothy 6:17 and 18.*) John 9:4 reminds us that we need to be diligent in our labor for the Lord: "I must work the words of him that sent me, while it is day: the night cometh, when no man can work."

Second, the farmer lives by faith. When a farmer plants a field, he does it believing that the seeds will grow and produce. A Christian farmer trusts God for rain and sunshine. When we work in God's harvest field of people, we have to work diligently, but we also have to trust God for the growth. Paul used a planting analogy. (*Read 1 Corinthians 3:6.*) Sometimes the rains don't come, or the wind and hail destroy what has started to grow. We can live by faith and be confident because we have learned to trust God and His Word in spite of circumstances. When we witness to others, sometimes they don't respond, and we become discouraged. But when we labor for God, we need to keep at it and not grow weary. We need to do our part and then leave the rest to God. We need to have faith like the farmer.

Third, the farmer waits patiently. A farmer plants his seed in the spring, waits all summer for it to grow, and harvests it in the fall. That is a long time to wait for a return. James talked about the farmer and how he patiently waits for the spring and summer rains for his crops. (*Read James 5:7.*) We, too, must be patient as we wait on the Lord for His return. He is coming back for us. (*Read Galatians 6:9.*) Wait patiently on the Lord.

The farmer should receive his share of the crops at harvesttime. Because the farmer has devoted himself to meeting his responsibilities, he will receive a share of the profit of new grain. As Christians, we, too, will receive rewards for work well done. (*Read 1 Corinthians 3:8 and 14.*) The Bible refers to our rewards as crowns; we will receive them for the good job we have done. The farmer's reward for a job well done is his share of the crops. Like the farmer, we will receive our reward in Heaven one day because we have faithfully worked hard in God's fields that are white unto harvest.

Nametags

Prizes

- Bag of candy corn
- Miniature pumpkins
- Indian corn
- Work gloves

Recipes

Corn Casserole

1 bunch green onions, chopped
1 stick margarine
1 can creamed corn
1 can whole corn, undrained
2 eggs, beaten
1/2 cup sour cream
1 Jiffy corn muffin mix

Sauté onion in margarine. Add all other ingredients and mix well. Bake at 350°F for about 45 minutes.

Apple Salad

1 cup white sugar
1 cup water
1 egg
1 tablespoon margarine
2 tablespoons flour
2 tablespoons vinegar
5–6 medium apples, cored and chopped
1 1/2 cups grapes, halved
1 (20 oz.) can pineapple tidbits, drained
2 bananas, sliced
1 cup miniature marshmallows

Mix sugar, water, egg, margarine, flour, and vinegar; cook until thick, stirring constantly. Cool; stir in rest of ingredients.

Pecan Pie

1 unbaked 9" pie shell
4 tablespoons margarine
1 cup sugar
3 tablespoons flour
3/4 cup white corn syrup
3 eggs, beaten
1 teaspoon vanilla
1 cup chopped pecans

Using a pie crust cutter, cream together the margarine, flour, and sugar. Stir in syrup and eggs. Add vanilla and pecans; stir until blended. Pour into pie shell and bake at 350°F for 45 minutes.

Overnight Rolls

4 cups water
1/4 cup sugar
1 cup oil
4 eggs, beaten
1 tablespoon salt
2 pkgs. active dry yeast
12–15 cups flour

1. Boil water and sugar for 5 minutes; cool. Add oil, eggs, salt, yeast, and flour. Mix ingredients and let rise (3:00 P.M. is a good starting time). Punch down after 2 1/2 hours (5:30 P.M.). Let rise 2 1/2 hours (8:00 P.M.).

2. For hamburger buns, form buns the size of a large egg and place on a greased cookie sheet. Cover pan. Let buns rise overnight. Bake at 350°F for 10 minutes.

3. For dinner rolls, form smaller pieces and place on a greased cookie sheet. Cover pan. Let rolls rise overnight. Bake at 350°F for 8–10 minutes.

Pumpkin Pie

1 unbaked 9" pie shell
3/4 cup sugar
1/2 teaspoon salt
1 teaspoon cinnamon
1/2 teaspoon ginger
1/4 teaspoon ground cloves
2 eggs
1 3/4 cups pumpkin
1 (12 oz.) can evaporated milk

Combine all ingredients in a blender. Mix until smooth and pour into pie shell. Bake at 425°F for 15 minutes. Reduce temperature to 350°F and bake for 40–50 minutes until knife inserted comes out clean.

Home Improvement

Theme and Decorations

- Decorate with all kinds of tools for building, such as hammers, pliers, nail aprons, and wrenches. Bring a stepladder, and on each step place items such as duct tape, paint cans, brushes, and tool belts.
- Use rosin paper or clean drop cloths for tablecloths.
- Decorate the tables with small pieces of wood, boxes of nails, carpenter pencils, tape measures, and levels. Sprinkle wood shavings among the decorations.
- Put boards on a sawhorse to use for your buffet table.
- Have a toolbox filled with tools that you will give away as prizes.

Food

- Taco Buffet
- Fresh fruit
- Oreo Cookie Ice Cream Dessert
- Cream Puff Dessert

Games

Hammering Contest

Divide into age groups. Have a contest in each age group to see who can hammer a nail into a piece of board with the fewest strokes. The nail needs to go completely into the board as straight as possible.

Word Builders

On pieces of construction paper, write large letters from which the players can build words (one letter per sheet of paper). It is important to have enough vowels. Attach yarn to each piece of paper so the player can wear his letter around his neck. Each player wears a letter.

The leader announces, "Build a six-letter word." All the players scramble to find letters that make a six-letter word. The leader gives them one minute to make a word. After one minute, any player who is not part of a word is out. The remaining players split up again, if needed, and wait for the leader to announce the next number of letters in a word. Keep playing until they can't build a word or until only one group can make a word. The last group to build a word is the winner.

Home Improvement

Give each man a sheet of paper and a pencil or pen. See who is the most skilled at measuring. Collect as many items as possible ahead of time to compare with the drawings.

1. Draw a straight line two inches long.
2. Draw a circle the size of a quarter.
3. Draw a circle the size of a number 9 nail head.
4. Draw a line the length of a number 9 nail.
5. Draw a circle the size of a paint can lid.
6. Draw a line the size of a new carpenter pencil.
7. Draw a rectangle the size of a dollar bill.
8. Draw a rectangle the size of an average electrical outlet.
9. Draw a line the length of your boot, without looking.
10. Draw a circle the size of a penny.

How Sharp Are You?

Choose your answers from the list below and write the letters on blanks. You'll need to use your imagination for this game.

1. Who was the first electrician? _____
2. Who was Jonah's guardian? _____
3. When was paper money first used? _____
4. How long did Cain wait for his brother? _____
5. What part of the day was Adam created? _____
6. Why would Samson have made a good actor? _____
7. Who were the two shortest men in the Old Testament? _____
8. How do we know Peter was a short man? _____
9. What were the two smallest things mentioned by Jesus? _____
10. When was the "auto" mentioned in the Bible? _____
11. Where did a rooster crow and all the world heard? _____
12. Who was the greatest financier? _____

Answers to Choose From

(a) A little before Eve; (b) the whale that brought him up; (c) Noah (he made the ark light on Mount Ararat); (d) because he slept on the watch; (e) when the dove brought the first green back; (f) he could easily have brought down the house; (g) Noah (he floated a limited company when the world was in liquidation); (h) in the ark; (i) the disciples were in one accord; (j) Nehemiah and Bildad, the Shuhite; (k) as long as he was "Abel"; (l) the widow's mite and the wicked flea.

Answers

(1) c; (2) b; (3) e; (4) k; (5) a; (6) f; (7) j; (8) d; (9) l; (10) i; (11) h; (12) g.

Songs

"Tools for the Trade"
"In the Service of the King"
"To the Work"
"Give of Your Best to the Master"
"Make Me a Blessing"

Devotions
Tools in God's Hand

So you have decided to work on that project you've been wanting to tackle. It's time for some home improvements. You start by seeing what materials you will need. If it's that shelf you want to make your daughter for her birthday, you need to find just the right lumber, a good jigsaw, and your tape measure. But if your project is that leaky faucet your wife has been after you to fix, you will need entirely different tools. It will take a pipe wrench, plumbing tape, and some sealer. Or maybe some siding on the house is loose, and all you need is a hammer and some nails. Each project takes time and planning and the use of different kinds of tools.

Each believer is equipped with gifts to use in the Body of Christ, which is the church. (*Read 1 Corinthians 12:18–20*). Some of the gifts God gives to His children were outlined by Paul in Romans 12:4–8. (*Read these verses.*)

You might say we're like many tools in a toolbox. When God needs a tool for a specific job, He reaches for the one He knows will do the job right. Sometimes it is easy to look around at the other "tools" and wonder why we can't be used like them or wish we could do great things for God like someone else.

On the other hand, sometimes we look around at the other tools in the church and wonder why they *don't* do anything. We start thinking we don't even need them. But *each* memeber of the Body is important. (*Read 1 Corinthians 12:21–25.*) As members, we need to respect and care for one another.

Maybe you are wondering what you can do with the gift God has given you. If we are willing, God will show us how we can be tools for Him. There are four ways that all of us can be God's tools.

First, we can pray. (*Read Philippians 4:6.*) Each believer can uphold others before God. We know God will hear and answer our prayers when we seek Him. We can be tools for God's use when we pray.

Second, we can be wise. (*Read James 1:5*). God's Word can make us wise. Second Timothy 3:16 and 17 reassure us of the profitability of the Bible. (*Read the verses.*) God's Word will equip us for every occasion. It will teach us, bring reproof when we need it and correction when we sin, and give instruction when we need wisdom from God. We can be tools for God's use when we study God's Word.

Third, we can encourage others. (*Read 1 Thessalonians 5:11.*) Hebrews 3:12 and 13 also command us to watch out for one another. (*Read the verses.*) We need to build one another up, encourage others to repent and believe, and be diligent in the faith. We can be tools for God's use when we encourage others.

Fourth, we can love. (*Read Matthew 22:37–39.*) We can be tools for God's use when we love God with all our hearts, souls, and minds and when we love our neighbors as ourselves.

We need to be ready and willing to be used by the Master Carpenter. As tools, each of us will be used differently, but when used, all will bring glory to Christ.

Nametags

Prizes

- Screwdrivers
- Tape measures
- Wood glue
- Sandpaper
- Carpenter pencils
- Chalk lines

Recipes
Taco Buffet

Provide hard and soft shells for tacos. On your buffet table, place bowls of seasoned ground beef, refried beans, shredded lettuce, chopped tomatoes, shredded cheese, sliced black olives, sour cream, and taco sauce or salsa.

Also have bowls of seasonal fresh fruit, such as grapes, bananas, or apples.

Oreo Cookie Ice Cream Dessert

$1/2$ gallon vanilla ice cream
1 (12 oz.) container frozen whipped topping, thawed
$1/2$ pkg. Oreos, broken into small pieces

Blend ice cream, whipped topping, and cookie pieces. Freeze and serve.

Cream Puff Dessert

FIRST LAYER
1 cup water
1 stick margarine
1 cup flour
4 eggs

SECOND LAYER
1 (8 oz.) pkg. cream cheese, softened
2 (3.4 oz.) pkgs. instant vanilla pudding and pie filling
3 cups milk

THIRD LAYER

   1 (8 oz.) container frozen whipped topping,
      thawed

  Chocolate syrup to taste

   1. Boil water and margarine together. Add flour and eggs, one at a time. Stir together with a fork. Pour mixture into a greased 10" x 15" glass baking dish. Bake at 400°F for 20 minutes. Cool.

   2. Combine cream cheese, dry pudding mix, and milk. Pour over cooled crust.

   3. Spread whipped topping over pudding mixture and drizzle topping with chocolate syrup. With a knife, cut through the syrup to decorate just before serving. Serves 12–15.

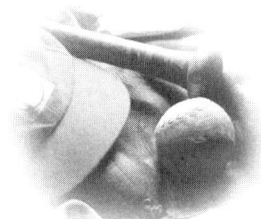

Hook, Line, and Sinker

Theme and Decorations

- Decorate with fishing poles and gear. Throw in some fishing vests and hats.
- Arrange on the tables sunglasses, bobbers, and inexpensive fishing lures with the hooks clipped off so no one gets caught.
- Make a splash with a canoe in the corner, if available. Around it, place tackle boxes, nets, and buckets.
- Clean and remove labels from tin cans, tape over any sharp edges, and fill with crushed Oreos. Dangle gummy worms out the sides.

Food

- Buckets of fried chicken
- Potato Salad
- Baked Beans
- Coleslaw
- KFC-Style Coleslaw
- Turtle Bars

Games
Fishing Puzzle
Use the words to fill in the puzzle.

Fishing Puzzle

Words to Use

LAKE	BASS	REPELLANT
KNIFE	TACKLE	FISH
VESTS	CANOE	POLE
BOBBER	BUCKET	SUNGLASSES
WORMS	CATFISH	FILET
LINE	SUNSET	BLUEGILL
NET	POND	LURE
CLEAN	REEL	

Answers: Fishing Puzzle

```
F I S H
    U   P O L E
R   N   O           R
E   S U N G L A S S E S
E   E   D   I       P       W
F I L E T   N       E       O
        B L U E G I L L   L U R E
        O           L         M
            V   C A T F I S H
    K   B U C K E T   N
C A N O E       S   T A C K L E
    I   R       T           A
    F   B A S S             K
C L E A N               N E T
```

What's in the Tackle Box?

Place a number of common fishing items in a tackle box. Give each person a few minutes to look at the items. Close the tackle box. Tell them the number of items you have shown them, and have them write from memory what they saw. The person who remembers the largest number of items wins!

Songs

"I Will Make You Fishers of Men"
"Follow On"
"Throw Out the Life Line"

Devotions

Be a Fisher of Men

What is more relaxing than a day down at the old fishing hole? Maybe you have one of those fa-vorite spots. It is the place you can't wait to get to on a warm afternoon. You grab your fishing pole, tackle box, lawn chair, and a cooler of cold pop and head to the pond. You know that today the fish'll be biting.

Fishing has been a favorite pastime and occupation of men for centuries. In Bible times, many were fishermen by trade. One day while Jesus was walking by the Sea of Galilee, He saw Peter and Andrew casting their nets into the sea. Jesus called out to them. *(Read Mark 1:17.)* Immediately they left their nets and followed Jesus. James and John were mending their nets when Jesus called to them. They also left their boats and nets and followed Christ.

Christ is our example to follow too. The more we follow Him, the more we will become like Him. The more we become like Him, the more successful we will be at winning others to Him. Jesus is still calling people to follow Him and to be His disciples. He wants us to be fishers of men.

To be fishermen, we must have certain characteristics. First, we must catch fish. As believers, we should want to bring people to Jesus. We have good news to share with our neighbors and friends. Are we telling others about the free gift of eternal life God offers through His Son? To be fishers of men, we need to be leading people to Christ. A good fisherman will be catching people for God.

Second, we must have fishing skills. A good fisherman knows the best time of day and the best place to go fishing. Maybe from experience he knows the right lure to use to attract a certain kind of fish. As believers, we need to be skilled in knowing God's Word so we can share the gospel with others. We must be sensitive to the Holy Spirit's leading for the best time and place to talk to someone about Christ. Do our lives lure, or attract, others to want to know more? Use your skills to be a good fisherman.

Third, we must have patience. Sometimes the fish don't bite; we don't even get a nibble. That can be discouraging, and we can grow tired of waiting. On one occasion Peter and his fellow fishermen had toiled all night and had caught nothing (Luke 5:5). Jesus told Peter to cast his net into the deep. When Peter did as Jesus said, he and his partners caught so many fish that their nets broke from the weight. The men were amazed. Sometimes we may be discouraged when we want to lead people to Christ and they don't respond in trusting Him as their Savior. Maybe you have relatives and friends you have witnessed to for years. Don't give up. The Lord is patient; He doesn't want any to perish but for all to repent (2 Pet. 3:9). A good fisherman is patient.

Fourth, we must endure. The old fishing hole isn't necessarily a comfortable place. There are always discomforts to endure: pesky mosquitoes, sunburn, or uncomfortable seating; but the discomfort is part of fishing.

The disciples were willing to endure by leaving all behind. They left their boats, nets, and families. *(Read Luke 9:23.)* Jesus said that we need to deny self daily, take up our cross, and follow Him. We need to leave behind the things that get in the way of our following Him and being the fishermen Christ wants us to be. A good fisherman will deny self and will endure.

So the next time you grab your fishing gear and head out to your favorite fishing spot, think about how Christ gave us the example of being good fishermen. A good fisherman is one who catches fish by leading people to Jesus. He has patience and never grows weary in telling the gospel. He uses the skills of relying on God's Word and the Holy Spirit's leading. He endures discomfort by denying self daily and picking up the cross to follow Christ.

Nametags

Prizes

- Lures
- Bobbers
- Tackle box
- Go Fish card games
- Coupons for fish sandwiches at a local restaurant

Recipes

Potato Salad

10 white potatoes
6 hard-boiled eggs, peeled and chopped
$\frac{1}{4}$ cup onion, chopped
$\frac{1}{2}$ lb. Velveeta cheese, cubed
1 cup pickle relish
$\frac{1}{4}$ cup sugar
1 teaspoon salt
$\frac{1}{2}$ teaspoon pepper
$1\frac{1}{2}$ cups Miracle Whip
1 tablespoon prepared mustard

1. Cook potatoes with skins on until soft but not mushy. Run under cold water and peel. Cut into small pieces.

2. Mix all ingredients and chill.

Baked Beans

2 (15.5 oz. each) cans pork and beans, drained

1 cup catsup

1$^1/_2$ cup brown sugar

$^1/_4$ cup chopped onion

2 tablespoons prepared mustard

$^1/_2$ cup mild molasses

Stir ingredients together and bake uncovered at 350°F for 50–60 minutes.

Coleslaw

2 cups Miracle Whip

1 cup sugar

2 tablespoons vinegar

Salt and pepper to taste

2 pkgs. shredded coleslaw mix or 1 head cabbage, shredded

Mix first four ingredients together, and let stand 1 hour. Add shredded cabbage and let stand 30 minutes. Stir again.

KFC-Style Coleslaw

$^1/_3$ cup sugar

$^1/_2$ teaspoon salt

$^1/_8$ teaspoon pepper

$^1/_4$ cup milk

$^1/_2$ cup Miracle Whip

$^1/_4$ cup buttermilk

1$^1/_2$ tablespoons white vinegar

2$^1/_2$ tablespoons lemon juice

1 head cabbage, finely chopped

1 medium carrot, shredded

Combine first eight ingredients. Beat until smooth. Add cabbage and carrots; mix well. Cover and refrigerate at least 2 hours.

Turtle Bars

BASE

1 German chocolate cake mix

$^1/_2$ cup evaporated milk

$^3/_4$ cup margarine, melted

MIDDLE

$^1/_3$ cup evaporated milk

1 (14 oz.) pkg. caramels, unwrapped

TOPPINGS

$^3/_4$ cup milk chocolate chips

1$^1/_2$ –2 cups chopped pecans

1. For base, combine cake mix, evaporated milk, and margarine. Pour half of batter into greased and floured 9" x 13" pan. Bake 5 minutes at 350°F. Base will look puffy but not done. Cool.

2. While base is cooling, place caramels and evaporated milk in a double boiler or microwave. Dribble over base.

3. Sprinkle chocolate chips onto the caramel mixture. Add pecans. Drop spoonfuls of remaining batter over top and bake 18–20 minutes. Don't overbake.

Mountain Men

Theme and Decorations

- Decorate tables with different-colored rocks in small piles. Put pine branches underneath the piles.
- Find moose or bear items to place on tables.
- Make a mountain backdrop with a rugged terrain.
- Place wool socks, long johns, work gloves, hiking boots, cooking gear, ropes, water bottles, and backpacks around the room.
- Add a few artificial Christmas trees to look like mountain pines.
- Put syrups and different kinds of butter on the tables.

Food

- Flapjacks
- Potato Pancakes
- Maple Syrup
- Pear Honey, Apple Butter, and Blueberry Butter
- Scrambled eggs
- Bacon or ham
- Orange juice
- Hot chocolate

Games

Lumberjack Test

1. What trees are straight to the line? _____
2. What tree is a good church leader? _____
3. What tree do you have in your hand? _____
4. What was the forbidden tree in the Garden of Eden? _____
5. What tree is stuffed? _____
6. What tree remains after a fire? _____
7. Under what tree would you seek shelter from rain? _____
8. What trees are always sad? _____
9. Which tree is well liked? _____
10. What tree likes to be clean and ready to go? _____
11. What tree did Elijah sit under? _____
12. Which tree keeps moths away? _____
13. What tree did the trees first want to anoint king? _____
14. What tree would Sir Isaac Newton have liked? _____
15. What kind of tree did Zacchaeus climb? _____
16. What tree would make a great couple? _____
17. What tree is always grouchy? _____
18. What tree is chewy? _____
19. What tree could be an insect? _____
20. What tree could be trim for a coat? _____
21. What tree might be used to seal a bottle? _____

Answers

(1) Lodge pole pines or plum; (2) elder; (3) palm;
(4) knowledge of good and evil; (5) olive;
(6) ash; (7) umbrella; (8) weeping willows;
(9) poplar; (10) spruce; (11) juniper or broom;
(12) cedar; (13) olive (Judg. 9:8); (14) fig;
(15) sycamore; (16) pear; (17) crab apple;
(18) gum; (19) locust; (20) fir; (21) cork.

Breakfast Is Ready Word Search

Find the items a man might eat for breakfast. Answers go all directions: up and down, left and right, and diagonally.

Breakfast Is Ready

```
J  A  B  C  O  F  F  E  E  C  A  K  E  E  S
S  U  L  J  M  H  N  G  P  R  U  N  E  S  Y
A  W  I  L  E  O  G  D  E  H  F  G  Q  T  R
U  A  E  C  L  S  W  O  N  O  S  B  R  I  U
S  P  X  E  X  M  V  U  T  T  A  B  U  P
A  D  M  X  T  E  A  B  U  C  J  C  I  C  T
G  M  A  H  F  R  E  N  C  H  T  O  A  S  T
E  P  R  W  U  V  O  C  Y  O  D  N  H  I  A
L  A  M  N  T  D  S  L  R  C  I  G  H  B  L
F  N  A  I  M  I  L  K  L  O  F  T  O  C  A
F  C  L  F  A  E  O  P  Q  L  E  D  N  B  E
A  A  A  F  J  N  S  E  P  A  R  G  E  G  R
W  K  D  U  K  T  B  U  T  T  E  R  Y  A  E
L  E  E  M  T  I  U  R  F  E  P  A  R  G  C
```

Words to Choose From

BACON	JELLY
BISCUITS	JUICE
BUTTER	MARMALADE
CEREAL	MELON
COFFEE CAKE	MILK
DONUT	MUFFIN
EGGS	OMELET
FRENCH TOAST	PANCAKE
GRAPEFRUIT	PRUNES
GRAPES	SAUSAGE
HAM	SWEET ROLL
HONEY	SYRUP
HOT CHOCOLATE	TEA
JAM	WAFFLE

Answers: Breakfast Is Ready Word Search

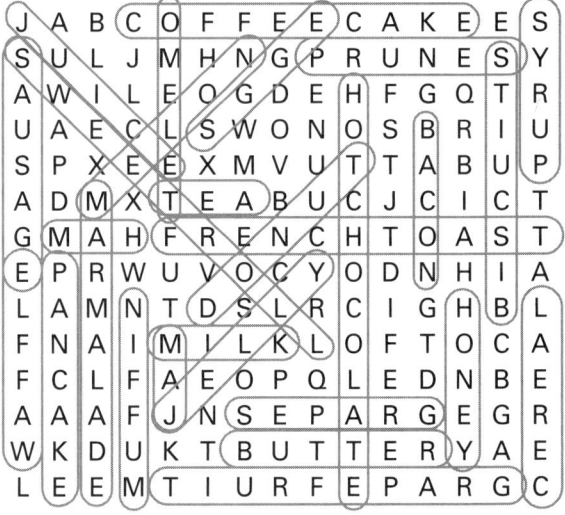

Mountain Match

Can you match the description or group name in the left column with the animals in the second column? For example, a skulk is a group of foxes. Draw a line from skulk to foxes. Put on your thinking cap. This game is a challenge!

	GROUP	ANIMALS
1.	cloud	birds
2.	skulk	locusts
3.	flock	fish
4.	gam	geese
5.	army	monkeys
6.	plague	ponies
7.	troop	cattle
8.	herd	flamingos
9.	stand	grasshoppers
10.	gaggle	whales
11.	string	foxes
12.	school	ants

Answers

(1) Cloud of grasshoppers; (2) skulk of foxes; (3) flock of birds; (4) gam of whales; (5) army of ants; (6) plague of locusts; (7) troop of monkeys; (8) herd of cattle; (9) stand of flamingos; (10) gaggle of geese; (11) string of ponies; (12) school of fish.

Songs

"True-Hearted, Whole-Hearted"
"Rise Up, O Men of God"
"Rock of Ages"
"The Rock That Is Higher Than I"

Devotions

Mountain Men

What comes to mind when you think of mountain men—strong, independent trappers, dressed in fur and a coonskin cap, alone in the woods or standing on a mountain and looking off into the distance? Mountain men were strong, rugged individuals. They had to be if they were going to survive the cold, unforgiving environment where they lived. They relied on their survival training.

As men, we have to be strong Christians and role models. Our world is as unforgiving as the world of the mountain men. Satan is trying to devour and disrupt our families everyday. We are being hit from all sides at once. As dads and sons, we have to be on the lookout daily. We have to be dependable and strong.

I mentioned earlier that we think of mountain men as living by their skills and training. Men, our skills and training alone are not going to cut it today. We cannot make it if we go it alone and rely on our own strength.

What is a strong man? Is it just someone who is strong physically? (*Read the last part of 1 Timothy 4:7.*) When we exercise godliness, we will profit not only now but also in the life to come. To be godly is to be strong on the *inside*.

Samson is a Biblical example of a strong man. Unfortunately, Samson did not always make godly choices, but he was a man whom God used.

First, Samson was a man sent from God. He was sent to judge the Israelite people and deliver them from the oppression of the Philistines. An angel appeared and told Samson's parents that they would have a son. This child was to be a Nazarite from his birth to his death. He was to ingest no wine, grapes, grape juice, or raisins. He was not to touch any unclean thing and was not to go near a dead body. He was not to cut his hair. Usually the vow of the Nazarite was made voluntarily by a man or a woman for about thirty days. In rare cases people made the vow for life. Samson was one of them. As long as he kept his vow, the Lord's blessing was upon him.

Second, Samson was a man of great strength. Samson killed a lion with his bare hands. He broke cords that bound him and killed a thousand men with the jawbone of a donkey. He escaped a trap of the Philistines by carrying away the gates to their city. He tied three hundred foxes' tails together and burned the Philistines' fields. He escaped Delilah's trap by breaking fresh boughs, snapping new ropes, and pulling out the pin that fastened his hair to a loom. He pushed down the pillars of a temple, killing more Philistines in his death than in his lifetime. Now there's a mountain man for you!

God used Samson to kill many Philistines who were oppressing God's people. Samson's mighty abilities and strength were all a part of God's plan. If we want to be strong dads, we have to depend on the Lord. We can draw our strength from Him through Bible study and prayer.

Third, Samson was a man of great weakness. If you have failed and are discouraged because you have messed things up in your life, once again think of Samson. As a young man, he chose the wrong friends and spent time with the Philistines. He dishonored his parents and didn't respect their wishes. He disobeyed God and broke the Nazarite vow. He lost his temper, and his wife was given to another man. He loved a Philistine woman named Delilah, who sold him out. He revealed the secret of his strength, lost his sight, and was taken prisoner.

God can still use us even when we sin. Samson had plenty of time to think about his life while he was blind and forced to grind grain for the Philistines. Perhaps he spent time talking to God and repenting for the mistakes he had made.

Fourth, Samson was a man of faith. Even though God did not approve of Samson's disobedience, God used Samson to deliver Israel. Samson showed faith in God when he prayed for water, and God provided it from a rock. God heard Samson's prayer for strength and honored his prayer by allowing him to push down the pillars that killed hundreds of Philistines. We know Samson had faith because God listed him in Hebrews 11:32 as a man of faith.

Samson was rugged and strong, a picture of a mountain man. God used Samson to deliver Israel

from God's enemies. He can use men of faith, who find their strength in Him.

Nametags

Prizes

- Beef jerky
- Bags of pretzels
- Water bottles
- Pocketknife
- Gummy bears

Recipes
Flapjacks

$1^1/_2$ cups flour
1 teaspoon salt
3 tablespoons sugar
$1^3/_4$ teaspoons baking powder
1 egg, beaten
3 tablespoons butter, melted
$1^1/_4$ cup milk

1. Heat griddle or large skillet. Grease lightly with oil. Griddle is ready when drops of water sizzle and disappear.

2. Mix dry ingredients in a medium-size bowl; add egg, butter, and milk. Stir until blended. Pour slightly less than $1/_4$ cup batter for each pancake on griddle.

3. Cook until bubbles break on top. Turn and cook an additional 1–$1^1/_2$ minutes or until golden brown.

Potato Pancakes

2 cups grated potatoes

3 eggs, beaten

1½ tablespoons flour

1¼ teaspoons salt

1–3 teaspoons grated onion

1. Extract as much moisture from the potatoes as possible with a muslin towel. Mix all other ingredients in a medium-size bowl; add potatoes. Shape potato mixture into small patties.

2. Heat griddle or large skillet. Grease lightly with oil. Cook until golden brown on both sides.

Maple Syrup

2 cups water

¼ teaspoon salt

1 cup sugar

2 cups dark corn syrup

1 teaspoon maple flavoring

Combine first four ingredients in a saucepan over medium heat. Stirring occasionally, let the mixture come to a full boil. Boil 7 minutes. Turn off heat an let syrup cool for 15 minutes. Stir in maple flavoring.

Pear Honey

4 cups pear pulp

2 tablespoons lemon juice

½ teaspoon cinnamon

1 pkg. Sure-Jell

5 cups sugar

In large pan (at least 5 quarts) mix first four ingredients and bring to a boil. Add sugar all at once. Stir and bring to boil again. Boil 1 minute. Remove from heat and pour into hot scalded pint jars. Seal with hot lids.

Apple Butter

16 cups apple, peeled, cored, cut

1 cup apple cider vinegar

8 cups sugar

4 teaspoons cinnamon

Cook apples until soft. Add rest of ingredients and cook about 15 minutes or until thick. Remove from heat and pour into hot scalded pint jars. Seal with hot lids.

Blueberry Butter

5 cups sugar

5 cups chopped rhubarb

1 can blueberry pie filling

2 (3 oz. each) pkgs. red raspberry gelatin dessert

Cook sugar and rhubarb until tender. Add pie filling. Cook 5–8 minutes; remove from heat. Add gelatin. Put in hot jars and seal, or store in freezer as freezer jam.

Take Me Out to the Ball Game!

Theme and Decorations

- Decorate with baseball caps, gloves, bats, and balls.
- Tell the guys ahead of time to wear their favorite baseball team shirt or cap.
- Make centerpieces with small flags, sparklers, and shiny red, white, and blue paper.
- Sprinkle miniature Baby Ruth candy bars down the middle of each table.

Food

- Hot dogs and bratwursts
- Nachos
- Popcorn
- Apple Pie
- Homemade Ice Cream
- Coolers of pop

Games

Father-Son Baseball Game

Have the sons take on their dads, or divide into teams of fathers and sons.

All-American Indoor Baseball Game

Divide into a red team and a blue team, with older and younger men on each team. Use a writing board, overhead projector, or computer to keep track of scores, strikes, and the players' positions on base.

Each question will be a single, double, triple, or home run. A single gets a player to first base. He stays there until the next player scores. If the next player gets a double, for example, the one on first base would also move two bases.

You will need two extra men, one as an umpire for questionable answers and one to keep score. Flip a coin to determine which team goes first.

Each wrong answer is a strike. After three strikes, the other team comes up to "bat." Play as many innings as you have time for.

SINGLES

1. What is the longest river in the U.S.?
2. The Mississippi River empties into what body of water?
3. In what U.S. city is the Liberty Bell located?
4. The people of what country gave the Statue of Liberty to the U.S.?
5. What two states in the U.S. are named for the same native American tribe?
6. Name the only state that grows coffee beans.
7. Who was the first person to walk on the moon?
8. Name one of the top two soybean-producing states in the U.S.
9. In what state is the Alamo?

DOUBLES

1. Which of the five Great Lakes is located entirely in the U.S.?
2. Who published the first American dictionary?

3. What mountain range is the largest on the continent?

4. In which U.S. harbor does the Statue of Liberty stand?

5. Who wrote the "The Star-Spangled Banner"?

6. Which state is known as the "Show Me State"?

7. Who was President of the U.S. when the stock market crashed in 1929?

8. What state leads the U.S. in beef production?

9. Where was the prison Alcatraz located?

TRIPLES

1. Name the four faces on Mount Rushmore.

2. What group of islands lies approximately 650 miles off the coast of North Carolina?

3. Where did the famous tea party of 1773 occur?

4. In what state is the Garden of the Gods located?

5. What state produces the most grapes?

6. In what state did Paul Revere make his famous ride?

7. In what state is the Air Force Academy?

8. What state in the U.S. leads in production of milk and butter?

9. Where are the Badlands located?

HOME RUNS

1. What small state was the first to spin cotton by machine in a factory?

2. In what state is the Henry Ford museum?

3. What year was Alaska entered into the Union?

4. What state grows more food than any other state?

5. Where was the famous gunfight at the OK Corral?

6. Name the city and state that produces the most chocolate and cocoa.

7. What university was first named the Collegiate School?

8. What famous poet read a poem at the inauguration of John F. Kennedy?

9. In what two states is the Okefenokee Swamp?

Answers: Singles
(1) Mississippi; (2) Gulf of Mexico; (3) Philadelphia; (4) France; (5) North Dakota and South Dakota; (6) Hawaii; (7) Neil Armstrong; (8) Iowa or Illinois; (9) Texas.

Answers: Doubles
(1) Lake Michigan; (2) Noah Webster; (3) Rocky Mountains; (4) New York; (5) Francis Scott Key; (6) Missouri; (7) Herbert Hoover; (8) Texas; (9) San Francisco.

Answers: Triples
(1) Washington, Lincoln, Jefferson, and Roosevelt; (2) Bermuda Islands; (3) Boston Harbor; (4) Colorado; (5) California; (6) Massachusetts; (7) Colorado; (8) Wisconsin; (9) South Dakota.

Answers: Home Runs
(1) Rhode Island; (2) Michigan; (3) 1959; (4) California; (5) Tombstone, Arizona; (6) Hershey, Pennsylvania; (7) Yale; (8) Robert Frost; (9) Georgia and Florida.

Songs

"Take Me Out to the Ball Game"
"The Star-Spangled Banner"
"You're a Grand Old Flag"
"America the Beautiful"
"God Bless America"

Devotions
Take Me Out to the Ball Game

Everyone loves to go to a good baseball game in the summer. Maybe you have a favorite team you like to support, or maybe you just like to get away and enjoy the atmosphere. The fans, the popcorn, the roasted peanuts, the hot dogs, and the soft drinks make for a fun day at the ballpark for a father and son. After the "The Star-Spangled Banner," the umpire yells, "Play ball!" and the players take to the field. There have been some great names in baseball, like Mickey Mantle, Babe Ruth, and Willie Mays. They could do it all. They were probably born with a bat in one hand. They were naturals. They played the game of baseball with greatness and finished their careers strong.

A great man of the Bible who finished strong was David. He is one of the heroes of faith listed in Hebrews 11. David was a winner in the game of life.

To be a winner, you need to do three things.

First, you need to spend time in training. In any sport, you train, prepare, and practice, or you won't be ready for the competition. It is the same way in the game of life. David put in practice time while tending his father's sheep. God trained David as a shepherd boy (1 Sam. 17:34–37). He spent time alone with God in the fields, developing his faith. With God, David killed a lion and a bear. When it came time for action against an enemy, David was ready. He may not have played baseball, but he did have a good arm and a great swing when he boldly faced Goliath. His was a perfect hit.

We Christians need to spend time in training too. We need to discipline ourselves to take time to study God's Word (the playbook) and to pray daily. That can be hard work. Many pressures and interruptions steal our time away. Practice and training are not easy for us, but they're required if we're going to play or compete successfully. It's in practice that we learn to handle the bunt down third or the high fly ball. By being in God's Word, we can learn to handle troubles wisely and learn how to trust God in all things. That is what David did.

Second, to be a winner, you need to keep trying even when you fail. You dropped the ball. You struck out. Your head just wasn't in the game. Your teammates were counting on you, and you

let them down. You had a really bad day.

David could relate. He failed miserably when he sinned with Bathsheba and tried to cover his sin by having her husband killed in battle. He really dropped the ball. He let down those who had counted on him. He didn't play by the rules. Coaches may say, "When the going gets tough, the tough get going." But we Christians say, "When the going gets tough, go to God." That is just what David did. He may have failed miserably, but he turned to God and repented of his sin.

Psalm 51 is a psalm of confession and forgiveness written by David. (*Read verses 1–4, 10, 16, and 17.*) When you fail, confess your sin. First John 1:9 promises, "If we confess our sins, he is faithful and just to forgive us our sins, and to cleanse us from all unrighteousness." When you fail, pick yourself up and keep trying. Encourage others also. The members of a team have different strengths and abilities, so they all have to work together to succeed. When those around you stumble, help them back up. (*Read Ecclesiastes 4:10.*)

David finished strong even though he had failed. He didn't quit, and we shouldn't either. Even if you drop the ball, confess your failure to God and get back in the game. You can do it.

Third, to be a winner, you need to be willing to listen to and obey the coach. Every good team needs a good coach, and, of course, the Christian's coach is God. It is from Him that we need to get directions. He has given us the rulebook, the Bible, to play by. We need to read and study it to be able to follow His plan.

The most important directions God gives us are about eternal life. He wants us to put our faith in Christ alone. That is the whole reason He sent His Son. (*Read or quote John 3:16.*) We need to realize we have sinned. Then we need to accept God's free gift of salvation. If you want to be on God's team, you need to make that decision. He will then be your coach to direct and guide you through life. David believed in God and trusted in Him. He looked to God for direction and spent time with Him in prayer.

Remember that to be a winner in the game of life, you need to obey God's leading by first trusting Him as your Savior. Spend time in training, by reading God's Word and praying. Keep trying when you fail. Confess your sins to God and don't quit. Listen to and obey the Coach. Look to God's Word for direction. When you do, you will honor God and finish strong.

Nametags

Prizes

- Cracker Jacks
- Bags of peanuts
- Bags of cotton candy
- Baby Ruth candy bars
- Baseball cards

Recipes
Apple Pie
CRUST
1 heaping cup flour
$\frac{1}{2}$ teaspoon salt
$\frac{1}{2}$ cup butter-flavored shortening (or $\frac{1}{4}$ cup butter-flavored shortening and $\frac{1}{4}$ cup lard)
$\frac{1}{4}$ cup cold milk

APPLE FILLING
7–9 baking apples (Jonathon, Winesap, Granny Smith)
1 cup sugar
3 tablespoons flour
1 teaspoon cinnamon
2 tablespoons margarine

1. For crust, cut flour and salt and shortening until crumbly. Stir in cold milk until dough forms a ball. Roll half out on floured surface for bottom crust and put in a 9" pie pan. Roll remaining crust for top.

2. Peel and slice apples. Mix together sugar, flour, and cinnamon. Sprinkle onto apples. Fill bottom crust with apple mixture. Dot with margarine. Add top crust and seal. Sprinkle with additional sugar. Bake at 375°F for 45–55 minutes or until bubbly in center.

Homemade Ice Cream
4 eggs
$2\frac{1}{2}$ cups sugar
1 quart half-and-half
2 quarts milk
1 tablespoon vanilla
1 teaspoon lemon extract
1 teaspoon salt
2 pkgs. dry Dream Whip

Beat eggs until light. Gradually add sugar, beating until thick. Add rest of ingredients, mix well, and freeze in ice cream freezer.

Nachos
Melt Velveeta cheese in a slow cooker. Add one or more of the following.
1 lb. ground beef, cooked and drained
1 small jar salsa
1 pkg. cream cheese
1 container sour cream
1 can cheddar or nacho cheese soup

Mother and Daughter Events

Come for Coffee; Let's Talk

Theme and Decorations

- Decorate with telephones of all kinds, especially antique ones if you can find them.
- Use grapevines or ivy on the tables to emphasize that news travels through the grapevine.
- Accent decorations with grape-scented candles.

Food

- Streusel-Filled Coffee Cake
- Fruit Dip
- Grapes and other fruit
- Flavored coffees

Games

Mailbox

News can travel through the mail. Unscramble these words—items you might find in your mailbox.

1. slibl _____
2. gloatac _____
3. yapcekhc _____
4. treelt _____
5. amazeing _____
6. vimendtreatse _____
7. dingdwe vatnniiiot _____
8. tribh tounemnnnaec _____
9. cihna ettlre _____
10. ribthyda cdar _____
11. agackpe _____
12. axt furend _____
13. poonscu _____
14. ylfre _____
15. knju aiml _____

Answers

(1) Bills; (2) catalog; (3) paycheck; (4) letter; (5) magazine; (6) advertisement; (7) wedding invitation; (8) birth announcement; (9) chain letter; (10) birthday card; (11) package; (12) tax refund; (13) coupons; (14) flyer; (15) junk mail.

Telephone

News travels on the telephone. Have everyone sit in a line or in a circle. Divide a large group into smaller groups. Tell one person a message to send down the line. Each person whispers the message to the next one. The last person says aloud what she heard whispered in her ear. The difference between the final message and the beginning message may surprise you and make you laugh.

Examples

Rob and Betty's daughter, who looks a lot like her grandmother, will be two years old on Friday.

The new department store on Main Street will open in January and will carry clothes for the entire family.

Game Variation

Divide into several groups. Send a question about a missionary that your church supports; for example, "Todd and Dawn Daily are missionaries who serve the Lord in Germany. How many children do they have?" Each group that sends the message correctly gets one point. They each get one point for answering the question correctly.

Songs

"I Love to Tell the Story"
"I Must Tell Jesus"
"I Found a Friend"
"What a Friend We Have in Jesus"

Devotions

Come for Coffee

At some time in our lives each of us, even you young girls, has wished for someone to talk to. And we are not alone. Many hurting or lonely people could use a word of encouragement or cheer. God can use us Christians, whether we're young or old, to show His love to others in need. Ecclesiastes 4:9 and 10 say, "Two are better than one. . . . For if they fall, the one will lift up his fellow." Maybe you know a woman struggling in her marriage, a family facing cancer, or a tired mother who wants to talk to someone besides children today. Maybe you know a girl who is having a hard time at school or isn't getting along with her friends or has family problems. Whatever the case, you can use God's Word, the Bible, to encourage others. How?

First, show patience. First Thessalonians 5:14 states, "Now we exhort you, brethren, warn them that are unruly, comfort the [fainthearted], support the weak, be patient toward all men." Invite your friend to talk about what has discouraged her. Let her set the pace, because she might not want to talk about the problem yet. Let her know you are available if she needs you. Just being with

someone who cares may be enough to encourage her. Don't be pushy; be patient.

Second, show kindness. Second Peter 1:7 instructs us to add "brotherly kindness" to godliness. Doing a kind deed provides encouragement. Take your friend a loaf of bread or a plate of cookies. A bouquet of flowers from your garden would brighten anyone's day.

Third, show love. In John 15:12 Jesus commands, "Love one another, as I have loved you." Tell your friend you love and care for her and that God cares for and loves her even more. He loved each of us so much that He gave His only Son to die on the cross for us. Share John 3:16 with her, filling in her name as you quote the verse. For example, "For God so loved [Josie], that he gave his only begotten Son, that [if Josie] believeth in him [Josie] should not perish, but have everlasting life."

Fourth, show that you are praying. (*Read Colossians 1:9.*) In times of trial or need we count on others to pray. How good to know we have a God Who hears and answers our prayers when we pray for His will. Let others know you are available to pray for them and to be with them in their time of need.

Fifth, encourage your friend to cast her cares upon God. (*Read 1 Peter 5:7 and Matthew 10:29–31.*) God knows what we are going through; He has compassion on us and wants us to lean on Him. You can encourage others in need to cast their cares on God and leave their problems in His almighty hands.

Sixth, encourage your friend to go to God for strength. (*Read Psalms 46:1 and 50:15.*) Going through difficult times can make us tired and weary. In God we can find strength to sustain us and see us through.

Seventh, trust God. (*Read Proverbs 3:5 and 6.*) God always wants the best for us, and He will guide us as we lean on Him and acknowledge Him in all we do.

Finally, encourage your friend to rejoice in the Lord. (*Read Philippians 4:4 and Romans 12:12.*) We can encourage each other to rejoice in God no matter what our circumstances. God is always good; we can rejoice in that truth!

Think of someone you could encourage. Share your patience, kindness, love; and prayerful concern by inviting your friend for cup of coffee—or a mug of hot chocolate. The time you give of yourself will be a blessing to her and to you.

Nametags

Prizes

- Grape-scented candles
- Doilies
- Flavored coffees

Recipes

Streusel-Filled Coffee Cake

STREUSEL FILLING AND TOPPING

- 4 teaspoons cinnamon
- 1 cup brown sugar
- 4 tablespoons margarine, melted
- 4 tablespoons flour
- 1 cup pecans (opt.)

CAKE

- 3 cups flour
- 1½ cups sugar
- ½ teaspoon salt
- 2 tablespoons baking powder
- ½ cup margarine
- 2 eggs, beaten
- 1 cup milk

1. In a small bowl, combine streusel ingredients. Set aside.

2. For the coffee cake, combine flour, sugar, salt, baking powder, and margarine with a pastry cutter. Stir eggs and milk into flour mixture.

3. Spread half the batter into a greased and floured 9" x 13" pan. Sprinkle half of the streusel mixture on top. Add the other half of the batter; sprinkle the remaining streusel on top. Bake at 350°F for 30–40 minutes.

Fruit Dip

- 1 pkg. (8 oz.) cream cheese, softened
- 1 (7.5 oz.) jar marshmallow creme
- 2 tablespoons honey

Beat ingredients together and serve with fresh fruit.

Heavenly Handbags

Theme and Decorations

- At each setting, place a handbag made out of sturdy paper such as wallpaper samples (see pattern on page 147). Fill with items you might carry in your purse.
- For the centerpiece at each table, make a representation of Heaven. Lay down an eight-inch square mirror tile to represent Heaven's glassy sea. On the mirror, place a glass bowl with fresh flowers, such as carnations. Run strings of pearls around the bowl to represent Heaven's pearly gates.
- Down the center of the table, scatter gold-wrapped candy to represent the street of gold.

Food

- Angel Food Cake
- Hot Fudge Topping
- Toppings for cake, such as whipped cream and peach, cherry, or blueberry pie filling
- Perfectly Divine Punch

Games

Purse Parade

Involve guests of varying ages. Give each a purse filled with things a person her age would carry. Start with the youngest, and have her show and tell what is in her purse and why she thinks it is important to carry it in her handbag.

Examples

A young girl might carry crayons, candy, baby dolls, play makeup, dress-up jewelry, and a notepad.

A teenage girl might carry makeup, a compact mirror, perfume, gel pens, a cell phone, a hairbrush and comb, keys, lots of money, a nail file, lotion, and lip balm.

A young mom might carry a diaper bag, not a purse. Her bag might contain diapers, wet wipes, extra clothes, crackers or dry cereal, bandage strips, pacifiers, a grocery list, coupons, sunglasses, a bank card, but no money.

A grandma might have pictures of her grandbabies, lists of what to do and where to go, Kleenex, aspirin, lipstick, breath mints, dental floss, glasses or contacts case, tweezers, checkbook, and some money.

Purse Essentials

If you have a small group, each lady and girl could choose an item from her purse and explain what it says about her and why she is carrying it.

Purse Relay

Divide the ladies and girls into at least two groups, each in a row of chairs sitting side-by-side. Start with four purses on the floor by the first chair in the row. The first lady in each line picks up a purse with her left arm through the straps, and passes it to the left arm of the lady sitting next to her. No hands allowed! The first team to pass all four purses down and back wins. More than one purse may be going at a time. If your group is large, you may also choose two teams and have them stand in front while the rest of the guests watch.

Purse Prizes

Give prizes to ladies and girls who have these items in their purses: a green tube of lipstick, a sewing kit, a phone card, a calculator, a nail file, a straw, a plastic spoon, tickets to a performance, a work identification badge, a contacts case, hand sanitizer gel.

Skits

The Bag Lady

You will need the following items for this skit: Bible; limp celery stalk; small rug; newspaper; paper towel tubes, cut in half; paper napkins; dead flowers or weeds; soda can; cookbook; can of chili; crackers; teabags; plastic forks; video tape; shoestring.

At the end of this skit, ask each guest to make a list of the items she remembers from the lady's bag. Do not tell the guests ahead of time that they will be doing this. The one who lists the most items wins!

The skit begins with a bag lady making an entrance. She should be loud and dressed in old, dirty clothes and heavy work boots. She might even have a tooth missing. Her hair should be ratted and tangled. Have the emcee meet her and welcome her in surprise.

MC: Well, hello . . . Can we help you? Are you lost?

BL: Is this the party for the old bags?

MC: No, this is a party where each lady or girl brings her old but cherished handbag. Who are you?

BL: Well, I live out of my bag. (*proudly holds up her grocery sack*) It has everything in it to have a party. I just love to entertain.

MC: That's really nice. . . . I think.

BL: (*pulls her Bible from sack*) God's Word tells me to be hospitable and to show others love and kindness. Don't you agree?

MC: Well . . . yes, but I have been so busy lately . . . with my job and everything; and my house is really small, so I don't have a lot of room for entertaining. Besides, some of my good plates are broken, and I don't have enough that match.

During the following speech, the emcee should respond with facial expressions and by ad-libbing whenever appropriate.

BL: Being hospitable doesn't mean everything has to be perfect. I think God just wants us to share what He has blessed us with. I try to keep things handy so I can entertain on the spur of the moment. First, you need to do a little house cleaning. I always start with dusting. (*pulls out a limp stalk of celery and uses it as a duster*) And then I shake out the welcome mat. (*pulls out an old rug and shakes it*) After you are done cleaning, you will need to think about setting the table. (*pulls out a newspaper and lays it out like a tablecloth*) This *Wall Street Journal* is perfect for a tablecloth. As we visit, we can catch up on the latest happenings in the world. I have these great napkin holders. (*holds up paper tubes with paper napkins stuffed in them*) Then you need a centerpiece. (*pulls out some dead flowers or weeds*) I picked these a few days ago, but they will perk up once I put them in water. (*pulls out a soda can for the vase*)

MC: That sounds really nice. . . . I guess.

BL: I have this great cookbook, *Cooking over an Open Fire.* (*pulls out a cookbook*) I love the warmth and cozy atmosphere a fire adds.

MC: So what are you going to serve?

BL: I have this can of chili, some crackers, and hot tea. (*pulls out chili, crushed crackers, and teabags as she talks*) Next we need utensils. (*pulls out plastic forks to eat soup with*) After we have finished eating, we can watch this video if the guests bring a VCR. (*pulls out a video*) Of course, if it needs electricity, that probably wouldn't work. We love to play Phase 10, but you have to pay real close attention because I'm a few cards short of a deck.

MC: I guess I didn't think about how you can show hospitality on a shoestring budget.

BL: I have one of those too! (*pulls out a shoestring*) Being hospitable is sharing what you have with others no matter what your resources. It's not hard to do when your sharing comes from your heart.

MC: *(sheepishly)* I am so glad you came today. I have learned a lot about hospitality, and I'll be more willing to have others into my home.

BL: Well, I'd better go. See you around town. Remember, my door is always open.

Why Do Women Carry Purses?

(Have several good readers read the following essay about purses.)

Reader 1: It alters the way you walk. It knocks things off store shelves. It gives you a backache from toting it everywhere you go. Yet we love it and treasure it and can't leave home without it. It's a purse!

You can use a purse as a beauty salon, lunch box, trash can, daily organizer, first-aid kit, candy store, diaper bag. Then we complain about how big it is and how much it weighs! How do you feel about your purse? Is it a security blanket or a ball and chain? Do you love it or hate it? I asked some of my friends what they thought about their purses.

Reader 2: I have to have a purse for every season and every occasion. I can hardly walk past purses in the mall without thinking, *I could use this purse with my new brown shoes.* Then I go and buy some new brown shoes!

Reader 3: I hate to go purse shopping! I have to have one with just the right compartments. I have to have a zipper closure so things don't fall out. I stand for *hours,* looking in the mirror, to see where the purse hits me. I don't want it to make my hips look big.

Reader 4: Why, I've carried a purse for years. It's just become a part of me. It's like a third arm. Sometimes I find myself checking to make sure it is still there—kind of like a child or something. It's almost like a security blanket. Sometimes I have to stop everything and just find it—especially if we are traveling. What if I left it in the restaurant? I just have to know where it is.

Reader 5: My purse is part of work. I pack everything into it. I have my day planner, checkbook, stamps and envelopes, pens and pencils, cell phone, business cards, and sunglasses. I have makeup and hairspray so I can freshen up before meetings. When a carpenter goes to work, he carries a toolbox. Me, I carry my purse!

Reader 6: I decided to clean out my purse the other day, so I dumped it all out on the table. I found bills to be mailed, papers to grade, checking pencils, red pens, pictures of my kids, grocery receipts, to-do lists, a calendar, and also my empty bottle of nail polish remover. Let me explain: If I carry the empty bottle with me, it will help me remember to buy more!

Reader 7: I have to have this *huge* purse. Not only do I have to carry *my* things, I have to carry stuff for my husband too. A man won't carry a purse, but as soon as we get going, my husband needs a stick of gum or lip balm or nail clippers or a place to put his sunglasses. Why don't men carry purses instead of big, old, fat wallets in their back pockets? I get so tired of lugging all this around. Maybe a purse is like a man—sometimes you want him around and sometimes you don't. No, I take that back. I'll always want my purse.

Songs

"Heavenly Sunshine"
"When We All Get to Heaven"
"Heaven Is a Wonderful Place"
"Let the Beauty of Jesus Be Seen in Me"

Devotions
Heavenly Handbags

Many women and girls carry purses wherever they go. Purses have in them everything they will need! Most feel lost without them. Today we are going to look inside our spiritual, or heavenly, handbags to see what we as Christian women and girls have inside that we can share with others. *(Hold up each item.)*

1. LIPSTICK. Lipstick reminds us to use our lips for good. First, we should speak the truth. (*Read Psalm 34:13 and Proverbs 13:3.*) Honesty is the best policy! Telling the truth and guarding our lips is a must. It sets an example to our families and friends. If we want others to see Christ in us, we must speak the truth. (*Read Proverbs 31:26.*) With our lips we should praise and honor God.

2. MIRROR. A mirror reminds us to reflect Christ to the world through how we act. Matthew 5:16 tells us to "let your light so shine before men, that they may see your good works, and glorify your Father which is in heaven." People will look at how we live and act. Sometimes actions speak louder than words. We need to let the light of Christ reflect off of us so others will see that the good things we do are because we want to serve God and honor Him. Reflecting the Son will glorify the Father, Who is in Heaven.

3. PERFUME. Perfume reminds us to be sweet fragrance of Christ to other people. (*Read 2 Corinthians 2:15.*) What kind of fragrance do others think of when we are around them? As Christians, we need an aroma that leads to refreshing, rejuvenating, everlasting life. Let's determine to be a fragrance that draws others to Christ.

4. GLASSES. We need to see clearly and study God's Word. (*Read 2 Timothy 3:16 and 17.*) As we study God's Word and use it in our lives, we become better equipped to serve God. The Scriptures are profitable for us in four ways: (1) for doctrine—to help us see the right path; (2) for reproof—to help us see when we get off the path; (3) for correction—to help us see how to get back on the path; (4) for instruction in righteousness—to help us see how to stay on the path.

5. DRIVER'S LICENSE. A driver's license reminds us that we are free to drive a vehicle. Being free is a good feeling. Because of what God's Son did for us on the cross, we are free from the bondage of sin. Romans 8:2 says, "For the law of the Spirit of life in Christ Jesus hath made me free from the law of sin and death." Because of the fall of Adam and Eve, we are all born as sinners and slaves of sin, but Christ died on the cross of Calvary to free us from that sin and to offer us eternal life.

6. HAND CREAM AND LIP BALM. These items remind us that we need to be soothing to others. It feels good to rub cream into our hands and lip balm onto our lips. We should have this kind of encouraging ministry to others. "Wherefore comfort yourselves together, and edify one another, even as also ye do" (1 Thess. 5:11).

7. COMB AND BRUSH. We want to have every hair in place, looking just so. When people look at us and see Christ, they will want to know what gives us hope. We should always be ready to share what Christ has done for us. (*Read 1 Peter 3:15.*) He shed His blood for us on the cross. He took our punishment. Because He rose again, we can have eternal life when we place our trust in Him.

8. OLD FACIAL TISSUE, OLD GROCERY LISTS, AND GUM WRAPPERS. These items of trash remind us to get rid of the old and put on the new. Second Corinthians 5:17 informs us that "if any man be in Christ, he is a new creature: old things are passed away; behold, all things are become new." Sometimes we Christians need to get rid of some things in our lives. Each of us can probably think of things we have kept around too long, such as a bad attitude or self-pity. Sometimes we worry instead of accepting God's control. Don't keep such things around. Throw away the old and put on the new, such as love, joy, peace, patience, kindness, goodness, faithfulness, gentleness, and self-control (Gal. 5:22, 23). You will be much happier—and so will those around you.

What we carry in our purses says a lot about us. What things do you carry with you? Do you need to get rid of a few things? Let's be sure the things we are carrying will glorify and honor God and will help others see Christ in us.

Nametags

Prizes

- Hand cream
- Nail files
- Lip balm
- Wet wipes
- Facial tissues
- LifeSavers or breath mints

Recipes

Perfectly Divine Punch

2 pkgs. raspberry Kool-Aid

2 cups sugar

$\frac{1}{2}$ gallon water

3 tablespoons lemon juice from concentrate

1 (46 oz.) can pineapple juice

1 (2 liter) bottle lemon-lime carbonated soft drink

1 quart raspberry sherbet

Mix Kool-Aid, sugar, and water. Add lemon and pineapple juices. Just before serving, add the soft drink and sherbet.

Angel Food Cake

$1\frac{1}{4}$ cups cake flour, sifted

$\frac{1}{2}$ cup sugar, sifted

2 cups egg whites, room temperature (10–12 eggs)

$\frac{1}{4}$ teaspoon salt

$1\frac{1}{4}$ teaspoons cream of tartar

1 teaspoon vanilla

$\frac{1}{4}$ teaspoon almond extract

$1\frac{1}{3}$ cups sifted sugar

1. Sift flour; then measure $1\frac{1}{4}$ cups. Add $\frac{1}{2}$ cup sifted sugar to the flour and sift together four times. Set aside.

2. Combine egg whites, salt, cream of tartar, vanilla, and almond extract. Beat with a mixer until the whites form soft peaks. Add the rest of the sugar ($1\frac{1}{3}$ cups) in four additions, about 5 tablespoons at a time. Beat with a wire whip, 25 strokes after each addition. Add flour in 4 parts and beat with wire whip 15 strokes after each addition. Pour into an ungreased angel food cake pan. Bake at 350°F for about 40 minutes.

3. Remove cake from oven. Invert pan; cool at least 1 hour. Loosen sides with knife before removing.

4. Garnish with hot fudge topping, whipped cream, or fruit pie fillings.

Hot Fudge Topping

3 (1 oz. each) squares semisweet baking chocolate

1 stick margarine

3 cups sugar

1 (12 oz.) can evaporated milk

Melt baking chocolate and margarine. Stir in sugar until dissolved. Slowly add evaporated milk. Cook on low for 30 minutes.

PURSE PATTERN

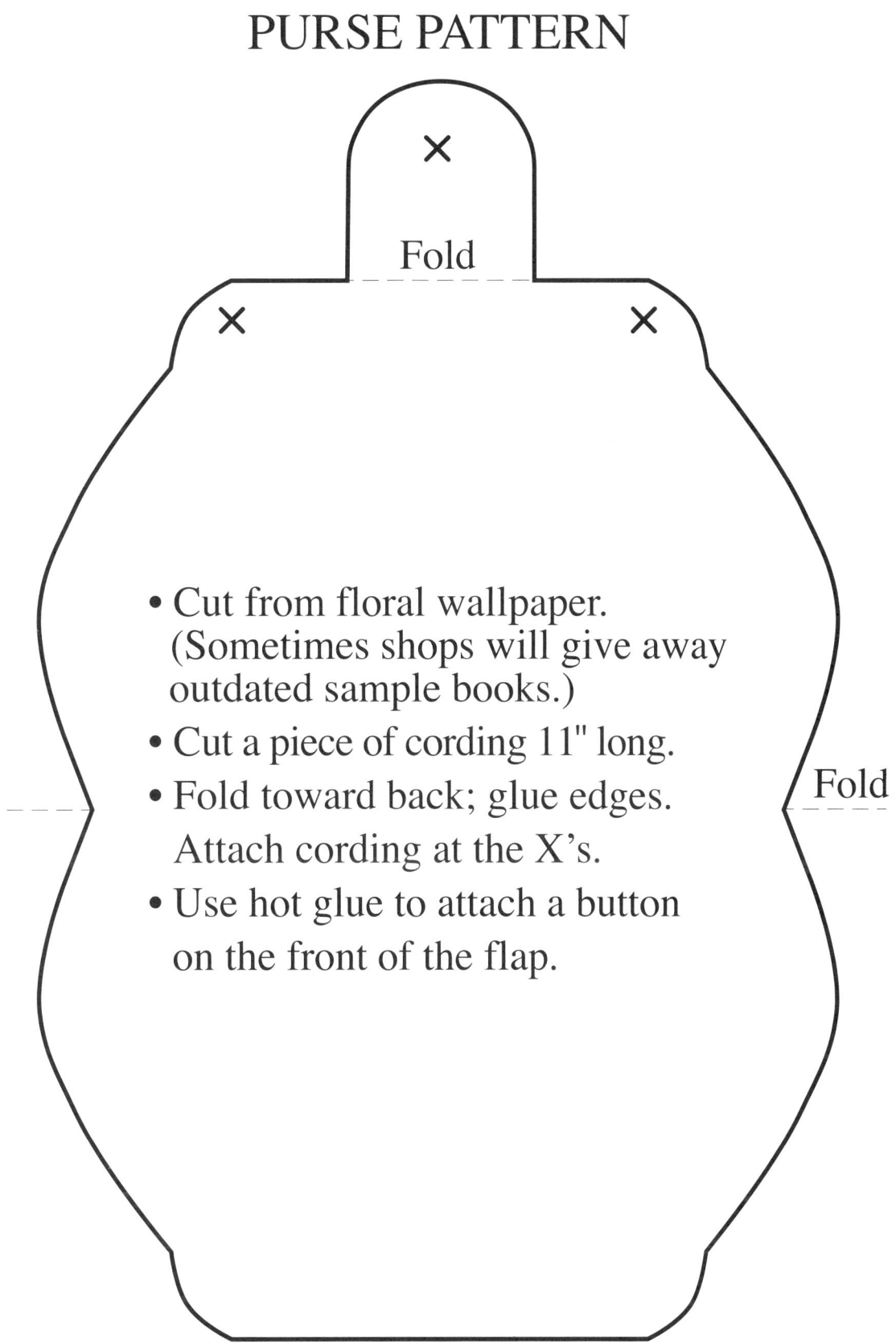

Fold

✕

✕   ✕

- Cut from floral wallpaper. (Sometimes shops will give away outdated sample books.)
- Cut a piece of cording 11" long.
- Fold toward back; glue edges. Attach cording at the X's.
- Use hot glue to attach a button on the front of the flap.

Fold

How about a Makeover?

Theme and Decorations

- Place a brightly colored place mat at each table setting. Use a splash of brightly colored purples and pinks for a fun, girlish atmosphere.
- Decorate tables with makeup kits or collections, stand-up mirrors, cotton balls and swabs, boxes of facial tissue, hairbrushes, combs, hairclips, nail polish, lipsticks, exercise videos, and towels.

Food

- "Makeup" Your Own Sub
- Hard rolls, variety of breads
- Chips and dip
- Fresh fruit and dip
- Homemade cookies

Games

Makeover Time

Have a beautician or another lady perform makeovers for anyone who would like one. Recruit teenagers to give manicures. Most teens love to do nails!

Name Game

Name the women who did the following.

1. Gave gifts to Solomon (1 Kings 10:1–10) _____

2. Assured King Joash that God would spare the king's people (2 Kings 22:13–20) _____

3. Was the first person to be buried in a cemetery (Gen. 23:19, 20) _____

4. Was a businesswoman known as a "seller of purple" (Acts 16:14) _____

5. Lied to her father to save her husband (1 Sam. 19:12–17) _____

6. Drove a nail through Sisera's head (Judg. 4:21) _____

7. Was a judge who held court under a palm tree (Judg. 4:4, 5) _____

8. Had John the Baptist beheaded (Matt. 14:6–10) _____

9. Appeared drunk while she prayed fervently (1 Sam. 1:12–15) _____

10. Protected spies for Israel (Josh. 2) _____

11. Stole her father's idols and sat on them (Gen. 31:19–35) _____

12. Deceived Samson and cut off his hair (Judg. 16:4–22) _____

13. Forged her husband's signature on an important document (1 Kings 21) _____

14. Was a citizen of Joppa known for her good deeds and was raised from the dead by Peter (Acts 9:36–40) _____

15. Saved the Jewish people from being sold and murdered (Esther 7:1–8) _____

16. Put her baby boy in a basket and placed him in the reeds of the Nile River (Exod. 2:1–10; 6:20) _____

17. Busied herself preparing food while her sister talked with Jesus; rebuked by Jesus (Luke 10:38–42) _____

18. Asked by Jesus for a drink of water (John 4:7) _____

19. Went to the tomb early to anoint Jesus' body (Luke 24:1–10) _____

20. Tricked her father-in-law after he wronged her; gave birth to twins (Gen. 38) _____

21. Saved her foolish husband from David (1 Sam. 25:2–42) _____

22. Had a son; was ministered to by an angel in the desert (Gen. 21:14–21) _____

23. With her husband was one of the first missionaries of the early church (Acts 18) _____

24. Looked back and became a pillar of salt (Gen. 19:2–26) _____

Answers

(1) Queen of Sheba; (2) Huldah the prophetess; (3) Sarah; (4) Lydia; (5) Michal; (6) Jael; (7) Deborah; (8) Herodias; (9) Hannah; (10) Rahab; (11) Rachel; (12) Delilah; (13) Jezebel; (14) Dorcas/Tabitha; (15) Esther; (16) Jochebed; (17) Martha; (18) Samaritan woman; (19) Mary Magdalene, Joanna, and Mary the mother of James; (20) Tamar; (21) Abigail; (22) Hagar; (23) Priscilla; (24) Lot's wife.

Makeup or Maine?

Answer each of the following with a word that begins with the "may" sound.

1. It holds letters _____
2. The head of a town or city _____
3. The Pilgrim's ship _____
4. What women put on their faces _____
5. A female head of a band _____
6. A young single woman _____
7. Perhaps _____
8. The long hair on the neck of a horse _____
9. To create or compose _____
10. A military officer _____
11. Indian corn _____
12. A married woman _____
13. What baby Jesus slept in _____
14. Pancake syrup _____
15. A companion _____
16. An old TV show town _____
17. Something children gather and sing around _____
18. A month that has 31 days _____
19. A confusing network of passages _____
20. The Pine Tree state _____
21. A bridal attendant _____
22. A salad dressing _____

Answers

(1) Mailbox; (2) mayor; (3) Mayflower; (4) makeup; (5) majorette; (6) maiden; (7) maybe; (8) mane; (9) make; (10) major; (11) maize; (12) matron; (13) manger; (14) maple; (15) mate; (16) Mayberry; (17) Maypole; (18) May; (19) maze; (20) Maine; (21) maid or matron of honor; (22) mayonnaise.

Skit

I Enjoy Being a Girl

Ask a group of girls or ladies to dress in bathrobes, curlers, and slippers. One or two should put cream on their faces and wrap their hair in towels. Have the girls or ladies sing "I Enjoy Being a Girl" from Rodgers and Hammerstein's musical *Flower Drum Song* while doing actions appropriate to the song. Order the music online by going to www.freesheetmusic.net and typing in "I Enjoy Being a Girl."

Songs

"Make Me a Blessing"
"More like the Savior"
"O to Be like Thee"
"I Enjoy Being a Girl"

Devotions

How about a Makeover?

It's a girl thing! We all want to be beautiful—inside and out! For ages women have pampered and colored and painted and exercised so they will look better and feel more confident about themselves. Women, teens, and girls today spend tons of money on beauty products. But beauty is only skin deep. No amount of money or primping can cover up on the outside what may be lacking on the inside. Before we work on fixing ourselves to look better on the outside, maybe we should work on fixing our attitudes and actions to make us more beautiful inside and out.

Have you ever noticed how many lotions, candles, and soaps are scented or named after a fruit? Apple Blossom, Strawberries and Cream, Cucumber Melon, Pearberry, and Candy Apple are just a few of the names.

Today we are going to look at the fruit of the Spirit to see how we can have beauty within. (Read Galatians 5:22 and 23.)

Fruit grows and matures on plants, trees, or vines. As Christians, we should grow and mature in Christ. The Holy Spirit develops in us the fruit, or characteristics, of Christ. We cannot produce it on our own. We need to abide in the Vine, the Lord Jesus. John 15:5 says, "I am the vine, ye are the branches: He that abideth in me, and I in him, the same bringeth forth much fruit: for without me ye can do nothing."

So if we abide in Christ, we will evidence fruit—the fruit of the Spirit. God will give us a spiritual makeover, so to speak, to use in our relationships, to please Him, to help others, and for our own good.

(Pick up each of the following items and show how to use it before you continue with the Biblical application. Or you could have volunteers do so. You will need moisturizer and a cosmetics sponge, foundation and applicator, face powder and a powder brush or puff, body lotion, hair spray, perfume [preferably with an applicator], nail polish and sealer, and a bowl of water and a towel.)

1. With a soft sponge, apply liberal amounts of LOVE (show moisturizer and cosmetics sponge). To love is to unselfishly meet the needs of someone else. First Corinthians 13 describes love as being supreme. There are different kinds of love: the love between a man and a woman, the love of a friend, and the love of God for people.

John 3:16 states, "For God so loved the world, that he gave his only begotten Son, that whosoever believeth in him should not perish, but have everlasting life." (Read or quote Romans 5:8.) God can help us to love one another, because God is love.

2. Next, apply a coat of JOY (show foundation and applicator). Joy is contentment and satisfaction in God and His plan for our lives. When we experience the joy of the Lord, our faces will show delight and pleasure, and we'll have a bounce in our step. Nehemiah 8:10 says, "The joy of the LORD is your strength." We can be like God when we show joy.

3. Next, powder lightly with PEACE (show powder and brush or puff). Peace is calmness within. Isaiah 26:3 tells what happens when we keep our minds focused on God: "Thou wilt keep him in perfect peace, whose mind is stayed on thee: because he trusteth in thee." When we keep our minds on God, He gives us peace. We will be like God when we have peace.

4. Rub in PATIENCE (show body lotion). Sometimes patience comes through our trials. Patience helps us remain calm and steadfast, and it helps us persevere through each trial. (Read Romans 15:5 and 6.) Rub in some patience and perseverance so you can be like God and glorify Him.

5. Spray all over with KINDNESS (show hair spray). Kindness is sympathy, pleasantness, and graciousness. The virtuous woman of Proverbs 31 spoke with words of kindness. Verse 26 describes her as having kindness on her tongue. We are like God when we show kindness.

6. Dab some GOODNESS here and there (show perfume). When we are good, we are agreeable, pleasant, true, sound, and attractive. Psalm 16:2 says that our goodness is nothing apart from God. We are like God when we show goodness.

7. Brush on a couple coats of FAITHFULNESS (show nail polish). Faithfulness is allegiance to a duty or a person. A faithful person is loyal and reliable. God is truly faithful to us. Psalm 92:1 and 2

praise God's faithfulness. *(Read the verses.)* We can be like God when we are faithful in whatever we say and do.

8. Add a layer of MEEKNESS *(show sealer)*. Meekness is a kind, soft, amiable spirit. Jesus described Himself as meek. *(Read Matthew 11:29.)* We can be more like God when we show meekness to others.

9. Last, rinse thoroughly with SELF-CONTROL *(show water and towel)*. Self-control is hard. It means exercising restraint of oneself. That means not losing our temper when we have been wronged or wanting something so much that we give into our desire for it. In 1 Corinthians 9:27 Paul described his self-control. *(Read the verse.)* We can be like God when we show self-control.

Do you want to have more fruit in your life and be more like God? Abide in Him, and you will have a makeover that gives you inner beauty.

Nametags

Prizes

- Tubes of lipstick
- Bottles of nail polish
- Nail files
- Cotton swabs
- Cotton balls
- Small mirrors

Recipes
Sub Sandwiches
Deli meats, such as roast beef, turkey, and ham

Different kinds of sliced cheese

Garnishes (lettuce, tomatoes, onions, cucumbers, pickles, green peppers, banana or jalapeño peppers, black olives, oil and vinegar, salt and pepper, mayonaise, salad dressings, mustard)

Betty's Best Cookies
$1\frac{1}{2}$ cups shortening

1 cup brown sugar

1 cup white sugar

3 eggs

$1\frac{1}{2}$ teaspoon vanilla

$3\frac{1}{2}$ cups flour

1 teaspoon salt

1 teaspoon baking soda

1 (10 oz.) pkg. Hershey's Mini Milk Chocolate Kisses

1 cup chopped pecans (opt.)

1 cup raisins (opt.)

Cream together shortening and sugars. Add eggs and vanilla. Stir in dry ingredients gradually. Add chips and pecans or raisins. Drop by teaspoons on cookie sheet. Bake at 375°F for 8–10 minutes.

ALTERNATE
1 pkg. orange slice candy

$\frac{1}{2}$ cup flour

With scissors, cut up the candy. Coat the candy with flour, and add them to the ingredients above, eliminating the chips, pecans, and raisins.

Peanut Blossom Cookies

$^1/_2$ cup margarine
$^1/_2$ cup sugar
$^1/_2$ cup brown sugar
$^1/_2$ cup peanut butter
1 egg
1 teaspoon vanilla
2 teaspoons milk
$1^3/_4$ cups flour
1 teaspoon baking soda
1 teaspoon salt
Chocolate star candy

Cream together margarine, sugars, and peanut butter. Add egg, vanilla, and milk. Stir in dry ingredients. Mix well. Roll into small balls and drop into sugar to coat. Bake at 375°F for 5–7 minutes. Press a chocolate star into the center of each cookie and bake 2 more minutes.

Sugar Dainties

1 cup margarine
1 cup white sugar
3 eggs
$3^3/_4$ cups flour
$^1/_2$ teaspoon salt
1 teaspoon baking soda
2 teaspoons cream of tartar
$1^1/_2$ teaspoons vanilla

Cream together margarine and sugar. Add eggs and blend well. Add dry ingredients and vanilla. Chill dough at least 30 minutes. Roll chilled dough on floured surface and cut with cookie cutters. Bake at 375°F for 6–8 minutes. Frost if desired.

Decorator's Frosting

$^1/_2$ cup shortening
$^1/_4$ cup milk
$^1/_4$ teaspoon vanilla
4 cups powdered sugar

Mix ingredients together, adding powdered sugar 1 cup at a time. Beat on high for 4–5 minutes.

Pecan Crispies

$^1/_2$ cup margarine
6 tablespoons brown sugar
6 tablespoons white sugar
1 egg
$^1/_2$ teaspoon vanilla
$1^1/_4$ cups flour
$^1/_4$ teaspoon baking soda
1 teaspoon baking powder
$^1/_4$ teaspoon salt
1 cup chopped pecans

Cream butter and sugars until fluffy. Beat in egg and vanilla. Add dry ingredients. Stir in pecans. Add extra flour if dough is too sticky. Drop by teaspoons on cookie sheet. Bake at 375°F for 10 minutes.

Chocolate Chip Cookies

$1^1/_2$ cups butter
1 cup brown sugar
1 cup white sugar
3 eggs
$1^1/_2$ tablespoons water
4 cups flour
$1^1/_2$ teaspoons baking soda
$1^1/_2$ teaspoons salt
1 pkg. (6 oz.) chocolate chips

Cream butter and sugars. Add eggs and water. Beat well. Add dry ingredients and chocolate chips. Drop by teaspoons on cookie sheet. Bake at 375°F for 10 minutes.

Oatmeal Raisin Cookies

1 cup raisins
1 cup margarine
1 cup sugar
2 eggs
1 teaspoon vanilla
2 cups quick oatmeal
2 cups flour
$1/_2$ teaspoon salt
1 teaspoon baking soda
$1/_2$ teaspoon nutmeg
1 teaspoon cinnamon
$1/_2$ cup pecans (opt.)

Cook raisins in 1 cup water until soft. Save $1/_3$ cup of the raisin juice. Blend together margarine and sugar. Stir in eggs and vanilla. Add the dry ingredients, raisins, pecans, and reserved raisin juice. Mix well. Drop by teaspoons on cookie sheet. Bake at 375°F for 8–10 minutes.

Corn Flake Cookies

$1/_2$ cup white sugar
$1/_2$ cup white corn syrup
1 cup peanut butter
2 cups corn flakes

Bring sugar and syrup to boil. Remove from heat. Add peanut butter and stir until smooth. Add corn flakes and drop by spoonfuls onto waxed paper. Cool.

Snickerdoodles

COOKIES
1 cup margarine
$1^1/_2$ cups sugar
2 eggs
$2^3/_4$ cups flour
2 teaspoons cream of tartar
1 teaspoon baking soda
1 teaspoon salt

COATING
1 teaspoon cinnamon
2 tablespoons sugar

Cream margarine and sugar. Add eggs. Mix thoroughly and add flour, cream of tartar, salt, and baking soda. Roll into balls the size of walnuts. Roll balls in a mixture of sugar and cinnamon. Bake at 375°F for 8–10 minutes.

How Does Your Garden Grow?

Theme and Decorations

- Decorate with flowers and flowerpots, gloves, wide-brimmed hats, rakes, hoes, and watering cans. Fill the watering cans with daisies or other cut flowers.
- Use flowered tablecloths and colored napkins to reflect a spring theme.
- Accent with light blue and yellow in the napkins and ribbons.
- Make Dirt Cakes (see "Recipes") in plastic flowerpots with artificial or fresh flowers arranged in the dessert. If you use real flowers, wrap the stems in wet paper towels and then aluminum foil before sticking them in the dessert. Place a new garden trowel beside each dessert to use for serving.

Food

- Ham and Pickle Roll-ups
- Tortilla Wraps
- Grapes, apples, and bananas
- Dirt Cake
- Lemonade

Games

Names of Flowers

Collect and display pictures (or the item itself) of the following list, numbering them from 1 to 20. Have each lady write down the name of the flower the item reminds her of. For example, a pan with a "z" in it is a "pansy."

1. A cup of butter _____
2. Two pitchers standing with lips touching _____
3. A clock set at 4:00 _____
4. Peas in a dish of sugar _____
5. Picture of a little boy or William Shakespeare or another "William" your guests will recognize; sprinkle sugar on the picture _____
6. A button _____
7. A man with children, indicating he is the father or grandfather _____
8. A woman's slipper _____
9. Small piece of pink material _____
10. Several soda straws _____
11. A pan with a "z" in it _____
12. A dignified little girl _____
13. A day calendar with the letters "zzz" written on it _____
14. A silver bell _____
15. Two or three stuffed sheep or lambs _____
16. A toy car on top of the map of a country _____
17. A picture of a lady's eyes _____
18. A toy dragon with a seamstress's snap by it _____
19. A pincushion full of pins _____
20. A toy elephant _____

Answers

(1) Buttercup; (2) tulip; (3) four-o'clock; (4) sweet pea; (5) sweet william; (6) bachelor's button; (7) poppy; (8) lady's slipper; (9) pinks; (10) strawflower; (11) pansy; (12) primrose; (13) daisy; (14) silver bell; (15) phlox; (16) carnation; (17) iris; (18) snapdragon; (19) pincushion; (20) forget-me-not.

Garden Quiz

1. What flower is a sugary vegetable? _____

2. What flower is in the song "A Bicycle Built for Two"? _____

3. What flower is a cooking utensil with a "z" in it? _____

4. What flower is a woman's house shoe? _____

5. What flower tells the time of day? _____

6. What flower do most girls hope to do? _____

7. What flower is a word for keeping a secret? _____

8. What flower reminds you of a herd of sheep? _____

9. What flower is like a jilted lover? _____

10. What flower is rooted in blood? _____

Answers

(1) Sweet pea; (2) daisy; (3) pansy; (4) lady's slipper; (5) four-o'clock; (6) marigold; (7) mum; (8) phlox; (9) bleeding heart; (10) bloodroot.

Songs

"In the Garden"
"The Beautiful Garden of Prayer"
"For the Beauty of the Earth"
"Learning to Lean"

Devotions
Learning and Growing in Jesus

(Show a photo of one of your guests as a baby, child, or young woman. Then show a more recent photo of her. Ask the girls in your audience, "What made the change in _____?" [Answer: She grew or she grew up or she grew older.])

Most of us enjoy a walk through a beautiful garden. We admire the lovely plants that grow there—whether it's a flower garden or a garden full of fresh vegetables. Whatever the case—flowers or vegetables—gardens start as little plants or seeds that are planted in fresh, black dirt. As a plant grows, it changes in size, develops new leaves, and produces fruits or seeds.

Christians are a lot like plants. Christians need to grow, and as they grow spiritually, change should be evident in their lives.

For most of us change is rarely easy. And for many, the stress of change is hard to cope with. Jesus knows all about change and stress, and He doesn't want us to try to deal with it on our own. He wants us to learn and grow in Him.

In Matthew 11:28–30 Jesus invited us to do three things: come unto Him, take His yoke, and learn of Him. *(Read the passage aloud.)*

First, in verse 28 Jesus invited us to come to Him. Before we can learn about Him, we need to come to Him alone for salvation. Our world is filled with sin, because each of us is a sinner (Rom. 3:23). Our sin wearies and burdens us. To find rest from the burden of sin, sinners need to receive Jesus as Savior (John 1:12), and He will give them rest.

Second, Jesus invites us to take up His yoke (Matt 11:29). We need to be willing to submit to God's ways and His leading. When we turn our lives over to God, we grow spiritually and become more like Him. Then as we grow in Him, we acknowledge that His way is best, and the yoke He has given us is light and easy to bear. It doesn't mean that Christians don't have problems or heartaches, but it does mean that when we are yoked together with the

One Who can give grace in our times of need, we won't have to bear our hurts alone.

Wearing Jesus' yoke is not bondage; it is freedom and victory, because Jesus shares our burdens with us and carries us through. We don't have to be alone when we are in Christ.

Third, in verse 29 Jesus invited us to learn of Him. Jesus wants to be our teacher. We need to read His Word daily and learn of Him through the guiding of His Holy Spirit. As He teaches us different lessons, we will grow closer to Him.

Jesus said that His yoke is easy and His burden is light (v. 30). So when change comes, remember that Jesus wants you to come to Him, take His yoke, and learn from Him.

As we heed the invitation of Jesus, we will know the truth of 2 Peter 3:18: "But grow in grace, and in the knowledge of our Lord and Saviour Jesus Christ."

Nametags

Prizes

- Sun visors
- Garden trowels
- Gardening gloves
- Flower seeds

Recipes

Ham and Pickle Roll-ups

16 oz. sliced ham

2 (8 oz. each) pkgs. cream cheese, softened

1 large jar dill pickles

Dry ham slices on paper towels. Spread cream cheese on ham slices. Add pickles. Roll up and slice. Chill.

Salsa Tortilla Wraps

1 (8 oz.) pkg. cream cheese, softened

$\frac{1}{4}$ cup salsa

1 (8–10) pkg. soft flour tortillas

Mix together cream cheese and salsa. Spread mixture on tortillas. Roll up and cut into slices. Chill.

Tortilla Wraps

1 (8–10) pkg. soft flour tortillas

1 (16 oz.) container sour cream

1 (8 oz.) pkg. cream cheese, softened

Garnishes and seasonings (chopped green onions, chopped black olives, pimentos, shredded cheddar cheese, garlic powder, dill weed)

Mix together sour cream and cream cheese; spread on tortillas. Add garnishes and flavorings according to your taste. Roll up and slice. Chill.

Dirt Cake

$^1/_2$ cup butter or margarine, softened

1 (8 oz.) pkg. cream cheese, softened

1 cup powdered sugar

$3^1/_2$ cups milk

2 (3.4 oz. each) pkgs. instant vanilla pudding and pie filling

1 (12 oz.) container frozen whipped topping, thawed

1 pkg. Oreo cookies, crushed

1 (8"–10") plastic flower pot

Gummy worms (opt.)

Fresh or artificial flowers (opt.)

1. Cream together butter or margarine, cream cheese, and powdered sugar. In another bowl, mix milk and dry pudding. Combine the two mixtures. Fold in whipped topping.

2. If the bottom of the flowerpot has a hole, cover it with a small piece of foil. In the bottom of the pot, put $^1/_3$ of the crushed cookies. Add $^1/_2$ of the filling mixture and another $^1/_2$ of the cookies. Add remaining filling and top with remaining cookies.

3. Refrigerate cake overnight. Before serving, add flowers and gummy worms, if desired. Serve with a garden trowel for an extra touch.

It Takes Two

Theme and Decorations

- Invite your mothers and daughters to come looking as much alike as possible. Award prizes to the pairs who look the most alike.
- Decorate with wildflowers of all kinds.
- Accent decorations with bumblebees and butterflies.
- Serve similar or look-alike foods on the same platter. (See "Food.")
- Obtain a copy of the song "Me and My Mom" by Mercer Mayer. (See "Songs.")

Food

- Waldorf Chicken Salad
- Tuna Salad and Chicken Salad Sandwiches
- Croissants, small buns
- Cracker-and-cheese duos
- Double Fudge Brownie Delight

Games

Go-Togethers

Ask ladies and girls to list as many pairs as they can think of in three minutes. The guest with the most pairs wins a package of Doublemint gum. Possible answers: cream and sugar, bread and butter, pork and beans, meat and potatoes, birds and bees, shoes and socks, cake and ice cream, bride and groom, husband and wife.

It's about Mom

Add some letters or a word to complete these "moms."

1. _____ mother (soon to be)
2. Mother _____ (native language)
3. Mother's _____ (holiday)
4. Mother _____ (a children's favorite nursery rhyme character)
5. Mother- _____ (mother by marriage)
6. Mother, _____ (children's game)
7. _____ mother (oversees college girls)
8. _____ mother (posed for a portrait)
9. Mother _____ (all mothers or the state of being a mother)
10. Mother _____ (vein of ore)
11. _____ mother (mom's mom)
12. Mother ___ _____ (used to make buttons or jewelry)
13. _____ mother (provides a temporary home)
14. Mother _____ (had a bare cupboard)
15. Mother _____ (site of your ancestry)

Answers

(1) Expectant; (2) tongue; (3) Day; (4) Goose; (5) in-law; (6) May I; (7) dorm; (8) Whistler's; (9) hood; (10) lode; (11) grand; (12) of pearl; (13) foster; (14) Hubbard; (15) country or land.

Songs

"Me and My Mom"
"O to Be like Thee"
"More like the Master"
"I Would Be like Jesus"

Devotions
"Bee" like God

Isn't it fun to look like someone else or to dream about being like someone we admire? Most little girls want to grow up to be mothers just like their moms. Even if you moms and daughters don't look alike, you probably have many similar actions and mannerisms. We tend to be like the people we spend the most time with. As Christians, we need to spend time with God so we can "bee" more like Him. Let's consider three ways in which we can be like God.

First, we are like God the Father when we forgive one another. Ephesians 4:32 tells us to be "kind one to another, tenderhearted, forgiving one another, even as God for Christ's sake hath forgiven you." God is our example for forgiveness. "He is faithful and just to forgive us our sins, and to cleanse us from all unrighteousness" (1 John 1:9). We need to have a forgiving heart toward others. We are like God the Father when we forgive.

Second, we are like God the Son when we love one another. *(Read 1 Thessalonians 4:9 and 1 John 4:7.)* Luke 10:25–37 records the parable Jesus taught of the Good Samaritan. The Good Samaritan showed love by helping a man who had been robbed and beaten and left for dead. A priest and a Levite had walked past the injured man without helping, but the Samaritan had compassion on the man. He bound the man's wounds, took him to an inn, and paid for his care. Jesus wants us to love as the Samaritan loved. Jesus said, "This is my commandment, That ye love one another, as I have loved you" (John 15:12). We can be most like God the Son when we love one another.

Third, we are like God the Holy Spirit when we encourage one another. First Thessalonians 5:11 tells us to comfort each other and build each other up. Hebrews 10:25 describes how we Christians should act: "[encouraging] one another: and so much the more, as ye see the day approaching."

Acts 4:36 presents Barnabas as an example of encouragement. *(Read Acts 11:22 and 23.)* Barnabas was used by God to console and encourage Christians in the early life of the church, and God can use us to encourage Christians today to remain true to the Lord. We will be like God the Holy Spirit when we encourage one another.

God can use us and make us more like Himself when we forgive, love, and encourage one another.

Nametags

Prizes

- Wildflower seeds
- Twix candy bars
- Doublemint gum

Recipes
Waldorf Chicken Salad

2 cups diced apples
2 tablespoons lemon juice
2 cups diced cooked chicken
1 cup finely chopped celery
$\frac{1}{2}$ cup chopped walnuts
$\frac{1}{2}$ cup white raisins or grapes
Miracle Whip to taste

Toss apples in lemon juice. Combine ingredients with enough dressing to hold the salad together. Refrigerate before serving.

Tuna Salad Sandwiches

2 cans chunk tuna, drained
$^1/_4$ cup diced celery
2 tablespoons sweet pickle relish
2 hard-boiled eggs, chopped
1 tablespoon lemon juice (opt.)
$^1/_2$ cup Miracle Whip

Mix ingredients together and spread on sandwich bread.

Chicken Salad Sandwiches

3 cups diced cooked chicken
1 cup seedless grapes, halved
$^3/_4$ cup diced celery
$^3/_4$ cup pineapple tidbits, drained
$^1/_2$ cup chopped pecans
1 cup salad dressing

Combine ingredients. Serve as a salad or spread on croissants.

Double Fudge Brownie Delight

BROWNIES

1 fudge brownie mix
2 pints vanilla ice cream, softened
$1^1/_2$ cups crushed peanuts

TOPPING

$^1/_2$ cup margarine
1 cup evaporated milk
2 cups powdered sugar
1 teaspoon vanilla

1. Prepare and bake a fudge brownie mix according to directions on package. Cool; then cover with softened ice cream and peanuts. Freeze several hours.

2. For topping, combine margarine, evaporated milk, and powdered sugar in a saucepan; boil for 8 minutes. Add vanilla. Cool 30 minutes; then pour over frozen dessert. Return to freezer. Remove from freezer 15–20 minutes before serving.

Let's Go Shopping

Theme and Decorations

- Set up the room with shopping games from the TV show *The Price Is Right*. Record the show's theme song; play it during the games.
- Hang yellow price tags around the room.
- As centerpieces, place on the tables old purses with play money sticking out.
- Cut out gold dollar signs ($) and scatter them between the purses. If your tablecloths are disposable, you could draw dollar signs on them.
- Borrow or rent grocery carts and fill them with grocery items, such as paper towels, cereals, crackers, laundry soap, and other dry goods. You might want to have the ladies bring these items to fill the cart and then to donate to a missionary cupboard, a family in need, a single lady, or a new couple.
- Because you will need more time for the setup of the games, a catered meal would be convenient. You could have the guests purchase tickets ahead of time. Or, as an alternative, hold a salad buffet.

Food

- Salad buffet
- Catered meal

Games
The Price Is Right

Set up and play some of the shopping games on *The Price Is Right*. As the guests come in, have them put their names in a box. When it is time to play, draw four names to identify the contestants for the show. Play the theme music. Call out, "_____ _____, come on down! You're the next contestant on *The Price Is Right!*" After each game, choose another player for contestants' row.

FIND A PLAYER

To determine the first player from contestants' row, display items such as a box of cereal, a bottle of dish soap, or any other items you have on hand. Each contestant guesses the price without going over. The one closest to the correct price gets to play and also wins the prize she bid on.

Award $1 to any contestants who guess the exact prices.

FIRST GAME

The first player goes up to the emcee to play the first game. The emcee announces, "You could win . . . a new car . . . wash! Get your car squeaky clean! You will get drive-through convenience and power brushes to make your vehicle shine. All this can be yours . . . if the price is right! Let's play the Higher or Lower game!"

Higher or Lower

Display six grocery items, each with the wrong price in front of it. Underneath the top card should be the right price on another card.

The contestant has to say whether the correct price is higher or lower. Show the correct price. If the contestant says lower and the price is higher, or vice versa, she is done. If she answers correctly, she can keep going. If she answers all six correctly, she wins the car wash. (The cost of this prize is the price of a standard car wash in your area.)

Find a Player

Go to contestants' row again and repeat the bidding procedure for finding the next player.

SECOND GAME

The emcee announces, "You could win . . . a fabulous trip to . . . _____ [name a favorite ice cream store]! Enjoy the cool, creamy soft ice cream topped with generous hot fudge and crunchy nuts! It's a yummy, delicious treat! And it can be yours . . . if the price is right! Let's play the Number 7 game."

Number 7

Describe a big item, such as a camper. Set a four-digit price for it, and give the contestant seven $1 bills. Tell her that the price contains four digits and that she needs to guess the first digit. Whatever number she guesses, she subtracts that amount from the real number of the price and gives back that many $1 bills. For example, if the contestant guesses a 3 for the first digit, and the actual first digit is 5, she has to give back two $1 bills. If she has any money left after guessing all four digits, she is a winner. (The cost of this prize is $3–$5.)

Find a Player

Go to contestants' row again and repeat the bidding procedure for finding the next player.

THIRD GAME

The emcee announces, "Our next prize will have you enjoying sand, surf, and fun in the sun! You and your friends will want to stay hours at the beach as you frolic in the sand with your new brightly colored . . . beach ball! It's a great catch, and it can be yours if the price is right! Let's play the Switch game!"

Switch

Show two items, such as suntan lotion and sunglasses, each with a price tag in front of it. The contestant may switch the prices if she wants to, or she may leave them the same. Reveal the correct price to see if the contestant won the beach ball. (The cost of this prize is $1–$3.)

Find a Player

Go to contestants' row again and repeat the bidding procedure for finding the next player.

FOURTH GAME

The emcee announces, "Our next prize will take you and a loved one on an all-expenses-paid ocean cruise. There you will find all kinds of fish from the ocean's deep waters. You will be the captain's special guest when you cruise in . . . and place your order at Long John Silver's [or other fast-food seafood place]. All this can be yours if the price is right! Let's play the Now or Then game."

Now or Then

Select five different grocery items and display them. Place a price tag in front of each item with a separate card underneath that says "now" or "then." Have the contestant guess if the price is current or from five years ago. If she misses one, she is done. She has to get all five correct to win the cruise to Long John Silver's. (The cost of this prize is $6–$8.)

Find a Player

Go to contestants' row again and repeat the bidding procedure for finding the next player.

FIFTH GAME

The emcee announces, "Our next prize will find you enjoying a world-renowned classic symphony. . . . Symphony candy bar, that is! Bits of Heath candy pieces and nuts covered with rich, creamy chocolate. It will start your taste buds singing! And it can be yours . . . if the price is right! [Contestant's name], step right up to play Squeeze Play."

Squeeze Play

Describe a large item, such as a dining room set or bedroom set. Display a five-digit number, and tell the contestant that the first number and the last number are correct. She has to "squeeze" out one number from the middle. If she chooses the right number to get rid of, she wins the candy bar. (The cost of this prize is $1–$3.)

Find a Player

Go to contestants' row again and repeat the bidding procedure for finding the next player.

SIXTH GAME

The emcee announces, "Our next prize could be . . . a beautiful new house! The furniture and accessories for each room are excellently detailed with color and are professionally designed. You will spend hours looking at the rooms in your new . . . House . . . *Beautiful* magazine. Your magazine will have you planning your next dream house! And this beautiful magazine can be yours . . . if the price is right! [Contestant's name], come on over to play In the Bag."

In the Bag

You need five small brown bags, each with a price listed on it. Give the contestant five items to place in front of the bags. She should place each item in front of the bag that she thinks has its right price. If she matches the first item, give her a quarter. She has the choice now to quit and keep her money or to go on to the second item. If the second item matches, she wins two quarters. She can quit there or go on. The money doubles each time. If she guesses incorrectly, she is done and loses all her money. (The cost of this prize is $4–$8.)

Make Your Move

(An alternate game for any of the others)

Describe three items, and print the name of the item on a piece of poster board. The first item's price should be a two-digit number, the second item a three-digit number, and the last item a four-digit number. For example, the two-digit prize could be a food processor worth $70, the three-digit prize could be a television worth $635, and the four-digit prize could be a snowmobile worth $2,440.

Arrange all the numbers into one large number, but keep the prices together. For example, for these three prizes, you would make this number: 702440635. The contestant has to place the items in order and circle what she thinks the price is. So to get this one right, she would put the food processor first and circle 70, the snowmobile second and circle 2,440, and the television third and circle 635. If she does it correctly, she wins.

Grocery Game

Wheel a cart of groceries around the tables, and ask the ladies to guess the total dollar amount of the items in the cart. The closest one wins the first prize; the second closest, the second prize; and so on.

Shopping for Produce

Here are names of produce. Put the correct fruit or vegetable by each one.

1. Red Delicious _____
2. Concord _____
3. Bing _____
4. Thompson _____
5. Romaine _____
6. Navy _____
7. Bartlett _____
8. Driscoll _____
9. Bell _____
10. Purple _____
11. Russett _____
12. McIntosh _____
13. Vidalia _____
14. Maraschino _____
15. Kidney _____
16. Dromedary _____
17. Honeydew _____
18. Navel _____
19. Colorado _____
20. Zucchini _____

Answers

(1) Apples; (2) grapes; (3) cherries; (4) grapes; (5) lettuce; (6) beans; (7) pears; (8) strawberries; (9) peppers; (10) plums; (11) potatoes; (12) apples; (13) onions; (14) cherries; (15) beans; (16) dates; (17) melons; (18) oranges; (19) peaches; (20) squash.

Songs

"Jesus Paid It All"
"I Have Decided to Follow Jesus"
"Living for Jesus"
"Nor Silver nor Gold"

Devotions
Making Choices

Making choices is just a part of life. We choose what clothes to wear: an ironed blouse, skirt, and heels, or comfy denim and a sweatshirt. We choose when to get up: at 6:00 to exercise or 7:30 to sleep in. We choose what to eat for breakfast: a granola bar or pancakes, eggs, and sausage. Then we remember it is Saturday! Yes! We sleep in, wear sweats, and make a big breakfast.

We make so many choices, both big and small. Since it is Saturday, should we do laundry or go shopping? Of course, we choose shopping. In shopping, we make more choices. Every day it is important to make good choices.

In Joshua 24:15 Joshua admonished the Israelites to serve the Lord. He wanted the best for the nation, and that meant choosing to serve God. "Choose you this day whom ye will serve; . . . but as for me and my house, we will serve the LORD."

The most important choice we can ever make is what to do with God. He wants us to decide to accept the free gift of His Son, Jesus Christ. God has planned a way for sinful people like you and me to have a choice of where to spend eternity. Will you choose to accept God's free gift of eternal life? John 1:12 says, "But as many as received him, to them gave he power to become the sons of God, even to them that believe on his name." The most important decision we will ever make is to choose Christ!

Luke 10:38–42 records how two sisters, Martha and Mary, welcomed Jesus into their home. Martha set out at once to make a wonderful feast for their guests. When Mary didn't help, choosing instead to sit at Jesus' feet and learn from Him, Martha became upset. Listen to what Jesus said to her. *(Read verse 41.)*

As women, and even as girls, we can relate to Martha. We can get so wrapped up in everyday living that we forget to choose the best; that is, time alone with Jesus, learning and growing and praising Him for what He has done in our lives. One day each of us will account for the choices we have made. Romans 14:10–12 tells us all about it. *(Read the verses.)* We need to make choices that will count for eternity: first to accept Christ as Savior and then to live our lives to honor Him.

Nametags

Prizes

- Grand prize: 100 Grand candy bar
- Symphony candy bar
- Coupons to car wash, restaurants
- Chocolate gold coins
- Grocery items, such as cereal, crackers, nuts, chips, bar soap, hand lotion, kitchen cleanser, kitchen towels, spatula

Recipes

Fudge Cookie Salad

1 (3.4 oz.) pkg. instant French vanilla
    pudding and pie filling
1 cup buttermilk
1 (8 oz.) container frozen whipped topping,
    thawed
1 (20 oz.) can crushed pineapple, drained
1 can mandarin oranges, drained
14–16 fudge striped cookies, broken into
    large pieces

Mix together the pudding, buttermilk, and topping. Add the fruit. Just before serving, fold in the cookie pieces.

Cauliflower Salad

1 head cauliflower, bite size
1 cup cashew halves
$1/4$ cup bacon bits
$1/2$ cup frozen peas
2 cups Miracle Whip

Combine all ingredients and chill.

Five-Cup Salad

1 cup miniature marshmallows
1 cup sour cream
1 small jar maraschino cherries, halved
1 cup chunk pineapple
1 cup mandarin oranges

Drain all fruits. Mix marshmallows and sour cream together and let stand several hours. When marshmallows are soft, add cherries, pineapple, and oranges. Stir well and then refrigerate.

Crab Salad

1 (8 oz) pkg. imitation crab
$1/4$ cup onion, finely chopped
$1/4$ cup celery, finely chopped
$1/2$ cup mayonnaise
$1/2$ cup sugar

Break crab meat into small pieces. Add onion and celery. Slowly add sugar to mayonnaise mixture until you have the flavor you want. Combine all ingredients. Refrigerate at least 30 minutes before serving.

Quick Bacon Broccoli Raisin Salad

1 lb. fresh broccoli, bite size
$1/2$ cup raisins
$1/3$ cup bacon bits
$1/4$ cup sunflower seeds
3 oz. coleslaw dressing

Combine all ingredients; refrigerate at least 30 minutes before serving.

Old-Fashioned Baskets

Theme and Decorations

- Decorate with different kinds of woven baskets, using seasonal colors; gather things to put in them, such as lilacs in the spring, garden produce in the summer, Indian corn in the fall, or pinecones in the winter. To make the baskets more attractive, fill them with potpourri, doilies, or old lace handkerchiefs.
- Accessorize with candles or old-fashioned oil lamps and old, worn, well-loved Bibles.
- Cut out shapes of fruits, and set one at each place setting. (See "Games.")
- Set up a clothesline, and hang children's clothes on it. (See "Games.")

Food

- Homemade breads and muffins
- Bagels and cream cheese
- Fresh fruit
- Coffee, tea, and hot chocolate

Games

Fruit Basket Upset

Cut out shapes of fruits, and set one at each place setting. Anytime during the program before the meal, when the emcee says a specific fruit, such as apples, all the people with an apple cutout have to exchange places with one another. When the emcee says, "Fruit Basket Upset," *everyone* has to find a new place to sit. No one is out . . . the guests just have different people to sit by and visit with.

Gathering Game

String a clothesline, and hang children's clothes on it. Have one lady at a time take clothes and clothespins off the line. The object is to see how many articles each lady can take down without dropping any clothes or clothespins. Invite girls to cheer their mothers on.

Gathering in the Clothes

Unscramble the following items from the clothesline that you might put in your clothesbasket.

1. kocss _____
2. jaaapms _____
3. thabbore _____
4. stanp _____
5. wthei sriths _____
6. srdes _____
7. waterse _____
8. dbe sthsee _____
9. shid wetosl _____
10. gurs _____
11. batlechotl _____

Answers

(1) Socks; (2) pajamas; (3) bathrobe; (4) pants; (5) white shirts; (6) dress; (7) sweater; (8) bed sheets; (9) dish towels; (10) rugs; (11) tablecloth.

Oldies but Goodies

Name these things that start with the word "old."
1. Been around forever
2. A Yellowstone geyser

3. American flag
4. Navy ship
5. A person who has been around awhile
6. Reference to the past
7. A merry old soul
8. Eccentric bits of advice
9. A children's favorite card game
10. First part of Bible
11. A favorite hymn
12. A clothing store
13. Continent of Europe
14. Keeping to old ways or ideas
15. Popular songs of the past

Answers

(1) Old as dirt; (2) Old Faithful; (3) Old Glory; (4) *Old Ironsides;* (5) old-timer; (6) old days; (7) Old King Cole; (8) old wives' tales; (9) Old Maid; (10) Old Testament; (11) "Old Rugged Cross"; (12) Old Navy; (13) Old World; (14) old-fashioned; (15) oldies.

Songs

"Bringing in the Sheaves"
"Bring Them In"
" 'Tis So Sweet to Trust in Jesus"
"Trusting Jesus"

Devotions

Old-Fashioned Baskets

How many of us collect baskets? Why do they fascinate us? Maybe it's their different shapes, sizes, and colors. Maybe it's the variety of ways we use them. Since Bible times baskets have served in or decorated our homes. We use them to hold and carry items. We store bread and fruit in baskets.

People in other countries and in Bible times carried their supplies in baskets. Even the Hebrew priests used baskets to store the bread and wafers in the tabernacle (Exod. 29:3, 23). In New Testament times, the disciples used baskets to gather the leftover bread and fish after Jesus fed the five thousand (Matt. 14:20). According to Acts 9:25, Paul rode in a large basket as his friends lowered him over a wall to escape the Jews.

Today baskets can be made from any material, but the most common is woven reed. Basket weaving, once a dying art, has become a popular hobby. Bible time baskets could have been made with reed, twigs, stalks, or any other natural material available.

One of the most precious baskets ever was the one that held baby Moses. Imagine the care and love Jochebed put into making that papyrus basket. She placed her baby boy into it and then carefully released it into the muddy waters of the Nile River. It was just an ordinary basket made by a woman of extraordinary faith, courage, and love. Let's consider those three things as demonstrated by Jochebed.

First, Jochebed showed faith. Hebrews 11:23 reports that by faith Jochebed and Amram hid their infant son because Pharaoh had issued a command to kill all the Hebrew baby boys. They trusted God and prayed. Maybe they remembered how God had spared Isaac, Abraham's son, from death and, therefore, believed God would protect their son too. Above all, Jochebed's faith in God allowed her to put Moses in a tar-pitched basket and push it out into the river.

Second, Jochebed showed courage. If you are a mother, can you imagine leaving your baby in a river and walking away? I am sure Jochebed knew if she didn't do something, Moses would soon be killed by Pharaoh's men. She determined to protect and spare her child, and she willingly gave him up to save his life. Mothers fear for their children both physically and spiritually. It is the job of parents to protect children from harm and to teach them the things of God. It is an awesome responsibility. In the midst of their fears, mothers need courage like Jochebed's. Girls, even as young as you are, you can show courage by doing the right thing no matter how hard it is.

Third, Jochebed showed love. She left her daughter, Miriam, to watch Moses. When Pharaoh's daughter found him, Miriam asked if she needed a nursemaid. Then Miriam ran home to get her mother. Can you imagine how overjoyed Jochebed was to hold little Moses again? Now she could tell him about her God and show him how God had answered their prayers. She educated him in the Hebrew faith before he came completely under Egyptian influence. Moses would be called the son of Pharaoh's daughter, but he had the love of Jochebed embedded in his heart. Girls, you can show love to your parents, sisters, brothers, and other family members.

God used Jochebed, a devoted mother, to start the plan He had for rescuing the Hebrew people from slavery. God has plans for each one of us mothers and daughters, although we might not understand them. We can be like Jochebed and Miriam and be a part of His plan. We, too, can show faith, courage, and love as we trust Him with our lives and let Him use us for His glory.

Nametags

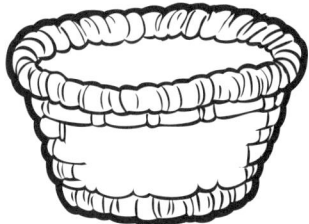

Prizes

Present each winner with a small basket filled with one or more of the following:

- Small loaves of bread
- Jars of jam or jelly
- Candles
- Potpourri

Recipes
Poppy Seed Bread

GLAZE

$1/4$ cup orange juice

$1/2$ teaspoon butter flavoring

$1/2$ teaspoon vanilla

$1/2$ teaspoon almond flavoring

$3/4$ cup powdered sugar

BREAD

$2^1/4$ cups sugar

$1^1/2$ cups oil

3 eggs

$1^1/2$ cups milk

3 cups flour

$1^1/2$ teaspoons salt

$1^1/2$ teaspoons baking powder

$1^1/2$ teaspoon vanilla

$1^1/2$ teaspoons butter flavoring

$1^1/2$ teaspoons almond extract

$1^1/2$ teaspoons poppy seeds

1. Mix together ingredients for glaze and set aside

2. In a large bowl, blend sugar, oil, eggs, and milk. Combine dry ingredients and add to egg mixture. Mix well.

3. Bake bread in two greased bread pans at 350°F for 55–60 minutes. The top will crack. Remove from oven and cool for 5 minutes; then make holes in the crust with a toothpick and add the glaze.

Lemon Bread

BREAD

$1/2$ cup margarine

1 cup sugar

2 eggs

Grated rind of 1 lemon

$1/2$ cup milk

$1^1/2$ cups flour

1 teaspoon baking powder

$1/2$ teaspoon salt

GLAZE

$1/4$ cup sugar

Juice of 1 lemon

1. Cream margarine and sugar. Add eggs and beat. Add lemon rind, milk, and dry ingredients. Mix well.

2. Pour batter into a well-greased loaf pan. Bake at 350°F for 45–55 minutes or until an inserted toothpick comes out clean. While bread is warm, drizzle it with the glaze.

Cranberry Nut Bread

2 cups flour

1 cup plus 2 tablespoons sugar

$1^3/4$ teaspoons baking powder

$1/2$ teaspoon baking soda

1 teaspoon salt

1 tablespoon oil or melted margarine

$1/3$ cup orange juice

$1/4$ cup water

1 egg, slightly beaten

2 cups fresh cranberries, cut in half

$3/4$ cup chopped pecans

1. Mix the first five ingredients together. Make a well in the center. Add the rest of the ingredients and mix only to moisten.

2. Pour batter into a lightly greased loaf pan. Bake at 350°F for 65–70 minutes or until an inserted toothpick comes out clean. Cool 10 minutes and remove from pan.

Apple Bread

$1/2$ cup margarine

$1/2$ cup sugar

2 eggs

1 teaspoon vanilla

1 teaspoon baking soda

2 tablespoons warm water

2 cups flour

$1/2$ teaspoon salt

1 teaspoon baking powder

1 cup peeled, diced apples

$1/4$ cup chopped pecans (opt.)

1. Cream together margarine and sugar. Add eggs and vanilla. Put soda in warm water and set aside. Stir flour, salt, and baking powder into creamed mixture; then add the soda water. Mix well. Fold in apples and nuts.

2. Bake bread in two small well-greased loaf pans at 350°F for 40–45 minutes or one large loaf pan for 50–60 minutes. Cool before slicing.

Cinnamon Bread

$1/4$ cup oil

1 cup sugar

1 cup buttermilk

1 egg

2 cups flour

1 teaspoon baking soda

$1/2$ teaspoon salt

TOPPING

$1/2$ teaspoon cinnamon

$1/2$ cup sugar

1. In a small bowl, mix together topping ingredients; set aside.

2. In a larger bowl, combine oil, sugar, buttermilk, and egg. Add dry ingredients and mix well. Pour half the batter into a greased loaf pan. Sprinkle with half the cinnamon-sugar mixture. Pour in rest of batter and add remaining cinnamon and sugar on top.

3. Bake at 350°F for 50–60 minutes.

Pumpkin Swirl Bread

1 (8 oz) pkg. cream cheese, softened
$1/4$ cup sugar
1 egg, beaten
$1^1/2$ cups sugar
1 (15 oz.) can pumpkin
$1/2$ cup margarine, melted
1 egg, beaten
$1/3$ cup water
$1^3/4$ cups flour
1 teaspoon baking soda
$1/2$ teaspoon salt
1 teaspoon cinnamon
$1/4$ teaspoon ground nutmeg

1. In a small bowl, blend together cream cheese, sugar, and egg. Set aside.

2. In a large bowl, mix together pumpkin, margarine, egg, and water. Combine dry ingredients and add to pumpkin mixture. Mix just until moistened.

3. Reserve 2 cups pumpkin batter. Pour remaining batter into greased and floured loaf pan. Pour cream cheese mixture over pumpkin batter. Top with reserved pumpkin batter. Cut through batter several times with knife for swirl effect.

4. Bake at 350°F for 1 hour and 10 minutes or until an inserted toothpick comes out clean. Cool 5 minutes. Remove from pan.

Zucchini Bread

1 cup oil
2 cups sugar
3 eggs
2 cups grated unpeeled zucchini
1 tablespoon vanilla
3 cups flour
1 teaspoon baking soda
1 teaspoon salt
$1/2$ teaspoon baking powder
1 tablespoon cinnamon

1. Combine oil, sugar, eggs, zucchini, and vanilla. Sift dry ingredients together and add to zucchini batter. Mix well.

2. Pour batter into greased loaf pan and bake at 350°F for 50–60 minutes or until done.

Queen for a Day

Theme and Decorations

- Decorate a head table for the queen and her court, using royal colors of gold and purple. Make crowns for the queen and her court; place the crowns on the head table. The queen will also need a purple robe, a golden scepter, and a royal bell to ring. (See "Games.")
- Cover table with gold table coverings. Or sprinkle gold confetti on the tables. Roll up purple napkins; encircle them with gold rings.
- Borrow ornate jewelry boxes and use them for centerpieces. Scatter and drape old costume jewelry around each jewelry box.

Food

- Royal pie buffet
- Coffee, tea, and hot chocolate

Games

Queen for a Day

Choose five ladies, or hide five gold stickers under the guests' plates. Choose the queen by asking questions of the five "finalists." When a finalist answers yes, she becomes a princess. The woman or girl remaining at the end of the questions is the queen.

The queen should be the one who has had the toughest day, so she will go from being a "poor Cinderella" to being a queen.

Possible Questions

1. Has anyone told you today how nice you look?

2. Did someone kiss you today?
3. Have you ever won anything in a prize give-away?
4. Have you eaten chocolate in the last five hours?
5. Have you bought or received any new clothes in the last week?

After you have chosen a queen, have her mother or her daughter crown her. Drape a purple robe around her, and give her a golden scepter. Play music suitable for a new queen (e.g., "Here She Comes, Miss America").

Have the queen walk around the tables and then take her royal seat at the head table with her princesses sitting on both sides.

The queen can make decrees during the evening. Suggest that when she wishes to make a decree, she (1) write it on a note, (2) hand the note to one of the princesses, and (3) ring her royal bell to get the emcee's attention. The princess will then give the royal decree to the emcee, who will, in turn, read it to the audience.

Examples of Royal Decrees

1. Everyone, take off your shoes.
2. We all need chocolate. Pass out Hershey's Kisses.
3. We all need to be happy. Let's sing (name a "happy" song that the group knows).

Songs

"Crown Him with Many Crowns" (use a trumpet trio, if possible)

"Stand Up, Stand Up for Jesus"

"Count Your Blessings"
"To God Be the Glory"
"Lavender Blue, Lavender Green"

Devotions
Queen for a Day

Most of us can only dream of what it would be like to live as royalty. Even if we tried to imagine it, I don't think we could. But other women know from firsthand experience. The Bible tells us about one of them, an orphan girl who grew up to become the queen of Persia. Her name was Esther.

Esther probably never imagined that the king's officials would one day appear at her door, but they did. Because they had heard about her beauty and virginity, they came to take her for the king's harem. Her cousin, Mordecai, had raised her after her parents died. No doubt he was alarmed and afraid for her, but he also knew that King Xerxes owned everything. He held absolute reign over a great empire.

For a year, along with other women in the harem, Esther was pampered with oils, perfumes, and baths. She learned about life in the palace, but she did not reveal to anyone that she was a Jew.

Finally Esther appeared before the king, who immediately fell in love with her (Esther 2:17). He crowned her queen and gave a royal banquet. Esther's life in the palace must have been more than she had ever dreamed. One day Mordecai sent word to her that he had overheard a plan to kill the king. Esther sent word to King Xerxes, and the conspirators were hanged.

Another day Esther's maids told her that Mordecai was mourning because of a decree issued by Haman and the king to murder all Jews. Haman hated the Jewish people. Mordecai, a Jew, had refused to bow when he walked by. This lack of respect angered Haman so much that he conspired to have a decree signed by King Xerxes to have all the Jews killed.

Mordecai sent a message to Queen Esther that she needed to go to the king to beg for mercy for her people.

Knowing that God must have put her in that position, for this reason, she agreed to go to the king, even though she could die for going to him without being called.

Esther had a plan. She, along with her handmaids and the Jews, fasted and humbled herself before God for three days and nights. Even as a queen, she knew the real power was in God's hands, not hers.

Putting on her royal robes, she entered the court and stood at the door to King Xerxes' throne room. What a relief it was as he stretched the gold scepter toward her, giving her permission to approach him. She asked him and his chief counselor, Haman, to attend a banquet she had prepared. At the banquet Xerxes told her she could have whatever she wanted up to half the kingdom. She asked the two men to attend another banquet. The next day the king again offered her up to half of his kingdom.

This time Esther asked him to spare her life and the lives of her people (Esther 7:3). The king was stunned. Who would do such a thing, to take the lives of her and her people? Esther told him it was Haman. Outraged, the king left the room; when he came back, he found Haman clinging to his wife for mercy.

The king summoned the guards, who hanged Haman on the very gallows he had built for Mordecai. The king then gave Esther permission to write another decree that would help spare the lives of her people.

God had a special plan for Esther's life. Maybe His plan for you or me isn't to save a nation, but we need to be willing to let God use us to fulfill His plan.

As women and girls, we can learn from Esther's example.

First, she was a woman of great courage. Esther was taken from her home and put into the king's harem. She must have been terrified. She was headed for a life she knew nothing about and was told not to reveal her identity as a Jew. She was also asked to go to the king and plead for the lives of her people at the risk of her own life. Esther's courage must have come from her belief that God had total control of the situation. The power to save herself and her people was not in her hands, but God's.

Second, she was a woman of great compassion. When Esther learned about the decree and her cousin Mordecai's mourning, no doubt her heart ached. Esther 4:4 says that the queen was deeply distressed. Reports came to her of the Jews' mourning and weeping and fasting as well. She was the queen, but she was also a Jew. She would do whatever it took to save her people. Esther 4:16 records her words, "If I perish, I perish."

Third, she was a woman of great character. She chose to go to God. She fasted and humbled herself and left the situation in God's hands. The best position she could take in the crisis was on her knees before God. She faced an impossible situation, but she knew God had used impossible situations before to bring honor and glory to Himself. Her faith and trust in God showed her true character.

Fourth, she was a woman of great confidence. With her confidence in God, Esther approached the king. The men in the court must have gasped and stared wide-eyed as she stepped into the room. Nevertheless she had confidence as she asked the king to attend a banquet. She would prepare a feast for him and show him he was important to her. Then Esther chose the right time and place to make her appeal. Showing respect, carefully choosing her words, and trusting God, she approached the king with great confidence.

Esther was a woman who showed courage, compassion, character, and confidence in God. We can learn from her example to do what God has called each of us as Christians to do—to share the gospel with those around us. We can pray and humble ourselves before God so He can use us.

We can then have courage to share the good news of God's gift of eternal life. We can have confidence in God to work in others' lives and bring them to a saving knowledge of His Son. Let God use you "for such a time as this."

Nametags

Prizes

- Box of chocolates
- Gold foil-wrapped candy
- Jewelry box
- Jewelry

Recipes

Pie Crust

2$\frac{1}{2}$–2$\frac{2}{3}$ cups flour

1 cup butter-flavored shortening

$\frac{1}{2}$ cup cold water

Cut flour and shortening together until crumbly. Stir in cold water until dough comes together in a ball. Divide dough. Roll on floured surface and put in a 9" pie pan. Makes top and bottom crusts.

Pumpkin Pie

³/₄ cup sugar
¹/₂ teaspoon salt
1 teaspoon cinnamon
¹/₂ teaspoon ginger
¹/₄ teaspoon ground cloves
2 eggs
1³/₄ cups pumpkin
1 (12 oz.) can evaporated milk
9" pie shell (unbaked)

In a blender, combine all ingredients. Mix until smooth. Pour into pie shell. Bake 15 minutes at 425°F. Reduce temperature to 350°F and bake for 40–50 minutes until an inserted knife comes out clean. Cool and serve.

Perfect Lemon Pie

1¹/₂ cups sugar
¹/₄ cup plus 2 tablespoons cornstarch
¹/₄ teaspoon salt
¹/₂ cup lemon juice
¹/₂ cup cold water
3 egg yolks, well beaten
2 tablespoons margarine
Grated rind of 1 lemon
1¹/₂ cups boiling water
9" pie shell (baked)

MERINGUE
1 tablespoon cornstarch
2 teaspoons water
¹/₂ cup boiling water
3 egg whites
¹/₄ teaspoon cream of tartar
6 tablespoons sugar
4 drops lemon flavoring

1. In a saucepan, mix sugar, cornstarch, and salt. Gradually add lemon juice and cold water. Mix well and add egg yolks, margarine, and lemon rind. Gradually add 1¹/₂ cups boiling water. Cook over medium heat and boil 1 minute. Stir constantly. Pour hot mixture into baked crust.

2. For meringue, mix together 1 tablespoon cornstarch and 2 teaspoons water in a saucepan. Stir in ¹/₂ cup boiling water and cook until thick. Cool.

3. Meanwhile, beat egg whites and cream of tartar. Gradually add sugar and lemon flavoring. Beat until stiff. Fold into cooled cornstarch mixture and spoon onto lemon filling. Make sure meringue reaches the edges of the crust.

4. Bake at 400°F for 8 minutes. Peaks should be lightly browned.

French Apple Pie

CRUST
2¹/₂ cups flour
¹/₄ teaspoon salt
Pinch of baking powder
1 cup lard or shortening
1 egg
1 tablespoon vinegar
1 tablespoon water

FILLING
2¹/₂ lbs. (7 cups) tart apples
1 cup sugar
2 tablespoons flour
¹/₂ teaspoon cinnamon
2 tablespoons lemon juice

TOPPING
¹/₂ cup sugar
¹/₂ cup flour
¹/₂ cup margarine

1. For crust, mix together flour, salt, and baking powder. Cut shortening into dry ingredients. Beat egg, vinegar, and water. Stir everything together to form a soft dough. Roll out crust on floured surface.

2. For filling, peel and slice apples. Mix with sugar, flour, and cinnamon. Put into pie shell and drizzle with lemon juice.

3. For topping, mix together ¹/₂ cup sugar and ¹/₂ cup flour. Sprinkle this mixture and margarine over apples. Slip pie into heavy paper sack. Fold the end over and set the bag on a cookie sheet. Bake at 400°F for 1 hour.

Coconut Cream Pie

$3/4$ cup sugar

3 tablespoons cornstarch

3 tablespoons flour

$1/2$ teaspoon salt

3 egg yolks, beaten

$1/2$ cup cold milk

2 cups hot milk

1 tablespoon margarine

1 teaspoon vanilla

3 egg whites

$3/4$ cup coconut

9" pie shell (baked)

1 (12 oz.) container frozen whipped
    topping, thawed

$1/4$ cup toasted coconut

1. Blend sugar, cornstarch, flour, and salt. Add egg yolks and cold milk. Mix well. In saucepan, heat 2 cups milk; do not scald. Add flour and egg mixture. Cook until thick, stirring constantly. Remove from heat. Add margarine and vanilla. Beat egg whites and add to the sauce mixture. Stir in coconut. Put mixture into pie shell and cool.

2. Top with whipped topping and toasted coconut. To toast coconut, bake at 375°F on cookie sheet until lightly browned (5–7 minutes).

Strawberry-Rhubarb Pie

1 cup strawberries

2 cups rhubarb

3 tablespoons flour

1 cup sugar (overflowing)

$1/2$ teaspoon cinnamon

9" pie shells, top and bottom (unbaked)

In a saucepan, stir together ingredients. Cook until thick, stirring constantly. If using fresh fruit, add a little water. Pour into unbaked pie shell. Dot with margarine. Add top crust and sprinkle with sugar. Seal and bake at 375°F for 35 minutes.

Cherry Pie

3 cups (overflowing) tart red cherries

$1 1/2$ cups sugar

3 tablespoons tapioca

Dash of salt

1 teaspoon almond extract

1 tablespoon margarine

9" pie shells, top and bottom (unbaked)

In a saucepan, mix together ingredients. Let set 15 minutes to soften tapioca. Cook until thick, stirring constantly. Pour into pie shell. Dot with margarine. Add top crust. Seal and sprinkle with sugar. Bake at 375°F for 35–45 minutes.

Pecan Pie

4 tablespoons margarine

3 tablespoons flour

1 cup sugar

$3/4$ cup white corn syrup

3 eggs, beaten

1 teaspoon vanilla

1 cup chopped pecans

9" pie shell (unbaked)

Cut margarine into flour and sugar with a pastry cutter. Stir in corn syrup and eggs. Add vanilla and pecans; stir until blended. Pour into pie shell and bake at 350°F for 45 minutes.

Peach Pie

$3/4$–1 cup sugar

4 tablespoons flour

$1/2$ teaspoon cinnamon

$3 1/2$ cups peaches, drained

$1/2$ cup peach juice (from drained peaches)

1 tablespoon margarine

9" pie shells, top and bottom (unbaked)

Mix together sugar, flour, cinnamon, and juice from drained peaches. Cook over medium heat, stirring constantly until thick. Lightly mix in peaches. Pour into crust. Dot with margarine. Add top crust and seal. Bake at 375°F for 35–45 minutes.

Sour Cream Raisin Pie

$^3/_4$ cup sugar
2 eggs, slightly beaten
$^1/_4$ teaspoon salt
1 teaspoon cinnamon
$^1/_4$ teaspoon cloves
$^1/_2$ teaspoon nutmeg
1 cup raisins
1 cup sour cream
8" pie shell (unbaked)

Combine ingredients and pour into crust. Bake at 450°F for 10 minutes, then at 350°F for 30 minutes or until an inserted knife comes out clean.

Strawberry Brunch

Theme and Decorations

- Decorate with strawberries piled high in small baskets. Make large red berries from poster board to hang from the ceiling and around the room.
- Tie big red bows on several teddy bears. Bring tricycles, wagons, or wheelbarrows to place the bears in.
- Arrange vases of flowers on each table. If your brunch takes place in the spring, use crabapple (pink) or apple (white) blossoms. Tie a red bow on each vase.
- Purchase plates and napkins with a strawberry theme to help make the room look "beary" special.

Food

- Overnight Egg Casserole
- Overnight Caramel Rolls
- Pancakes and waffles topped with strawberries, blueberries, and/or raspberries

Games

Teddy Bear Parade

Recruit a few older ladies ahead of time to dress up and act like kids. They will each need to carry a teddy bear. Have them sing "Me and My Teddy Bear" or "Fuzzy Wuzzy Was a Bear" or a similar children's song as they parade around entertaining the rest of the guests. For example, one might sing extra bold and loud. One might act shy. A couple might push each other out of line or try to steal the show.

Culinary Activity

Work in groups of two, and be sure to use a pencil because you will erase!

Choose the correct word to finish the sentence.

1. _____ the pie.
2. _____ the flour.
3. _____ the cinnamon rolls.
4. _____ the eggs.
5. _____ the bananas.
6. _____ the raspberries.
7. _____ the apple.
8. _____ the can.
9. _____ the rolls.
10. _____ the pan.
11. _____ the cookies.
12. _____ the water.
13. _____ the batter.
14. _____ the dough.
15. _____ the coffee.
16. _____ the nuts.
17. _____ the bowl.
18. _____ the strawberries.
19. _____ the waffles.
20. _____ the spatula.

Words to Choose From

Open	Frost	Core	Warm
Slice	Butter	Scramble	Stem
Boil	Chop	Lick	Peel
Bake	Mix	Scrape	Grease
Pick	Sift	Knead	Brew

Answers

(1) Slice; (2) Sift; (3) Frost; (4) Scramble;
(5) Peel; (6) Pick; (7) Core; (8) Open; (9) Warm;
(10) Grease; (11) Bake; (12) Boil; (13) Mix;
(14) Knead; (15) Brew; (16) Chop; (17) Scrape;
(18) Stem; (19) Butter; (20) Lick.

Berry Bear Game

Fill in these blanks with the names of bears and berries.

1. An Australian bear that has gray fur, large ears, sharp claws, and feeds on the leaves of eucalyptus trees._____ bear
2. A spiny shrub having sour, edible, greenish red berries. _____berry
3. A big brown bear of northwest North America. _____ bear
4. A tart red berry used in sauces, jellies, and beverages. _____berry
5. A common North American bear that lives in forests and has a glossy black coat. _____ bear
6. A type of blackberry that grows low to the ground and produces a dark berry. _____berry
7. A large white furred bear living in Arctic regions. _____ bear
8. A prickly shrub from the rose family that bears edible red fruit. _____berry
9. A large black-and-white bear from China with black circles around its eyes. _____ bear
10. A shrub having large prickly thorns with black or deep purple fruit. _____ berry
11. A plant that has white blossoms and red edible seedy fruit. _____berry
12. A common name for plants with berries that are eaten by bears. _____berry
13. A child's stuffed toy, usually one to cuddle. _____ bear
14. A plant that has white tubular flowers and edible blue or blue-black berries. _____ berry
15. A brown bear that lives on the coastal areas of Alaska. _____bear

Answers

(1) Koala; (2) goose[berry]; (3) grizzly; (4) cran-[berry]; (5) black; (6) dew[berry]; (7) polar; (8) rasp[berry]; (9) panda; (10) black[berry]; (11) straw[berry]; (12) bear[berry]; (13) teddy; (14) blue[berry]; (15) Kodiak.

Songs

"When Love Shines In"
"Love Lifted Me"
"O Perfect Love"
"God Will Take Care of You"

Devotions

Ruth and Naomi

Mother's Day is a special day we set aside once a year to honor our mothers. A mother is often a very precious friend. She is a woman who listens, encourages, and keeps confidences. She knows how to laugh and cry with you. She is loyal, loving, and forgiving. Godly mothers are wonderful treasures!

In the book of Ruth we read about a young widow who loved her mother-in-law so much that she was unwilling to leave her. The widow, Ruth, made a promise to her mother-in-law, Naomi, on the road back to Naomi's hometown. Although made from one woman to another, this promise is often quoted at wedding ceremonies. It has become an expression of love and loyalty between two people: "Whither thou goest, I will go; and where thou lodgest, I will lodge: thy people shall be my people, and thy God my God" (Ruth 1:16).

Ruth had no way of knowing what would happen in her life, but God did, and He had it all planned. Because Ruth was faithful to Naomi, God blessed Ruth with a husband, a son, and a place to call home. Ruth's name means "friendship." It is easy to imagine Ruth as her mother-in-law's friend, probably her best friend. We could all wish for a good friend like Ruth. Let's consider Ruth's promises to Naomi.

First, Ruth promised Naomi she would share in her journey. She told Naomi, "Whither thou goest, I will go." Ruth wanted to be where Naomi was and to help care for her needs. She willingly looked for food for the two of them (Ruth 2:2, 3).

How good are we at spending time with our mothers or mothers-in-law, or, if you're a girl, your grandmothers? We get so busy with our own family's concerns that we don't have time to check in on them or to take them shopping or out for lunch, to make something for them, or to send them an e-mail. Remember, "Where you go, I will go." Share in their journey through life.

Second, Ruth promised Naomi she would share her family. "Thy people shall be my people," Ruth said. Naomi may have been a loving mother-in-law, but she was bitter because of the death of her husband and two sons. Ruth could have gone back to live with her own parents. They probably could have provided well for her, but Ruth loved her mother-in-law and her God. Naomi had become Ruth's family.

As we grow older, our families grow. Children grow up and marry, and we have extended families. Whether you're a woman or a girl, you may find it hard to love certain people in your family. Ruth accepted Naomi's family as her own. We should accept all of our family members too.

Third, Ruth promised Naomi she would share her spiritual values. "Thy God [shall be] my God," she said. Ruth had a strong love for Naomi, but she was also drawn in her heart to Naomi's God, the God of Israel. She had learned about Him when she married into Naomi's family. Ruth wanted to obey God. Whatever gods or idols she had worshiped, she was willing to turn away from them to worship the one true God with Naomi.

Hebrew law provided for widows who had no one to care for them. A close relative, or kinsman, could come to the aid of a family member. To redeem the widow's inheritance, the kinsman had to pay the redemption price in full. Boaz became Ruth's kinsman-redeemer.

Today Christ is our Kinsman-Redeemer. He paid the price in full when He died on the cross for our sins. We need to choose Christ as our Savior. Ruth chose God to be her God and shared Naomi's spiritual heritage.

Fourth, Ruth's promise to Naomi implied that Ruth would stay with Naomi no matter what happened. She didn't have any idea that Boaz or anyone else would redeem her and take her as his wife. When Ruth married Boaz, Naomi went with her. Ruth also included her mother-in-law in the care of her baby boy, Obed. Naomi's neighbor women told her that Ruth, who loved her, was better than seven sons (Ruth 4:14, 15). Ruth had devoted herself to care for her mother-in-law, and Naomi then helped her care for her home and family. We can share our lives with our families by sharing our children with them. God made us a family unit, and we can be there for one another.

We can honor our mothers today as Ruth did her mother-in-law. We can do this by sharing life's journey, by sharing and accepting family, by sharing spiritual values, and by sharing life with them until death. How good God is to give us the mother-daughter relationship. How great God is to give us His Son as our Kinsman-Redeemer.

Nametags

Prizes

- Gummy bears
- Berry-scented candles
- Teddy Grahams
- Strawberry jam
- Small teddy bears

Recipes

Overnight Egg Casserole

6–8 slices buttered bread, cubed

1 lb. American cheese, sliced or cubed

3 cups milk

8 eggs, well beaten

$3/4$ teaspoons salt

2–3 cups ham, cubed

Mix ingredients in a 9" x 13" pan. Refrigerate overnight. Bake at 350°F for 1 hour.

Overnight Caramel Rolls

1 pkg. dry yeast

3 cups warm water

1 cup sugar

$2^1/_2$ teaspoons salt

1 stick margarine, melted

2 eggs

8 cups flour

Margarine, melted

Brown sugar

Cinnamon

TOPPING

$3/_4$ cup margarine

$1^1/_2$ cups brown sugar

6 tablespoons white corn syrup

3 tablespoons water

1. Start dough at 4:00 or 5:00 in the afternoon. In a large bowl, mix together yeast and warm water. Stir in sugar, salt, margarine, and eggs. Add the flour until stiff. Do not knead. Let rise.

2. Mix topping ingredients together in a saucepan. Bring to a boil. Pour topping into two 9" x 13" pans.

3. Make into rolls at 9:00 or 10:00 P.M. Start by rolling half the dough into a rectangle (about 16" x 24"). Brush with melted margarine. Cover with brown sugar and sprinkle on cinnamon to suit your taste. Roll up and seal. Cut into 12 slices. Place each slice on the topping in the pan. Cover with a damp towel overnight. Repeat the procedure with the other half of the dough.

4. Bake rolls the next morning at 375°F for 20–25 minutes. Immediately invert pans. Makes 24 rolls.

Sugar 'n' Spice

Theme and Decorations

- Decorate with a country apple theme. Put apples in baskets lined with navy blue checkered napkins or towels.
- Accent the theme with apple-red candles.
- Add old blue or antique Mason jars filled with long cinnamon sticks.
- Serve ice cold water or iced tea in old-fashioned tin pitchers. Use pint Mason jars for your cold drinks.

Food

- Summer sausage
- Cheddar cheese
- Crackers and cheese spread
- Betty's Apple Pie
- Vanilla or cinnamon ice cream
- Iced tea

Games

Spice Game

Select several spices. Put a tablespoon of each spice into small plastic bags. Number the bags, and ask the ladies to identify the spices by sight and smell only. Have ladies write their answers on pieces of paper. Whoever has the most correct answers wins.

Spice of Life Game

From the list below, match the word ending to the word beginning of the following spices.

1. Cinn _____	iander
2. Ore _____	weed
3. Pe _____	sil
4. Cor _____	ram
5. Cl _____	age
6. Pap _____	rika
7. S _____	amon
8. Nut _____	pice
9. Alls _____	gano
10. Th _____	pper
11. Dill _____	lt
12. Gin _____	nel
13. Ga _____	tar
14. Marjo _____	rlic
15. Sa _____	oves
16. Ba _____	ger
17. Tar _____	meg
18. Fen _____	yme

Answers

(1) amon; (2) gano; (3) pper; (4) iander; (5) oves; (6) rika; (7) age; (8) meg; (9) pice; (10) yme; (11) weed; (12) ger; (13) rlic; (14) ram; (15) lt; (16) sil; (17) tar; (18) nel.

Songs

"The Name of Jesus"
"His Name Is Wonderful"
"Why Do I Sing about Jesus?"
"The Sweetest Name"

Devotions

Our Fragrance to God

(Ask the ladies and girls to tell you some of the scents and smells they love. Share some that you enjoy.)

Second Corinthians 2:15 identifies Christians as "the [aroma] of Christ, in them that are saved, and in them that perish." What fragrance are we to God and to those we meet every day? Do others know we are Christians?

As mothers and daughters, we want to be to God the fragrance of Christ. Proverbs 31:30 describes a woman who has a sweet fragrance. She is a women who fears the Lord. Her secret is her godly character. Proverbs 31:10–31 describes a woman who depicts the honor and dignity of womanhood. The woman in this chapter is ultimately praised for her fear of God—not for her sewing, cooking, or home decorating.

Proverbs 31:10–12 describes this woman as a wife. She is rare and valuable: "Who can find a virtuous woman? for her price is far above rubies" (v. 10). She is trustworthy: "The heart of her husband doth safely trust in her, so that he shall have no need of spoil" (v. 11). She is submissive: "She will do him good and not evil all the days of her life" (v. 12).

Proverbs 31:13–24 describes this woman as a homemaker. She is conscientious. According to verses 13–15, she works with her hands; she prepares food; she provides for her household. Verses 16–19 talk of her as industrious. She buys land; she raises crops; she works hard.

Finally, verses 25–31 describe the inner character of this woman. She is strong in character: "Strength and honour are her clothing; . . . she openeth her mouth with wisdom; and in her tongue is the law of kindness. She looketh well to the ways of her household" (vv. 25–27). She is praiseworthy: "Her children arise up, and call her blessed; her husband also, and he praiseth her. Many daughters have done virtuously, but thou excellest them all" (vv. 28, 29). She will be re-warded: "Give her of the fruit of her hands; and let her own works praise her in the gates" (v. 31).

This was definitely a woman who had a sweet-smelling fragrance to God and others! As mothers and daughters, we can have that fragrance, too, as others see that we love and fear God and want to serve Him.

Nametags

Prizes

- Dried apple snacks
- Jars with cinnamon sticks
- Apple-red candles
- Baskets with apples

Recipes

Homemade Ice Cream

4 eggs
2$\frac{1}{2}$ cups sugar
1 quart half-and-half
$\frac{1}{2}$ gallon milk
1 tablespoon vanilla
1 teaspoon lemon extract
1 teaspoon salt
2 pkgs. dry Dream Whip

Beat eggs until light. Gradually add sugar; blend until thick. Add half-and-half, milk, vanilla, lemon extract, salt, and Dream Whip. Mix well and freeze.

Cheese Spread
2 cups shredded cheddar cheese
$1/2$ lb. bacon, browned and crumbled
2 tablespoons finely chopped green onion
1 small pkg. slivered almonds
$2/3$ cup Miracle Whip
Mix ingredients together; spread on crackers.

Betty's Apple Pie
CRUST
   $2^1/_2$–$2^2/_3$ cups flour
   1 cup butter-flavored shortening
   $1/2$ cup cold water

FILLING
   4 cups baking apples, peeled and sliced
   $1/2$ cup sugar
   $1/2$ cup brown sugar
   Salt
   1 teaspoon cinnamon
   3 tablespoons flour
   2 tablespoons margarine

1. For crust, cut flour and shortening together until crumbly. Stir in cold water until dough comes together in a ball. Divide dough in half. Roll on floured surface and put in a 9" pie pan. Makes top and bottom crust.

2. Combine apples, sugars, dash of salt, cinnamon, and flour. Put in a 9" pie crust and dot with margarine. Add top crust; seal and sprinkle with sugar. Bake at 375°F for 60–90 minutes or until bubbly in center.

Game Index

Mother and Daughter Events

Recipe Index

Topical Recipe Index

Contents of Let's Plan a Party! CD-ROM

Included on the accompanying CD-ROM are numerous items to help you plan, promote, and have a successful church event. Clip Art images in GIF files are intended for electronic use (such as PowerPoint or Web pages); images in TIF files are designed for print media. Some items are samples only; you will need to customize the announcement or flyer for your specific event. If you do not have Adobe Acrobat Reader, you will need to install the included program to view any PDF files.

To see more church educational resources from Regular Baptist Press, visit our Web site: www.regularbaptistpress.org.

- Games and Puzzles
- Clip Art Files
- Print-Ready Name Tags
- PowerPoint Backgrounds
- Event Organizer and Planning Sheet
- Assignment Sheet
- Bulletin Announcements and Inserts
- Adobe Acrobat Reader